COMPUTERS AND THE PROFESSIONAL

(A series of publications intended to help the computer professional, and other professionals involved in computing, in dealing with problems associated with the various tasks for which they are responsible.)

Factfinder 11: Verified Software Products — A Catalogue

This book contains a catalogue of 199 computer program abstracts covering a wide range of topics and which, because they have all been subjected to examination by the NCC Software Verification process, can be classed as identifiable and usable products.

Following a description of the Verification process, the catalogue contains an index allowing program abstracts to be retrieved according to subject area, computer series, mode of operation and method of release.

The book is particularly aimed at those potential users who are searching for a software product — including computer professionals and other professionals concerned with computer applications.

Other titles in the 'Computers and the Professional' series

Factfinder 1:   Visible Record Computers
Factfinder 2:   Keyboard/Printer Terminals
Factfinder 8:   Program Testing Aids
Factfinder 9:   Generalised Data Management Systems
A System Documented
Decision Tables in Data Processing
Systems Documentation Manual

The National Computing Centre Limited is a non-profit organisation supported by industry, commerce and government. It is dedicated to promoting the wider and more effective use of computers throughout the economy. In realising its objectives the Centre

gives *information* and *advice*

provides *education* and *training*

promotes *standards* and *codes of practice*

co-operates with, and *co-ordinates* the work of, other organisations concerned with computers and their use.

Any interested company, organisation, or individual can support the work of the Centre by subscribing as a member. Throughout the country facilities are provided for members to participate in working parties, study groups, and discussions and to influence NCC policy. A regular newsletter keeps members informed of new developments and NCC activities. Special facilities are offered for courses, training material, publications and software packages.

For further details about membership get in touch with the Centre at Quay House, Quay Street, Manchester M3 3HU. Telephone: 061-832 9731

or at one of the following regional offices:

BELFAST	1st Floor 117 Lisburn Road	Telephone: 0232 665997
BIRMINGHAM	Prudential Buildings St. Philips Place Colmore Row	Telephone: 021-236 7149
BRISTOL	Royal Exchange Building 6th Floor 41 Corn Street BS1 1HG	Telephone: Bristol 27077
GLASGOW	Claremont House North Claremont Street C3	Telephone: 041-332 0117
LONDON	Audrey House Ely Place EC1	Telephone: 01-242 1044

Factfinder 11: Verified Software Products — A Catalogue

PUBLISHED BY THE NATIONAL COMPUTING CENTRE LIMITED

Keywords for information retrieval
drawn from *NCC Thesaurus of
Computing Terms:* program abstracts,
software verification.

*All enquiries concerning the information contained in this publication
should be addressed to: Information Operations, The National Computing
Centre Limited, Quay House, Quay Street, MANCHESTER M3 3HU
(Telephone: 061-832 9731, Telex: 668962 NCC MANCHESTER)*

SBN 85012 068 3

This book is set in Univers series
by Wright's (Sandbach) Limited
Sandbach, Cheshire, England

Foreword

This present publication, containing a catalogue of items of Verified Software, brings to fruition the first stage of an important and new concept concerned with the quality of information about computer software.

First introduced in April 1971, the Software Verification process breaks new ground because, at last, items of computer software are treated as products in just the same way that items of computer hardware have been treated in the past.

Although the work on Software Verification is far from complete, I fully support NCC in raising the status of information about software — a process which can only serve to raise the status of software itself, to the benefit of the computing community as a whole.

I now look forward to a widening of the scope of this activity in terms of an increasing number of products and their subjection to closer scrutiny by means of the more advanced stages of Verification.

Therefore I would encourage both the suppliers and users of computer software to support the work that this first publication represents.

There is nothing to lose and much to gain if, as I believe, the quality of computing can be thereby improved.

The Rt. Hon. Ernest Marples M.P.

Preface to the First Edition

This publication is the first of a projected series containing information about software products — all of which have successfully undergone an examination process called Software Verification.

As such, it was considered important to devote a part of the publication to an explanation of the Verification process itself and to describe the method for submitting new material about software products to software suppliers, who would like their products to be included.

By this means, together with an extension of the Verification process itself, it is intended that future issues will contain an extending catalogue of Verified Software and that editorial material concerned with the many and varied aspects of interchanging software will be included.

To those who have supported Software Verification, we give our thanks; particularly those who have supplied information and who are listed in the catalogue section.

Finally, we would like to say to those potential software users who cannot find what they want in this publication, please ask us — we may have received other useful information after publication.

And to those suppliers of software who have not yet submitted software for Verification — the remedy is in your own hands.

Contents

Part I

Introduction to
Software Verification

The Publication

A significant aspect of the work which The National Computing Centre Limited carries out is concerned with the provision of information on computing topics to the community as a whole.

This it achieves by operating an on-demand information service based on several indexes of information concerned with the following computer subjects:
- software
- hardware
- installations
- services and background
- literature
- education courses

From time to time NCC provides publications, magnetic tapes, etc., which either summarize the information in a particular index or extract the information about a particular sub-topic for special consideration. A list of current services and publications is given in the Appendix.

This present publication contains a catalogue of information about items of computer software, all of which have been subjected to an examination process called Software Verification and all of which are contained in the NCC computer software index.

In this introductory part of the publication, and in order to provide an understanding of the information contained in the catalogue proper, the meaning of the term Software Verification will be defined and its potential value to both the supplier and user of software should become apparent.

In the second part the mechanics of submitting an item of software for Verification will be outlined, in order that those suppliers who would like their products to be included can be made aware of the requirements of Verification.

The third part of the publication explains how the potential software user can search the catalogue of Verified Software which is the substance of Part IV, according to particular requirements.

What is Software Verification?

We define Software Verification as follows:

> "Software Verification is a process which identifies, in detail, the questions which an experienced potential user should ask about a computer program. Software Verification should then provide the answers to those questions."

It will be shown later that the process of Verification involves requesting the appropriate information from the software supplier and then measuring the information against relevant and defined criteria.

Basically then, Software Verification is concerned with being able to assign a value to a computer program so that the potential user can choose which, of a number of similar programs, suits his requirements best — and always with the knowledge that the right questions have already been asked.

This it does by presenting the information about every program of a given type by identical means and thus, by subjecting each to an identical examination, can allow direct comparisons between similar programs.

In this respect Software Verification can be considered to be similar to consumer testing, although it is understandably a much more complex process than that would suggest.

Accordingly there can be no attempt to recommend a 'best buy' in general terms, for this will be very dependent upon the user's particular circumstances. Rather, what we would hope to achieve with Verification is to identify the particular characteristics of a software product in a consistent manner. And then, by identical presentation of those products, to allow the potential user to choose a particular one.

We have used the term 'software product' deliberately. For, although a computer program is rather intangible compared with, say, an item of hardware, there is no reason why it cannot be defined precisely, particularly to a potential user. We do not intend that the words 'product' and 'for sale' be used synonymously. We know of some programs which are 'for sale' but which cannot be regarded as defined products at all. Conversely we know programs which are 'free' but which will cost the user a great deal of money and time to implement, because they are not products either.

Finally, in our preamble to Software Verification, it is important to understand that the process is not the same as Software Validation, the latter being a process involving practical testing of the software. There is no practical testing involved in Verification, although it will refer to the results of such tests, if they are available.

The Process of Verification

In order to introduce Verification it has been necessary for NCC to carry out the following preliminary work:

1 Identify and list all the basic classes, or types, of software such as compilers, utilities, applications, etc.
2 Identify and list the component parts which together comprise a detailed definition of each type of software.
3 Establish criteria against which the answers to questions about the component parts for each type can be measured.
4 Establish a method of presenting the resulting information to the enquirer.

The work has so far resulted in the design of a questionnaire, the establishment of a measurement technique, the standardisation of terminology and the presentation of Verified information in the form of abstracts.

The mechanical process can then be simply resolved into:

1 Asking software suppliers to complete a questionnaire about each of their software products.

2 Measuring the answers supplied against the Verification criteria.

3 Re-contacting the supplier if the information is unsatisfactory in any respect.

4 For satisfactory information — creating a Verified abstract and, with the supplier's permission, providing the information to enquirers and potential users of the software.

In case that there is a suggestion that this is a theoretical approach, it must be stressed that it is the intention that Verification information shall be of a very practical nature indeed.

For, in addition to gathering information about a program as a program, Verification is very much concerned with the practical details of its operation. As an example we are concerned to know on which computer configuration(s) the program has *actually* run, rather than those on which it is thought that it ought to run.

We would now like to introduce the Software Verification questionnaire and show the manner in which an abstract of a Verified program is created.

The Software Verification Questionnaire

The method of collecting information for possible Verification, is by means of a standard questionnaire. A copy of such a questionnaire is contained in the pocket at the back of this publication.

At this early stage of the Verification process a single type of questionnaire is used to gather the very basic information about all types of computer programs. We will show later, that in the later stages of Verification, several kinds of questionnaire related to the particular type of program will have to be used but this need not concern us at this stage.

It will be seen that the Stage 1 Software Verification questionnaire requests information on the following subjects:

1 The name, address, telephone number and telex number of the supplier and the organisation by which he is employed.
2 The name, address, telephone number and telex number of any agent who has been appointed to act on the supplier's behalf.
3 The type of software, e.g. operating system, compiler, utility, etc.
4 The name of the software.
5 The purpose of the software.
6 The computer(s) on which the software has run successfully.
7 The mode of usage, e.g. batch, interactive, etc.
8 The programming language(s) in which it is written.
9 Its availability, e.g. bureau, for sale, etc.
10 Extra comment.
11 The supplier's signature.

As far as Verification is concerned this last item — the supplier's signature — is very important. For it is here that we ask the supplier to verify that the information which has been given on the questionnaire is a correct representation of the software.

The Verification Procedure

Upon receipt of completed questionnaires the Verification procedure is started. A record of all questionnaires is kept by means of the questionnaire reference number which is added to each questionnaire.

Completed questionnaires are thus recorded and immediately keypunched. Thus they are placed on temporary computer file until Verified. This allows easy editing of the information and automatic printing of a Verified abstract the format of which is discussed in the next section.

The Verification procedure consists of:

1 Determining whether the program is already on file. This can happen, in which case the supplier is queried.
2 If not already on file, allocating an abstract number which will be used as a reference for retrieval and updating purposes.

3 Determining whether the information is acceptable according to certain criteria. At this early stage of Verification this is reasonably straight-forward and consists of:

  a Scanning to determine if the information is complete, e.g. if computer details are missing the information cannot be Verified.

  b Scanning for minor errors such as spelling mistakes.

  c Scanning for anomalies such as non-existent computer types or programming languages.

  d Examination by an expert in the particular area of activity represented by the information.

These examinations are carried out upon the abstracted form of the information, which is printed from the temporary files at regular intervals. The form of the abstract is already, at this stage, the one represented by the abstracts in PART IV, although as yet unverified.

Minor errors, such as spelling mistakes, are corrected on-line to the computer by the use of a standard Editor.

More serious anomalies are referred back to the supplier for action, or explanation, and the procedure is then repeated.

Satisfactory abstracts are classed as Verified information with the approval of the Head of Information Division at NCC, and are then transferred from temporary file to NCC's master file of Verified Software. The supplier is informed accordingly.

One additional matter which has not yet been mentioned, is that each abstract is indexed for the purposes of retrieval. The indexing is carried out using terms obtained from The NCC Thesaurus of Computing Terms* together with other appropriate non-computing terms such as the supplier's name and address. The indexing terms currently used are:

Supplier's organisation
Agent (if any)
Name of Software
Machine(s)
Language(s)
Other terms

The 'other terms' (average about six) are selected from the abstract material to allow precise indexing.

The indexing terms are also placed on computer file and are used in an on-line retrieval mode to select abstracts, in particular for answering enquiries to NCC in an on-demand mode.

For details of the telephone answering service, covering other information as well as software, see Appendix.

The Verified Software Abstract

Reference has already been made, several times, to a standard abstract format. The information contained in a Verified Software abstract is listed under a number of subject headings. All the abstracts contained in Section 3 of the catalogue, contained in PART IV, are in the following standard format:

Abstract title
NCC Software Verification abstract (number)
Name of software
Type of software
Purpose of software

---

*"The NCC Thesaurus of Computing Terms" is published quarterly on a subscription basis or for outright sale. It has application in areas other than Computer Software. Further details may be had on request.

Configuration and operating system
Mode of usage
Language
Availability
Supplier's comments (if any)

Verification so far

Software Verification was launched in April 1971, at which time the membership of NCC was informed by letter, which also included a copy of the questionnaire.

Since that time a number of other selected organisations have also been requested to provide software information.

The general statistics of the situation in April 1972 are as follows:

    No. of questionnaires returned = 254
    No. of abstracts verified   = 199
    No. of abstracts rejected   =   10
    No. of abstracts in process   =   45

We feel that these figures are low but not disappointing. They reflect, more than any other factor, the care which has been taken to ensure that the information is correct by means of a rigorous procedure.

The low figure of rejects (10) is not surprising either, for in many cases we have re-contacted the supplier many times, helping him to raise his information to the required level before Verifying. At this stage the rejects tend to indicate the number of suppliers who were not willing to co-operate.

It is interesting to note that, before Verification, NCC operated an index of information about computer programs called the National Computer Program Index (NCPI). This contained information on about 6,000 programs and can still be referenced. However, very little of that information is now of value, particularly when it is compared with Verified information.

In other words, it is easy to collect information about software. It is not as easy to collect information of quality about software.

The Next Steps

At an early stage in our planning for Verification, it was decided to introduce the process in easy stages. The figures which have been given, and the information contained in our catalogue, relate to the basic level of Verification which we call Stage 1 Verification. In July 1972 the second stage of Verification will be introduced. This Stage 2 Verification asks for more detailed information about a software product, and if it reaches the required level it will be published as a Stage 2 abstract.

The subject matter of Stage 2 will include the following:

    Compiler(s) used to compile the program
    Library routines used
    Storage overlay details
    Core storage requirements
    Legal agreement on sale
    Constraints on use of program
    Availability of documentation
    Documentation standards used
    Method of release

Medium of release
Charges
Availability for bureau use
Maintenance provided
Installation support
Provision of demonstrations
Test data and results
Extent of current use
List of current users

Similarly, Stage 3, which is now being planned, will reach an even more detailed level of information and it is probable that different versions of the Stage 3 questionnaire will be produced for different types of software.

In addition it is important, we feel, that information should be updated at regular intervals of not less than one year and preferably six months. The regularisation of information collection, verification and dissemination assists in this area of updating.

Part II

Submitting Software
for Verification

Submission of Material

It is in the interest of the users of software products, and hence in the interest of suppliers, that as many products as possible are submitted for Verification and included in the catalogue.

Because of the wide circulation of the catalogue it is hoped that the software supplier will regard it as an inexpensive means of publicising his products.

All we ask the supplier to do is to spend a little time completing a questionnaire about each product. We have already mentioned that this publication contains a sample questionnaire. NCC would be pleased to receive these back, complete with product information and will then submit them to Verification.

The questionnaire is self-explanatory and contains the address of NCC for postal purposes.

If, for any reason, the sample questionnaire is missing from the pocket in the back of this catalogue, please ask for further copies, either by letter or by telephone. The address is:

Information Operations
The National Computing Centre Limited
Quay House
Quay Street
MANCHESTER
M3 3HU
Telephone: 061-832 9731   Telex: 668962

Completed and returned questionnaires will be acknowledged and the supplier kept informed of the progress in Verifying the information.

We will also be pleased to assist if difficulty is encountered in completing the questionnaire.

Part III

Using Verified
Software Information

In this part, the method of searching for and using the Verified Software Information, contained in PART IV, in the form of a catalogue, will be explained.

PART IV contains:

Section 1:   a main subject index which lists appropriate abstracts and their titles.

Section 2:   a list of abstract numbers and titles in numerical order.

Section 3:   a list of complete abstracts in abstract number order.

Section 4:   a list of organisations which have supplied information.

Searching for a Product

The main method of searching is to use the main subject index in Section 1. In this section the abstracts are classified in terms of:

a   The type of software, e.g. accounting, statistical application, compiler, etc.

b   The main computer series on which they run, e.g. IBM 360, ICL 1900, HONEYWELL 200, etc.

c   The mode of usage, i.e. batch, interactive, real-time.

d   The availability, i.e. bureau, for sale — or both.

For each index term there is a list of abstract numbers and, in the case of (a) above, titles which are relevant.

Having obtained an abstract number the main body of abstracts contained in Section 3 may then be referenced.

If the searching requirement is more complex, for example an *accounting* program, running on *IBM 360* in *batch* mode then an abstract number which appears separately under all three terms must be isolated. Since in general the lists of abstract numbers are small, this is not considered to be a very onerus operation. This simple method avoids printed combinatorial indexing, which might well be more confusing and has therefore been avoided.

If all that is required is a quick browse through all the abstracts, the list of abstract numbers vs abstract titles, contained in Section 2 will be useful, since some effort has been made to make the titles meaningful.

Assuming that an abstract has been isolated and referred to, it will be seen that the information that it contains is in the standard abstract format described in PART I.

Contact with Supplier

The abstracts in Section 3 do not contain supplier information. Should you wish to contact the supplier of, or agent for, a software product in the catalogue we request that you should contact NCC giving the abstract number. The required information will then be supplied.

This procedure is necessary in order that we can keep a record of the utilisation of our information.

The address to contact is:

Information Operations
The National Computing Centre Limited
Quay House
Quay Street
MANCHESTER
M3 3HU

or telephone: 061-832 9731 and ask for the telephone answering service;

or telex: 668962 — NCC MANCHESTER — including: "For the attention of Information Operations".

A list of those organisations which have supplied information resulting in Verified Software abstracts is given in Section 4 of the Catalogue.

NOTE: The catalogue of abstracts in Section 3 is in numerical order of abstract number. However, there are gaps in the sequence of numbers. These gaps are caused by abstracts which have not yet reached the Verification level.

Part IV

A Catalogue of
Verified Software

Subjects and abstract numbers

ACCOUNTING

a **General**

A34023	Laundry Accounting System
A34026	Institutional Management System, INFORM
A34027	Accountants Time Ledger, ACT
A34095	Actuarial and Financial Language, ACT

b **Cost Accounting**

A34038	Transport and Plant Costing System, TRP
A34048	Menu Costing
A34056	Management Job Cost Control Program, JCP
A34103	Payroll and Job Costing System
A34105	Job Cost Control, GREGBC
A34106	Job Cost Control, WAPJCC
A34109	Smiths Industries Stock Evaluation, SISTER
A34119	Professional Cost Accounting, PATOCAP
A34177	Cost Build Up and Presentation
A34227	Auditors Time Billing System

c **Sales**

A34014	Sales Package, CAMSALES
A34017	Sales Analysis Package
A34024	Sales Ledger System
A34040	Sales Package
A34051	I.C.D.P. Sales Ledger Package
A34066	Economic Data Services Sales Ledger Package
A34098	Sales Ledger Package, PK 17
A34111	Smiths Industries Group Sales Ledger
A34113	Smiths Industries Sales Analysis, C.A.
A34132	Sales Ledger and Credit Control
A34155	Sales Ledger Accounting, NOR-SAL, NOR-PLAN
A34228	Sales Ledger and Analysis Package

d **Purchase and Other Ledgers**

A34052	I.C.D.P. Purchase Ledger Package
A34096	Incomplete Records Package, PK 35
A34100	Purchase Ledger Package, PK 34
A34133	Bought and Nominal Ledger
A34156	Purchase Accounting System, NOR-PURLA, NOR-PURLAN
A34160	Nominal Ledger with Budgetary Control
A34229	Purchase Ledger and Analysis Package

e **Investments/Shares**

A34006	Share Register
A34022	Share Registration Package
A34025	Investment Management System, INVEST
A34131	Portfolio Performance

f **Miscellaneous**

A34099	Budgetary Control Package, PK 32
A34108	Smiths Industries Group Invoice Package
A34134	Cash Transfer Tape Conversion for Interbank Transactions
A34136	Arlington Inventory Management System, AIMS
A34173	Discounted Cash Flow, CASHFLO
A34212	File Interrogation and Reporting System
A34217	AUDITFIND — Information Retrieval with Auditing Requirements

EDUCATION

A34012	11 + Results Analysis
A34071	Business Simulation-Dynamic Restaurant MODELS 1, 2
A34174	Business Game — Dynamic Restaurant Model Series 3
A34188	Business Game — Dynamic Hotel Model Series 1

ENGINEERING APPLICATIONS

a   Structural Engineering/Design

(i) General

A34013	Structural Analysis by Finite Elements, ELFIN
A34054	General Purpose Structural Analysis Program, LEAP
A34135	R.C. Design, Detailing, ABCONS
A34182	Structural Analysis System, ASAS
A34211	Dynamic and Static Analysis by Finite Element Techniques

(ii) Walls

A34060	Plane Shear Wall Analysis
A34061	Plane Shear Wall Analysis

(iii) Joists, Beams, Spans

A34082	Section Constants for Joists
A34084	Bending Moments, Rolling Load, Simply Supported Span
A34093	Plastic Constants for Joists
A34094	Max. End Reaction — Rolling Loads over Adj. Spans
A34122	Continuous Beam Analysis by Influence Coefficients, SINCOF
A34125	Continuous Beam Influence Lines, INFLIN
A34126	Prestressed Beam Design, PRESBEAM
A34127	Standard Prestressed Beam Design, STANBEAM

(iv) Other Structural Parts

A34057	Tower Design Suite, DCTOWER, SCTOWER, FOUNDATION, SAGTENS
A34081	Floor Design (Simply Supported Beams)
A34083	Section Constants for built-up columns
A34085	Properties of Crane Girders
A34086	Axial Column Stress to BS 449 Table 17
A34087	Frame Analysis by Flexibility Method
A34088	Column Design
A34089	Section Constants for Rolled Steel Angles
A34090	Section Constants for Rolled Steel Channels
A34091	Section Constants for Bulb Flats with Plate
A34092	Section Constants for Bulb Flats
A34123	Interactive Pile Group Analysis, PINT
A34128	Section Design and Optimisation, SECTION
A34129	Westergaard Analysis of Slabs, WESTGARD
A34147	Shell, Space-frame, Finite-element Package, FESS 2

b   Detailing/Schedules

A34053	R.C. Detailing Suite, BARSHED, BEAMDET, COLDET, PLANE
A34055	Optimised Reinforcement Bar Cutting, CUTSHED, SORTSHED
A34124	Bar Bending Schedules, BENSCH

c   Quantity Surveying

A34028	Quantity Surveyors Bills of Quantity
A34058	Bills of Quantities and their Re-analysis
A34064	Quantity Surveying Package, MULTIBILL 2, SLID, EPC, BILLING
A34121	Quantity Surveying Package

d   **Gases**
           A34141   Viscosity of a Gas at a High Pressure
           A34142   Density and Viscosity of Water and Steam
           A34143   Gas Deviation Coefficient for Air
           A34144   Specific Heat Ratio of a Mixture of Gases
           A34145   Density of Moist Gases
           A34146   Fluid Flow to B.S. 1042

e   **Chemical**
           A34152   Resource Allocation, Piping Isometrics, RAPID

FILE HANDLING

a   **Report Generators/Information Retrieval**
           A34015   System for Audit Technical Assistance, STRATA
           A34075   Filetab Report Generator, FILETAB
           A34078   Listing, Updating, Sorting, and Totalling Package, LUST
           A34138   Master File Interrogation, PSB
           A34139   File Retrieval and Reporting System, RSVP
           A34158   Select and Copy Utility, SELCOPY
           A34170   Thesaurus Management System
           A34212   File Interrogation and Reporting System
           A34217   AUDIT FIND — Information Retrieval with Auditing Requirements

b   **File Manipulation**
           A34016   File Maintenance System, POLYFILE
           A34110   File Processing in Cobol using Plan Routines
           A34178   File Management Program, DATAFLIP

c   **Other**
           A34010   Tabulation Suite, SIEVE, TABL, TEST
           A34020   Operating System, Supervisory Program
           A34037   Data Vetting Program Generator, Data Filter
           A34039   Survey Data Analysis
           A34042   Management Information System, EMPRENT
           A34059   Transaction Retrieval from Card File, CASH PULL
           A34069   CBH Schedule Program, SPS
           A34097   Membership Directory Package, PK 05
           A34120   Direct Mail Labelling Package
           A34134   Cash Transfer Tape Conversion for Interbank Transactions

LOCAL GOVERNMENT

           A34185   Employment Survey Program
           A34186   Population Projection Program
           A34195   Employment Tape Analysis
           A34196   Retail Sales Allocation Model
           A34197   Lowry Model, Urban Development
           A34198   Urban Plan Evaluation Model
           A34199   Population Forecasting
           A34200   Shopping Model
           A34201   Employment Statistics
           A34202   Sub-regional Activity Allocation Model
           A34203   Gravitational Attraction and Interaction between Locations
           A34208   Population Projection
           A34222   Shopping Model
           A34223   Population Projection

MANAGEMENT INFORMATION SYSTEMS

A34056	Management Job Cost Control Program, JCP
A34069	CBH Schedule Program, SPS
A34070	CBH General Schedule Program, GSP

OPERATIONAL RESEARCH APPLICATION

A34019	Delivery Route Scheduling, TRANSIT
A34043	Road Network Analysis, ROADNET
A34030	Depot Location Program, DEPSIT
A34071	Business Simulation-Dynamic Restaurant Models 1, 2
A34073	Sira Forecasting Suite
A34140	TRIPLAN — Vehicle Scheduling
A34174	Business Game, Dynamic Restaurant Model Series 3
A34188	Business Game — Dynamic Hotel Model Series 1
A34196	Retail Sales Allocation Model
A34197	Lowry Model, Urban Development
A34198	Urban Plan Evaluation Model
A34199	Population Forecasting
A34200	Shopping Model
A34202	Sub-regional Activity Allocation Model
A34208	Population Projection
A34220	Linear Programming Matrix Generator for Distribution Problems
A34222	Shopping Model
A34223	Population Projection

PAYROLL

A34005	Professional Salary Service, PROCESS
A34021	Salary Payroll System
A34029	General Purpose Payroll System, UNIPAY
A34045	Odhams (Watford) Payroll
A34050	I.C.D.P. Payroll Package
A34103	Payroll and Job Costing System
A34112	Smiths Industries Modular Bonus and Weekly Payroll
A34114	S.I. Pension Payroll, POPSI
A34153	Modular Accounting, Weekly, Monthly Payroll
A34159	Weekly, Monthly Payroll, EASYPAY
A34230	Payroll Package

PRODUCTION AND PROJECT MANAGEMENT

a   General

A34009	Production Control for Weaving Industry, Sunnyside System
A34069	CBH Schedule Program, SPS
A34070	CBH General Schedule Program, GSP
A34080	Workshop Analysis and Scheduling Procedure, WASP
A34104	Project Control System
A34161	Project Control Package, PROJECT-MASTER
A34192	Burroughs Production Control System
A34193	PROMIS — Project Oriented Management Information System

b   Costing

A34056	Management Job Cost Control Program, JCP
A34103	Payroll and Job Costing System
A34105	Job Cost Control, GREGBC
A34106	Job Cost Control, WAPJCC
A34119	Professional Cost Accounting, PATOCAP
A34177	Cost Build up and Presentation
A34227	Auditors Time Billing System

c   **Network**
      A34042   Management Information System, EMPRENT
      A34068   Precedence Diagram Analysis ,PDA
      A34171   Project Network Analysis, CAPSTAN
      A34172   Project Engineer Scheduling, PEST
      A34193   PROMIS — Project Oriented Management Information System

d   **Stock Control**
      A34065   Economic Data Services Stock Control Package
      A34108   Smiths Industries Group Invoice Package
      A34109   Smiths Industries Stock Evaluation, SISTER
      A34136   Arlington Inventory Management System, AIMS

e   **Parts Explosion**
      A34067   Economic Data Services Parts Explosion Program
      A34107   Smiths Industries Breaking and Netting Routines, BANG

RESERVATION AND TICKETING
      A34008   Reservation and Ticketing System, TICKETRON

SCIENTIFIC APPLICATION
      A34046   Dietary Analysis by Ingredients
      A34047   Dietary Analysis by Standard Recipes
      A34048   Menu Costing
      A34049   Random Menu Generation
      A34141   Viscosity of a Gas at a High Pressure
      A34142   Density and Viscosity of Water and Steam
      A34143   Gas Deviation Coefficient for Air
      A34144   Specific Heat Ratio of a Mixture of Gases
      A34145   Density of Moist Gases
      A34146   Fluid Flow to B.S. 1042
      A34148   Automatic Programming and Scaling of Equations, APSE
      A34168   Batch Distillation

STATISTICAL APPLICATION (COMMERCIAL)
      A34010   Tabulation Suite, SIEVE, TABL, TEST
      A34017   Sales Analysis Package
      A34018   Job Evaluation and Wages Drift System
      A34039   Survey Data Analysis
      A34095   Actuarial and Financial Language, ACT
      A34113   Smiths Industries Sales Analysis, C.A.
      A34116   Smiths Industries Sales Analysis 2, UA
      A34138   Master File Interrogation, PSB
      A34185   Employment Survey Program
      A34195   Employment Tape Analysis
      A34201   Employment Statistics

STATISTICAL APPLICATION (SCIENTIFIC)
      A34063   Multiple Regression with Element Analysis, MRAEA
      A34073   Sira Forecasting Suite
      A34074   Sira Regression Package
      A34169   Statistical Computing Package, ASCOP
      A34186   Population Projection Program
      A34204   Component Score Program
      A34206   Correlation Matrix
      A34209   Multiple Stepwise Regression Analysis

SYSTEMS PROGRAMS

A34002	Spooling System, GRASP 2
A34003	Telecommunications Access Method, TAM
A34020	Operating System, Supervisory Program
A34062	Assembler for Philips 500, U30
A34148	Automatic Programming and Scaling of Equations, APSE
A34190	Real Time Executive for Modular One

UTILITIES

a   **Module and Program Testing**

A34004	Test Data File Generation, TDFG
A34007	Program Module Testing System, MTS
A34011	Program Module linking program, ASSEMBLER PLUS
A34041	ICL 1900 Testing Software
A34101	Independent Module Development Package, IMD
A34115	Royal Program Module Tester
A34162	DOS 360 Module Test Bed, M TEST 360
A34163	Program Module Test Bed, MTB 360

b   **Validation/Checking**

A34037	Data Vetting Program Generator, DATA FILTER
A34077	Input, Validate, Output and Report Subroutine, IVOR
A34079	Data Field Checking Routine
A34102	Record Validation Language
A34117	Smiths Industries General Card Batch Validation, SMBV
A34154	Automatic Input Validation, NORVET

c   **Input**

| A34036 | Utility Routines for Tape Encoder Input, ENCOSUB |
| A34164 | Card Input Program |

d   **Print**

A34118	S.I. Simulated Off-line Print Program, SMPR
A34165	Tape Edit Pattern Search
A34166	Magnetic Tape Print Program
A34175	Paper Tape Listing, SMPT

e   **Flowchart/Crossreference Listings**

| A34149 | Cobol Source Deck Cross-Referencing, CROSS-REF |
| A34150 | Cobol Source Deck Flowcharting, COBOLDIAGRAMMER |

f   **Plotting**

| A34167 | Graphplotting System |
| A34183 | Lineprinter Mapping System, SYM1 |

g   **Sort**

| A34130 | General Purpose Core Sort (ICL 1900) |
| A34137 | Std. Mag. Tape Sort Timings |

h   **Miscellaneous**

A34000	Check Digit Generation
A34044	Translation of 4100 Algol to 1900 Algol, EDALG
A34134	Cash Transfer Tape Conversion for Interbank Transactions

BURROUGHS B500 SERIES
A34020   A34024   A34025   A34153   A34192   A34193

CDC 1700
A34008

CDC 3300
A34152

CDC 3600
A34138

CDC 6600
A34053   A34054   A34057   A34068   A34069   A34070   A34080
A34095   A34147   A34211

COMPUTER TECHNOLOGY MODULAR ONE
A34190

DEC PDP SERIES
A34010

HONEYWELL 200 SERIES
A34005   A34012   A34021   A34024   A34025   A34026   A34027
A34028   A34029   A34050   A34051   A34052   A34120   A34121
A34202   A34203   A34204   A34206   A34208   A34209   A34227
A34228   A34229   A34230

HONEYWELL G-200 SERIES
A34068

HONEYWELL G-600 SERIES
A34068   A34148

IBM 1130
A34105   A34220

IBM 1400 SERIES
A34029

IBM 1620
A34046

IBM 360 SERIES
A34002   A34003   A34004   A34007   A34011   A34013   A34015
A34016   A34019   A34029   A34037   A34040   A34043   A34045
A34053   A34054   A34055   A34056   A34057   A34059   A34064
A34077   A34079   A34080   A34095   A34096   A34097   A34098
A34099   A34100   A34101   A34102   A34103   A34104   A34106
A34115   A34119   A34131   A34136   A34139   A34147   A34148
A34149   A34150   A34154   A34155   A34156   A34158   A34159
A34160   A34161   A34162   A34163   A34169   A34171   A34172
A34173   A34178   A34182   A34183   A34195   A34196   A34197
A34198   A34199   A34200   A34201   A34212

IBM 370 SERIES
A34002   A34029   A34201   A34212

IBM 7094
A34095

ICL 1500
A34029

ICL 4100 SERIES
A34022   A34042   A34073   A34074

ICL 1900 SERIES
A34000   A34006   A34009   A34014   A34018   A34019   A34021
A34029   A34036   A34038   A34039   A34040   A34041   A34043
A34044   A34046   A34047   A34048   A34049   A34060   A34061
A34065   A34066   A34067   A34071   A34075   A34077   A34078
A34080   A34081   A34082   A34083   A34084   A34085   A34086
A34087   A34088   A34089   A34090   A34091   A34092   A34093
A34094   A34095   A34104   A34107   A34108   A34109   A34110
A34111   A34112   A34113   A34114   A34116   A34117   A34118
A34130   A34132   A34133   A34134   A34135   A34140   A34141
A34142   A34143   A34144   A34145   A34146   A34147   A34148
A34152   A34154   A34155   A34156   A34159   A34167   A34169
A34170   A34171   A34174   A34175   A34177   A34183   A34185
A34186   A34188   A34217   A34222   A34223

ICL 503
A34168

ICL 803
A34058   A34168

ICL ATLAS
A34122   A34123   A34124   A34125   A34126   A34127   A34128
A34129   A34135   A34169

ICL KDF9
A34148

ICL SYSTEM 4
A34007   A34011   A34017   A34029   A34037   A34101   A34137
A34154   A34155   A34156   A34164   A34165   A34166   A34173
A34183

MARCONI-ELLIOTT 900
A34023   A34063

PHILIPS DATA
A34062

RCA SPECTRA 70
A34137

UNIVAC 1100 SERIES
A34030   A34054   A34080   A34095   A34146   A34147   A34148
A34152   A34182

XDS SIGMA SERIES
A34053   A34182

BATCH

A34000	A34004	A34005	A34006	A34007	A34009	A34010
A34011	A34012	A34013	A34014	A34015	A34016	A34017
A34018	A34019	A34020	A34021	A34022	A34023	A34024
A34025	A34026	A34027	A34028	A34029	A34030	A34036
A34037	A34038	A34039	A34040	A34041	A34042	A34043
A34044	A34045	A34046	A34047	A34048	A34049	A34050
A34051	A34052	A34053	A34054	A34055	A34056	A34057
A34058	A34059	A34060	A34061	A34062	A34064	A34065
A34066	A34067	A34068	A34069	A34070	A34071	A34073
A34074	A34075	A34077	A34078	A34079	A34080	A34081
A34082	A34083	A34084	A34085	A34086	A34087	A34088
A34089	A34090	A34091	A34092	A34093	A34094	A34095
A34096	A34097	A34098	A34099	A34100	A34101	A34102
A34103	A34104	A34105	A34106	A34107	A34108	A34109
A34110	A34111	A34112	A34113	A34114	A34115	A34116
A34117	A34118	A34119	A34120	A34121	A34130	A34131
A34132	A34133	A34134	A34135	A34136	A34137	A34138
A34139	A34140	A34141	A34142	A34143	A34144	A34145
A34146	A34147	A34148	A34149	A34150	A34152	A34153
A34154	A34155	A34156	A34158	A34159	A34160	A34161
A34162	A34163	A34164	A34165	A34166	A34167	A34168
A34169	A34170	A34171	A34172	A34173	A34174	A34175
A34177	A34178	A34182	A34183	A34185	A34186	A34188
A34190	A34192	A34193	A34195	A34196	A34197	A34198
A34199	A34200	A34201	A34202	A34203	A34204	A34206
A34208	A34209	A34211	A34212	A34217	A34220	A34222
A34223	A34227	A34228	A34229	A34230		

INTERACTIVE

A34002	A34003	A34020	A34055	A34056	A34057	A34063
A34068	A34095	A34123	A34126	A34190		

REAL-TIME

A34002	A34008	A34020	A34122	A34124	A34125	A34127
A34128	A34129	A34190				

BUREAU OR SALE

A34000	A34003	A34005	A34007	A34008	A34010	A34011
A34013	A34014	A34015	A34016	A34017	A34018	A34020
A34021	A34022	A34024	A34025	A34026	A34027	A34028
A34029	A34030	A34036	A34037	A34038	A34041	A34043
A34050	A34051	A34052	A34053	A34054	A34055	A34056
A34057	A34059	A34064	A34065	A34066	A34067	A34068
A34069	A34070	A34073	A34074	A34075	A34077	A34078
A34080	A34094	A34095	A34096	A34097	A34098	A34099
A34100	A34101	A34103	A34104	A34105	A34106	A34107
A34108	A34109	A34111	A34112	A34113	A34114	A34116
A34117	A34118	A34119	A34124	A34127	A34128	A34129
A34131	A34132	A34133	A34134	A34136	A34137	A34139
A34140	A34147	A34148	A34149	A34150	A34152	A34153
A34154	A34155	A34158	A34159	A34160	A34161	A34162
A34163	A34164	A34165	A34166	A34167	A34168	A34169
A34170	A34171	A34172	A34173	A34175	A34177	A34182
A34183	A34202	A34203	A34204	A34206	A34208	A34209
A34212	A34220	A34222	A34223	A34227	A34228	A34229
A34230						

BUREAU SERVICE ONLY

A34009	A34040	A34042	A34046	A34047	A34048	A34049
A34058	A34060	A34061	A34071	A34081	A34082	A34083
A34084	A34085	A34086	A34087	A34088	A34089	A34090
A34091	A34092	A34093	A34120	A34121	A34122	A34123
A34125	A34126	A34135	A34174	A34188	A34192	A34193
A34211						

FOR SALE ONLY

A34002	A34004	A34006	A34012	A34019	A34023	A34039
A34044	A34045	A34062	A34063	A34079	A34102	A34110
A34115	A34130	A34138	A34141	A34142	A34143	A34144
A34145	A34146	A34156	A34178	A34185	A34186	A34190
A34217						

NOTE: The use of the word 'sale' does not imply the possibility of outright sale but may mean that the program can be licensed. For detailed conditions the supplier should be contacted via NCC. This is particularly true of the following abstracts:

A34195, A34196, A34197, A34198, A34199, A34200, A34201.

Abstract numbers and titles

LIST OF SELECTED ABSTRACT NUMBERS AND TITLES PRINTED ON 19/04/72

NUMBER   TITLE

A34000 CHECK DIGIT GENERATION

A34002 SPOOLING SYSTEM,GRASP 2

A34003 TELECOMMUNICATIONS ACCESS METHOD,TAM

A34004 TEST DATA FILE GENERATION,TDFG

A34005 PROFESSIONAL SALARY SERVICE,PROCESS

A34006 SHARE REGISTER

A34007 PROGRAM MODULE TESTING SYSTEM,MTS

A34008 RESERVATION AND TICKETING SYSTEM,TICKETRON

A34009 PRODUCTION CONTROL FOR WEAVING INDUSTRY,SUNNYSIDE SYSTEM

A34010 TABULATION SUITE,SIEVE,TABL,TEST

A34011 PROGRAM MODULE LINKING PROGRAM,ASSEMBLER PLUS

A34012 11+ RESULTS ANALYSIS

A34013 STRUCTURAL ANALYSIS BY FINITE ELEMENTS,ELFIN

A34014 SALES PACKAGE,CAMSALES

A34015 SYSTEM FOR AUDIT TECHNICAL ASSISTANCE,STRATA

A34016 FILE MAINTENANCE SYSTEM,POLYFILE

A34017 SALES ANALYSIS PACKAGE

A34018 JOB EVALUATION AND WAGES DRIFT SYSTEM

A34019 DELIVERY ROUTE SCHEDULING,TRANSIT

A34020 OPERATING SYSTEM,SUPERVISORY PROGRAM

A34021 SALARY PAYROLL SYSTEM

A34022 SHARE REGISTRATION PACKAGE

A34023 LAUNDRY ACCOUNTING SYSTEM

A34024 SALES LEDGER SYSTEM

A34025 INVESTMENT MANAGEMENT SYSTEM,INVEST

A34026 INSTITUTIONAL MANAGEMENT SYSTEM,INFORM

A34027 ACCOUNTANTS TIME LEDGER,ACT

A34028 QUANTITY SURVEYORS BILLS OF QUANTITY

A34029 GENERAL PURPOSE PAYROLL SYSTEM,UNIPAY

A34030 DEPOT LOCATION PROGRAM,DEPSIT

A34036 UTILITY ROUTINES FOR TAPE ENCODER INPUT,ENCOSUB

A34037 DATA VETTING PROGRAM GENERATOR,DATA FILTER

A34038 TRANSPORT AND PLANT COSTING SYSTEM,TRP

A34039 SURVEY DATA ANALYSIS

A34040 SALES PACKAGE

A34041 ICL 1900 TESTING SOFTWARE

A34042 MANAGEMENT INFORMATION SYSTEM,EMPRENT

A34043 ROAD NETWORK ANALYSIS,ROADNET

A34044 TRANSLATION OF 4100 ALGOL TO 1900 ALGOL,EDALG

A34045 ODHAMS (WATFORD) PAYROLL

A34046 DIETARY ANALYSIS BY INGREDIENTS

A34047 DIETARY ANALYSIS BY STANDARD RECIPES

A34048 MENU COSTING

A34049 RANDOM MENU GENERATION

A34050 I.C.D.P. PAYROLL PACKAGE

A34051 I.C.D.P. SALES LEDGER PACKAGE

A34052 I.C.D.P. PURCHASE LEDGER PACKAGE

A34053 R.C. DETAILING SUITE,BARSHED,BEAMDET,COLDET,PLANE

A34054 GENERAL PURPOSE STRUCTURAL ANALYSIS PROGRAM,LEAP

A34055 OPTIMISED REINFORCEMENT BAR CUTTING,CUTSHED,SORTSHED

A34056 MANAGEMENT JOB COST CONTROL PROGRAM,JCP

A34057 TOWER DESIGN SUITE,DCTOWER,SCTOWER,FOUNDATION,SAGTENS

A34058 BILLS OF QUANTITIES & THEIR RE-ANALYSIS

A34059 TRANSACTION RETRIEVAL FROM CARD FILE,CASH PULL

A34060 PLANE SHEAR WALL ANALYSIS

A34061 PLANE SHEAR WALL ANALYSIS

A34062 ASSEMBLER FOR PHILIPS 500,U30

A34063 MULTIPLE REGRESSION WITH ELEMENT ANALYSIS,MRAEA

A34064 QUANTITY SURVEYING PACKAGE,MULTIBILL 2,SLID,EPC,BILLING

A34065 ECONOMIC DATA SERVICES STOCK CONTROL PACKAGE

A34066 ECONOMIC DATA SERVICES SALES LEDGER PACKAGE

A34067 ECONOMIC DATA SERVICES PARTS EXPLOSION PROGRAM

A34068 PRECEDENCE DIAGRAM ANALYSIS,PDA

A34069 CBH SCHEDULE PROGRAM,SPS

A34070 CBH GENERAL SCHEDULE PROGRAM,GSP

A34071 BUSINESS SIMULATION-DYNAMIC RESTAURANT MODELS,1,2

A34073 SIRA FORECASTING SUITE

A34074 SIRA REGRESSION PACKAGE

A34075 FILETAB REPORT GENERATOR,FILETAB

A34077 INPUT,VALIDATE,OUTPUT,&REPORT SUBROUTINE,IVOR

A34078 LISTING,UPDATING,SORTING,& TOTALLING PACKAGE,LUST

A34079 DATA FIELD CHECKING ROUTINE

A34080 WORKSHOP ANALYSIS &SCHEDULING PROCEDURE,WASP

A34081 FLOOR DESIGN(SIMPLY SUPPORTED BEAMS)

A34082 SECTION CONSTANTS FOR JOISTS

A34083 SECTION CONSTANTS FOR BUILT UP COLUMNS

A34084 BENDING MOMENTS,ROLLING LOAD,SIMPLY SUPPORTED SPAN

A34085 PROPERTIES OF CRANE GIRDERS

A34086 AXIAL COLUMN STRESS TO BS 449 TABLE 17

A34087 FRAME ANALYSIS BY FLEXIBILITY METHOD

A34088 COLUMN DESIGN

A34089 SECTION CONSTANTS FOR ROLLED STEEL ANGLES

A34090 SECTION CONSTANTS FOR ROLLED STEEL CHANNELS

A34091 SECTION CONSTANTS FOR BULB FLATS WITH PLATE

A34092 SECTION CONSTANTS FOR BULB FLATS

A34093 PLASTIC CONSTANTS FOR JOISTS

A34094 MAX. END REACTION -ROLLING LOADS OVER ADJ. SPANS

A34095 ACTURIAL AND FINANCIAL LANGUAGE,ACT

A34096 INCOMPLETE RECORDS PACKAGE,PK 35

A34097 MEMBERSHIP DIRECTORY PACKAGE,PK 05

A34098 SALES LEDGER PACKAGE,PK 17

A34099 BUDGETARY CONTROL PACKAGE,PK 32

A34100 PURCHASE LEDGER PACKAGE,PK 34

A34101 INDEPENDENT MODULE DEVELOPMENT PACKAGE,IMD

A34102 RECORD VALIDATION LANGUAGE

A34103 PAYROLL &JOB COSTING SYSTEM

A34104 PROJECT CONTROL SYSTEM

A34105 JOB COST CONTROL,GREGBC

A34106 JOB COST CONTROL,WAPJCC

A34107 SMITHS INDUSTRIES BREAKING & NETTING ROUTINES,BANG

A34108 SMITHS INDUSTRIES GROUP INVOICE PACKAGE

A34109 SMITHS INDUSTRIES STOCK EVALUATION,SISTER

A34110 FILE PROCESSING IN COBOL USING PLAN ROUTINES

A34111 SMITHS INDUSTRIES GROUP SALES LEDGER

A34112 SMITHS INDUSTRIES MODULAR BONUS & WEEKLY PAYROLL

A34113 SMITHS INDUSTRIES SALES ANALYSIS,C,A,

A34114 S.I. PENSION PAYROLL,POPSI

A34115 ROYAL PROGRAM MODULE TESTER

A34116 SMITHS INDUSTRIES SALES ANALYSIS 2,UA

A34117 SMITHS INDUSTRIES GENERAL CARD BATCH VALIDATION,SMBV

A34118 S.I. SIMULATED OFF-LINE PRINT PROGRAM,SMPR

A34119 PROFESSIONAL COST ACCOUNTING,PATOCAP

A34120 DIRECT MAIL LABELLING PACKAGE

A34121 QUANTITY SURVEYING PACKAGE

A34122 CONTINUOUS BEAM ANALYSIS BY INFLUENCE COEFFICIENTS,SINCOF

A34123 INTERACTIVE PILE GROUP ANALYSIS,PINT

A34124 BAR BENDING SCHEDULES,BENSCH

A34125 CONTINUOUS BEAM INFLUENCE LINES,INFLIN

A34126 PRESTRESSED BEAM DESIGN,PRESBEAM

A34127 STANDARD PRESTRESSED BEAM DESIGN,STANBEAM

A34128 SECTION DESIGN AND OPTIMISATION,SECTION

A34129 WESTERGAARD ANALYSIS OF SLABS,WESTGARD

A34130 GENERAL PURPOSE CORE SORT (ICL 1900)

A34131 PORTFOLIO PERFORMANCE

A34132 SALES LEDGER AND CREDIT CONTROL

A34133 BOUGHT AND NOMINAL LEDGER

A34134 CASH TRANSFER TAPE CONVERSION FOR INTERBANK TRANSACTIONS

A34135 REINFORCED CONCRETE DESIGN,DETAILING,ABCONS

A34136 ARLINGTON INVENTORY MANAGEMENT SYSTEM,AIMS

A34137 STD. MAG. TAPE SORT TIMINGS

A34138 MASTER FILE INTERROGATION,PSB

A34139 FILE RETRIEVAL AND REPORTING SYSTEM,RSVP

A34140 TRIPLAN - VEHICLE SCHEDULING

A34141 VISCOSITY OF A GAS AT A HIGH PRESSURE

A34142 DENSITY AND VISCOSITY OF WATER AND STEAM

A34143 GAS DEVIATION COEFFICIENT FOR AIR

A34144 SPECIFIC HEAT RATIO OF A MIXTURE OF GASES

A34145 DENSITY OF MOIST GASES

A34146 FLUID FLOW TO B.S. 1042

A34147 SHELL,SPACE-FRAME,FINITE-ELEMENT PACKAGE,FESS 2

A34148 AUTOMATIC PROGRAMMING & SCALING OF EQUATIONS,APSE

A34149 COBOL SOURCE DECK CROSS-REFERENCING,CROSS-REF

A34150 COBOL SOURCE DECK FLOWCHARTING,COBOLDIAGRAMMER

A34152 RESOURCE ALLOCATION,PIPING ISOMETRICS,RAPID

A34153 MODULAR ACCOUNTING,WEEKLY,MONTHLY PAYROLL

A34154 AUTOMATIC INPUT VALIDATION,NORVET

A34155 SALES LEDGER ACCOUNTING,NOR-SAL,NOR-PLAN

A34156 PURCHASE ACCOUNTING SYSTEM,NOR-PURLA,NOR-PURLAN

A34158 SELECT & COPY UTILITY,SELCOPY

A34159 WEEKLY,MONTHLY PAYROLL,EASYPAY

A34160 NOMINAL LEDGER WITH BUDGETARY CONTROL

A34161 PROJECT CONTROL PACKAGE,PROJECT-MASTER

A34162 DOS 360 MODULE TEST BED, M TEST 360

A34163 PROGRAM MODULE TEST BED,MTB 360

A34164 CARD INPUT PROGRAM

A34165 TAPE EDIT PATTERN SEARCH

A34166 MAGNETIC TAPE PRINT PROGRAM

A34167 GRAPHPLOTTING SYSTEM

A34168 BATCH DISTILLATION

A34169 STATISTICAL COMPUTING PACKAGE,ASCOP

A34170 THESAURUS MANAGEMENT SYSTEM

A34171 PROJECT NETWORK ANALYSIS,CAPSTAN

A34172 PROJECT ENGINEER SCHEDULING,PEST

A34173 DISCOUNTED CASH FLOW,CASHFLO

A34174 BUSINESS GAME,DYNAMIC RESTAURANT MODEL,SERIES 3

A34175 PAPER TAPE LISTING,SMPT

A34177 COST BUILD UP AND PRESENTATION

A34178 FILE MANAGEMENT PROGRAM,DATAFLIP

A34182 STRUCTURAL ANALYSIS SYSTEM,ASAS

A34183 LINEPRINTER MAPPING SYSTEM,SYM1

A34185 EMPLOYMENT SURVEY PROGRAM

A34186 POPULATION PROJECTION PROGRAM

A34188 BUSINESS GAME-DYNAMIC HOTEL MODEL SERIES 1

A34190 REAL TIME EXECUTIVE FOR MODULAR ONE

A34192 BURROUGHS PRODUCTION CONTROL SYSTEM

A34193 PROMIS - PROJECT ORIENTED MANAGEMENT INFORMATION SYSTEM

A34195 EMPLOYMENT TAPE ANALYSIS

A34196 RETAIL SALES ALLOCATION MODEL

A34197 LOWRY MODEL, URBAN DEVELOPMENT

A34198 URBAN PLAN EVALUATION PROGRAM

A34199 POPULATION FORECASTING

A34200 SHOPPING MODEL

A34201 EMPLOYMENT STATISTICS

A34202 SUB REGIONAL ACTIVITY ALLOCATION MODEL

A34203 GRAVITATIONAL ATTRACTION AND INTERACTION BETWEEN LOCATIONS

A34204 COMPONENT SCORE PROGRAM

A34206 CORRELATION MATRIX

A34208 POPULATION PROJECTION

A34209 MULTIPLE STEPWISE REGRESSION ANALYSIS

A34211 DYNAMIC AND STATIC ANALYSIS BY FINITE ELEMENT TECHNIQUES

A34212 FILE INTERROGATION AND REPORTING SYSTEM

A34217 AUDITFIND - INFORMATION RETRIEVAL WITH AUDITING REQUIREMENTS

A34220 LINEAR PROGRAMMING MATRIX GENERATOR FOR DISTRIBUTION PROBLEMS

A34222 SHOPPING MODEL

A34223 POPULATION PROJECTION

A34227 AUDITORS TIME BILLING SYSTEM

A34228 SALES LEDGER AND ANALYSIS PROGRAM

A34229 PURCHASE LEDGER AND ANALYSIS

A34230 PAYROLL PACKAGE

Numerical list of verified abstracts

NCC STAGE 1 SOFTWARE VERIFICATION ABSTRACT A34000

NAME OF SOFTWARE
  ACCOUNT AND STOCK NUMBER GENERATION

TYPE OF SOFTWARE
  ACCOUNTING

PURPOSE OF SOFTWARE
  PRINTS LISTS OF NUMBERS TOGETHER WITH EITHER MODULUS 10 OR
  MODULUS 11 CHECK DIGIT ACCORDING TO NUMBER RANGES, LINE
  SPACE AND NUMBER OF COLUMNS SPECIFIED. MODULUS AND/OR
  WEIGHTING FACTORS ARE VARIABLE

CONFIGURATION AND OPERATING SYSTEM
  ICL 1900 SERIES

  HAS RUN SUCCESSFULLY ON ICL 1902
  AMOUNT OF PRIMARY STORAGE 4K-8K WORDS
  1 LINE PRINTER
  1 PAPER TAPE READER
  RUN UNDER OPERATING SYSTEM EXECUTIVE

MODE OF USAGE
  BATCH

LANGUAGE
  PLAN

AVAILABILITY
  PROGRAM MAY BE AVAILABLE FOR USE OUTSIDE SUPPLIERS
  ORGANISATION. PROGRAM AVAILABLE AS A BUREAU SERVICE

SUPPLIERS COMMENT
  INFORMATION IS FREELY AVAILABLE. PROGRAM MAY BE USED ON
  SUPPLIERS MACHINE (AT MODEST COST) OR ELSEWHERE
  N.B. LINE PRINTER TYPE 1933/2

      COPYRIGHT NCC 1972   PRINTED ON 19/04/72

NCC STAGE 1 SOFTWARE VERIFICATION ABSTRACT A34002

NAME OF SOFTWARE
  GRASP II

TYPE OF SOFTWARE
  OPERATING SYSTEM/SPOOLING SYSTEM

PURPOSE OF SOFTWARE
  PROVIDES SPOOLING OF SLOW I/O DEVICES ON AN IBM 360 UNDER DOS.
  ALSO CONTAINS FEATURES FOR SYSTEM ACCOUNTING AND USER PROGRAM
  RELOCATABILITY AND SUPPORT FOR REMOTE-JOB-ENTRY TERMINALS

CONFIGURATION AND OPERATING SYSTEM
  IBM 360,IBM 370

  HAS RUN SUCCESSFULLY ON IBM 360/25, IBM 360/30, IBM 360/40,
  IBM 360/50
  AMOUNT OF PRIMARY STORAGE 4K-8K BYTES, OVERLAYS USED
  1 DISC DRIVE, 10K-100K BYTES STORAGE
  1 LINE PRINTER
  RUN UNDER DISC OPERATING SYSTEM (DOS)
  (TESTED UP TO RELEASE 25)

  HAS RUN SUCCESSFULLY ON IBM 370/145
  AMOUNT OF PRIMARY STORAGE 65K-128K BYTES ,OVERLAYS USED
  1 DISC DRIVE,10K-100K BYTES STORAGE
  1 LINE PRINTER
  1 LINE PRINTER IS MINIMUM-OTHER DEVICES MAY BE SUPPORTED
  RUN UNDER DISC OPERATING SYSTEM (DOS)

  HAS RUN SUCCESSFULLY ON IBM 370/155
  AMOUNT OF PRIMARY STORAGE 65K-128K BYTES,OVERLAYS USED
  1 DISC DRIVE,10K-100K BYTES STORAGE
  1 LINE PRINTER
  1 LINE PRINTER IS MINIMUM-OTHER DEVICES MAY BE SUPPORTED
  RUN UNDER DISC OPERATING SYSTEM(DOS)

MODE OF USAGE
  INTERACTIVE, REAL-TIME

LANGUAGE
  BASIC ASSEMBLER (MACROS)

AVAILABILITY
  PROGRAM MAY BE AVAILABLE FOR USE OUTSIDE SUPPLIERS
  ORGANISATION

SUPPLIERS COMMENT
  OVER 200 INSTALLATIONS THROUGHOUT THE WORLD USE GRASP.
  AVAILABLE FOR RENT OR PURCHASE

      COPYRIGHT NCC 1972   PRINTED ON 19/04/72

NCC STAGE 1 SOFTWARE VERIFICATION ABSTRACT A34003

NAME OF SOFTWARE
  TELECOMMUNICATIONS ACCESS METHOD

TYPE OF SOFTWARE
  COMMUNICATION CONTROL PACKAGE

PURPOSE OF SOFTWARE
  TAM IS A MODULARLY CONSTRUCTED PROGRAM DESIGNED TO PROVIDE A
  CONTROL PROGRAM FOR TERMINAL BASED DATA PROCESSING SYSTEMS

CONFIGURATION AND OPERATING SYSTEM
  IBM 360 SERIES

  HAS RUN SUCCESSFULLY ON IBM 360/30, IBM 360/40
  AMOUNT OF PRIMARY STORAGE 17K-32K BYTES
  1 DISC DRIVE 10K-100K BYTES STORAGE
  1 LINE PRINTER
  1 CARD READER
  1 CARD PUNCH
  V.D.U.'S
  RUN UNDER IBM 360 DISK OPERATING SYSTEM (DOS) RELEASE 21

MODE OF USAGE
  INTERACTIVE

LANGUAGE
  BASIC ASSEMBLY LANGUAGE (BAL)

AVAILABILITY
  PROGRAM MAY BE AVAILABLE FOR USE OUTSIDE SUPPLIERS
  ORGANISATION. PROGRAM AVAILABLE AS A BUREAU SERVICE

SUPPLIERS COMMENT
  TAM USES THE IBM BTAM PROGRAM. TAM HAS BEEN DESIGNED TO
  REDUCE IMPLEMENTATION TIME OF TERMINAL BASED DP SYSTEMS, TO
  REDUCE CORE OCCUPANCY OF THE COMMUNICATION CONTROL PROGRAM
  TO REDUCE THE AMOUNT OF TELEPROCESSING FAMILIARITY AND TO
  OPTIMISE RESPONSE TIMES.

NCC STAGE 1 SOFTWARE VERIFICATION ABSTRACT A34004

NAME OF SOFTWARE
   TEST DATA FILE GENERATOR PROGRAM

TYPE OF SOFTWARE
   UTILITY

PURPOSE OF SOFTWARE
   CREATES DATA FILES FOR IBM 360 PROGRAM TESTING

CONFIGURATION AND OPERATING SYSTEM
   IBM 360 SERIES

   HAS RUN SUCCESSFULLY ON IBM 360/30
   AMOUNT OF PRIMARY STORAGE 17K-32K BYTES, OVERLAYS USED
   1 DISC DRIVE, 101K-1M BYTES STORAGE
   1 PAPER TAPE READER
   1 LINE PRINTER
   1 CARD READER
   DATA FILES ON MAGNETIC TAPE OR DISC
   RUN UNDER OPERATING SYSTEM IBM 360 DOS

   HAS RUN SUCCESSFULLY ON IBM 360/40
   AMOUNT OF PRIMARY STORAGE 17K-32K BYTES, OVERLAYS USED
   1 DISC DRIVE, 101K-1M BYTES STORAGE
   1 PAPER TAPE READER
   1 LINE PRINTER
   1 CARD READER
   DATA FILES ON MAGNETIC TAPE OR DISC
   RUN UNDER OPERATING SYSTEM IBM 360 DOS

MODE OF USAGE
   BATCH

LANGUAGE
   IBM 360 BAL

AVAILABILITY
   PROGRAM MAY BE AVAILABLE FOR USE OUTSIDE SUPPLIERS
   ORGANISATION

SUPPLIERS COMMENT
   SUPPORTS FIXED AND VARIABLE LENGTH DISC AND TAPE FILE
   ORGANISATIONS UNDER IBM 360 DOS. INPUT WRITTEN IN NATURAL
   LANGUAGE RATHER THAN LOWER LEVEL OF CODING.

NCC STAGE 1 SOFTWARE VERIFICATION ABSTRACT A34005

NAME OF SOFTWARE
  PROCESS-PROFESSIONAL COMPUTER SALARY SERVICE

TYPE OF SOFTWARE
  PAYROLL

PURPOSE OF SOFTWARE
  PRODUCTION OF PAYSLIPS, PAYROLL, CREDIT TRANSFERS AND ALL
  STATUTORY YEAR ANALYSES

CONFIGURATION AND OPERATING SYSTEM
  HONEYWELL 200 SERIES

  HAS RUN SUCCESSFULLY ON HONEYWELL 1200
  AMOUNT OF PRIMARY STORAGE 17K-32K CHARACTERS, OVERLAYS USED
  5 MAGNETIC TAPE DRIVES
  1 LINE PRINTER
  1 CARD READER

MODE OF USAGE
  BATCH

LANGUAGE
  COBOL

AVAILABILITY
  PROGRAM MAY BE AVAILABLE FOR USE OUTSIDE SUPPLIERS ORGANISATION.
  PROGRAM AVAILABLE AS A BUREAU SERVICE

SUPPLIERS COMMENT
  THIS SOFTWARE HAS BEEN OPERATIONAL FOR 4 YEARS AND IS USED BY
  MORE THAN 100 FIRMS

NCC STAGE 1 SOFTWARE VERIFICATION ABSTRACT A34006

NAME OF SOFTWARE
  SHARE REGISTER

TYPE OF SOFTWARE
  ACCOUNTING

PURPOSE OF SOFTWARE
  TO CREATE, MAINTAIN AND ACCESS THE COMPANYS SHARE REGISTER.
  ALL NORMAL FACILITIES FOR DIVIDENDS, ISSUES, REPAYMENT OF STOCK
  AND CAPITAL RE-ORGANISATION ARE PROVIDED

CONFIGURATION AND OPERATING SYSTEM
  ICL 1900

  HAS RUN SUCCESSFULLY ON ICL 1902A
  AMOUNT OF PRIMARY STORAGE 17K-32K WORDS
  4 MAGNETIC TAPE DRIVES
  1 LINE PRINTER
  1 PAPER TAPE READER
  RUN UNDER OPERATING SYSTEM ICL 1900 EXECUTIVE

MODE OF USAGE
  BATCH

LANGUAGE
  ICL 1900 PLAN 3

AVAILABILITY
  PROGRAM MAY BE AVAILABLE FOR USE OUTSIDE SUPPLIERS
  ORGANISATION

      COPYRIGHT NCC 1972   PRINTED ON 19/04/72

NCC STAGE 1 SOFTWARE VERIFICATION ABSTRACT A34007

NAME OF SOFTWARE
  MODULE TESTING SYSTEM

TYPE OF SOFTWARE
  UTILITY

PURPOSE OF SOFTWARE
  MTS PROVIDES A MEANS OF TESTING MODULES AND MODULE STRUCTURES
  IN MODULAR PROGRAMS,IT ALLOWS REPEAT TESTING OF MODULES PER
  RUN AND HAS FACILITIES FOR SIMULATION,AUTOMATIC RESULT CHECKS,
  FILE CREATION,ETC.

CONFIGURATION AND OPERATING SYSTEM
  IBM 360 SERIES, ICL SYSTEM 4

  HAS RUN SUCCESSFULLY ON IBM 360/40, IBM 360/50
  AMOUNT OF PRIMARY STORAGE 33K-64K BYTES, OVERLAYS USED
  1 DISC DRIVE, 10K-100K BYTES STORAGE
  1 LINE PRINTER
  1 CARD READER
  RUN UNDER OPERATING SYSTEM IBM 360 DOS

  HAS RUN SUCCESSFULLY ON ICL SYSTEM 4/40, 4/70
  AMOUNT OF PRIMARY STORAGE 33K-64K BYTES, OVERLAYS USED
  1 DISC DRIVE, 10K-100K BYTES STORAGE
  1 LINE PRINTER
  1 CARD READER
  RUN UNDER OPERATING SYSTEM ICL SYSTEM 4J

MODE OF USAGE
  BATCH

LANGUAGE
  BAL AND SYSTEM 4 USERCODE

AVAILABILITY
  PROGRAM IS AVAILABLE FOR USE OUTSIDE SUPPLIERS ORGANISATION.
  PROGRAM AVAILABLE AS A BUREAU SERVICE.

SUPPLIERS COMMENT
  MTS IS AVAILABLE FOR IBM 360 DOS/OS AND ICL SYSTEM 4 REGIME J,
  FOR LANGUAGES ASSEMBLER,USERCODE,COBOL,FORTRAN,PL/1.

     COPYRIGHT NCC 1972   PRINTED ON 19/04/72

NCC STAGE 1 SOFTWARE VERIFICATION ABSTRACT A34008

NAME OF SOFTWARE
  TICKETRON RESERVATION AND TICKETING SYSTEM

TYPE OF SOFTWARE
  REAL TIME APPLICATION

PURPOSE OF SOFTWARE
  THE SYSTEM PROVIDES A DEDICATED SYSTEM, FOR REAL-TIME SALES FROM
  AN INVENTORY AND THE CONTROL OF CASH RECIEVED AT UP TO 512 REMOTE
  OUTLETS

CONFIGURATION AND OPERATING SYSTEM
  CDC 1700

  HAS RUN SUCCESSFULLY ON CDC 1700
  AMOUNT OF PRIMARY STORAGE 17K-32K WORDS/OVERLAYS USED
  4 DISC DRIVES, 11M-100M WORDS STORAGE
  2 MAGNETIC TAPE DRIVES
  1 LINE PRINTER
  1 CARD READER
  1 DRUM
  1 TELETYPE
  TERMINALS HAVE KEYBOARD/TICKET PRINTER/TELETYPE, SYSTEM CONTAINS
  ITS OWN OPERATING SYSTEM

MODE OF USAGE
  REAL-TIME

LANGUAGE
  SYSTEM IS WRITTEN IN 50% ASSEMBLER, 50% FORTRAN

AVAILABILITY
  PROGRAM IS AVAILABLE FOR USE OUTSIDE SUPPLIERS ORGANISATION.
  PROGRAM AVAILABLE AS A BUREAU SERVICE

SUPPLIERS COMMENT
  THE SYSTEM MAY BE USED ON ANOTHER COMPANYS EQUIPMENT ON A
  HIRING BASIS ONLY. IT IS NOT AVAILABLE FOR OUTRIGHT PURCHASE.

NCC STAGE 1 SOFTWARE VERIFICATION ABSTRACT A34009

NAME OF SOFTWARE
  SUNNYSIDE SYSTEM (WEAVING EFFICIENCIES)

TYPE OF SOFTWARE
  PRODUCTION CONTROL

PURPOSE OF SOFTWARE
  TO PROVIDE WEAVING MANAGEMENT WITH LATEST INFORMATION
  ON PRODUCTION EFFICIENCIES AND ACHIEVEMENTS

CONFIGURATION AND OPERATING SYSTEM
  ICL 1900 SERIES

  HAS RUN SUCCESSFULLY ON ICL 1904A, ICL 1904, ICL 1903
  AMOUNT OF PRIMARY STORAGE 9K-16K WORDS
  1 DISC DRIVE, 101K-1M WORDS STORAGE
  1 LINE PRINTER
  1 PAPER TAPE BEADER
  RUN UNDER OPERATING SYSTEM ICL GEORGE 2

MODE OF USAGE
  BATCH

LANGUAGE
  PLAN

AVAILABILITY
  PROGRAM AVAILABLE AS A BUREAU SERVICE

NCC STAGE 1 SOFTWARE VERIFICATION ABSTRACT A34010

NAME OF SOFTWARE
   TABULATION SUITE - COMPRISING SIEVE, TABL . TEST

TYPE OF SOFTWARE
   STATISTICAL APPLICATION, FILE HANDLING, MARKET RESEARCH
   TABULATION

PURPOSE OF SOFTWARE
   FROM ALPHANUMERIC CHARACTER DATA ON MAGNETIC TAPE, DISC
   (CARD IMAGE OR BLOCKED): DOES LOGICAL EDIT TO SECOND
   TAPE, DISC: CROSS TABULATES SELECTED FIELDS OF ANY
   NUMBER OF SELECTED RECORDS: WEIGHTS, FILTERS, %, MANY
   OPTIONS: INDIVIDUAL SCORES, SCHOOL AND OTHER TESTS

CONFIGURATION AND OPERATING SYSTEM
   DIGITAL EQUIPMENT CORP PDP 15

   HAS RUN SUCCESSFULLY ON DEC PDP 15/30
   AMOUNT OF PRIMARY STORAGE 9K-16K WORDS, OVERLAYS USED
   1 DISC DRIVE,101K-1M WORDS STORAGE
   2 MAGNETIC TAPE DRIVES
   1 LINE PRINTER
   1 CARD READER
   1 TELETYPE
   RUN UNDER OPERATING SYSTEM ADVANCED MONITOR KM15V5A

MODE OF USAGE
   BATCH

LANGUAGE
   STANDARD FORTRAN IV

AVAILABILITY
   PROGRAM MAY BE AVAILABLE FOR USE OUTSIDE SUPPLIERS ORGANISATION
   PROGRAM AVAILABLE AS A BUREAU SERVICE

SUPPLIERS COMMENT
   COULD BE MODIFIED BY THE SUPPLIER (DOCUMENT READING SERVICES LTD)
   TO RUN ON ANY MACHINE WITH SUITABLE FORTRAN COMPILER UNDER BATCH
   CONTROL. FULLY DOCUMENTED IN SECTIONS (A) GENERAL (B) USER
   (C) OPERATING (D) PROGRAMMING
   16K WORDS OF PRIMARY STORAGE. 250K WORDS DISC
   STORAGE. ONE 7-TRACK, ONE 9-TRACK MAGNETIC TAPE
   DRIVES.

      COPYRIGHT NCC 1972   PRINTED ON 19/04/72

NCC STAGE 1 SOFTWARE VERIFICATION ABSTRACT A34011

NAME OF SOFTWARE
   ASSEMBLER PLUS

TYPE OF SOFTWARE
   PROGRAMMING PRODUCTIVITY AID

PURPOSE OF SOFTWARE
   AN INTEGRATED SET OF STANDARDS IN THE FORM OF A MACRO
   FRAMEWORK FOR HIERARCHICAL LINKING OF PROGRAM MODULES COMBINED
   WITH A MACRO-BASED HIGH-LEVEL PRINT LANGUAGE, A DECISION
   TABLE PROCESSING OPTION, AND A MODULE TESTING PACKAGE

CONFIGURATION AND OPERATING SYSTEM
   IBM 360 SERIES

   HAS RUN SUCCESSFULLY ON IBM 360/30, IBM 360/40, IBM 360/50
   AMOUNT OF PRIMARY STORAGE 9K-16K BYTES
   1 LINE PRINTER
   1 CARD READER
   RUN UNDER OPERATING SYSTEM DOS

   HAS RUN SUCCESSFULLY ON ICL SYSTEM 4/50
   AMOUNT OF PRIMARY STORAGE 9K-16K BYTES
   1 LINE PRINTER
   1 CARD READER
   RUN OPERATING SYSTEM 5J

MODE OF USAGE
   BATCH

LANGUAGE
   BASIC ASSEMBLER

AVAILABILITY
   PROGRAM MAY BE AVAILABLE FOR USE OUTSIDE SUPPLIERS
   ORGANISATION. PROGRAM AVAILABLE AS A BUREAU SERVICE

SUPPLIERS COMMENT
   CURRENTLY THE PACKAGE IS BEING TESTED ON THE UNIVAC 9400
   MACHINE.FULL DETAILS OF THIS PACKAGE CAN BE OBTAINED
   FROM COMPUTER SYSTEMS INTERNATIONAL AND DEMONSTRATIONS CAN
   BE ARRANGED WITH EXISTING USERS.

NCC STAGE 1 SOFTWARE VERIFICATION ABSTRACT A34012

NAME OF SOFTWARE
   11+

TYPE OF SOFTWARE
   PRODUCTION OF 11+ RESULTS

PURPOSE OF SOFTWARE
   TAKES EACH CHILDS SCORE AND PRODUCES VARIOUS ANALYSES FOR
   ASSESSMENT OF EACH CHILDS ABILITY

CONFIGURATION AND OPERATING SYSTEM
   HONEYWELL 200 (SPECIAL)

   HAS RUN SUCCESSFULLY ON H200
   AMOUNT OF PRIMARY STORAGE 17K-32K CHARACTERS
   4 MAGNETIC TAPE DRIVES
   1 LINE PRINTER
   1 PAPER TAPE READER

MODE OF USAGE
   BATCH

LANGUAGE
   COBOL D

AVAILABILITY
   PROGRAM MAY BE AVAILABLE FOR USE OUTSIDE SUPPLIERS ORGANISATION.

SUPPLIERS COMMENT
   HONEYWELL 200 (SPECIAL) HAS 2 CHARACTERS IN SET DIFFERENT FROM
   HONEYWELL 200 (STANDARD)

NCC STAGE 1 SOFTWARE VERIFICATION ABSTRACT A34013

NAME OF SOFTWARE
   STRUCTURAL ANALYSIS BY FINITE ELEMENTS

TYPE OF SOFTWARE
   ENGINEERING APPLICATION

PURPOSE OF SOFTWARE
   GENERALISED ANALYSIS OF STATIC STRESSES AND DISPLACEMENTS IN
   STRUCTURES, USING MATRIX DISPLACEMENT METHODS AND FINITE ELEMENT
   TECHNIQUES.

CONFIGURATION AND OPERATING SYSTEM
   IBM 360 SERIES

   HAS RUN SUCCESSFULLY ON IBM 360/65
   AMOUNT OF PRIMARY STORAGE 65K-128K BYTES, OVERLAYS USED
   3 DISC DRIVES, 10K-100K BYTES STORAGE
   1 LINE PRINTER
   1 CARD READER
   1 GRAPH PLOTTER
   RUN UNDER OPERATING SYSTEM IBM 360 O/S MFT2

MODE OF USAGE
   BATCH

LANGUAGE
   IBM 360 ALGOL

AVAILABILITY
   PROGRAM MAY BE AVAILABLE FOR USE OUTSIDE SUPPLIERS ORGANISATION.
   PROGRAM AVAILABLE AS A BUREAU SERVICE

NCC STAGE 1 SOFTWARE VERIFICATION ABSTRACT A34014

NAME OF SOFTWARE
   SALES PACKAGE

TYPE OF SOFTWARE
   ACCOUNTING

PURPOSE OF SOFTWARE
   OPEN ITEM SALES LEDGER SYSTEM WITH FULL CASH MATCHING
   FACILITIES. CREDIT CONTROL, TURNOVER ANALYSES. PROVIDES
   FACILITIES FOR PRINTING INDIVIDUAL ACCOUNT HISTORIES.

CONFIGURATION AND OPERATING SYSTEM
   ICL 1900 SERIES

   HAS RUN SUCCESSFULLY ON ICL 1903A, ICL 1903
   AMOUNT OF PRIMARY STORAGE 17K-32K WORDS
   1 DISC DRIVE, 1.1M-10M CHARACTERS STORAGE
   4 MAGNETIC TAPE DRIVES
   1 PAPER TAPE READER
   1 LINE PRINTER
   RUN UNDER OPERATING SYSTEM GEORGE 1 OR 2

MODE OF USAGE
   BATCH

LANGUAGE
   PLAN AND COBOL

AVAILABILITY
   PROGRAM IS AVAILABLE FOR USE OUTSIDE SUPPLIERS
   ORGANISATION. PROGRAM AVAILABLE AS A BUREAU SERVICE.

SUPPLIERS COMMENT
   THE PACKAGE CAN BE ADAPTED TO RUN ON A 16K MACHINE. THE
   SYSTEM WAS DESIGNED IN CONJUNCTION WITH THE INTERNATIONAL
   COMMERCIAL AND FINANCE CORPORATION FOR AN APPLICATION WITH
   80,000 ACCOUNTS WHICH HAS BEEN RUNNING SUCCESSFULLY SINCE
   MID-1969. HOWEVER IT IS EQUALLY SUITABLE FOR SMALL APPLICATIONS
   AND HAS FACILITIES TO ENABLE MORE THAN ONE COMPANYS DATA TO
   BE PROCESSED IN ONE RUN.

      COPYRIGHT NCC 1972   PRINTED ON 19/04/72

NCC STAGE 1 SOFTWARE VERIFICATION ABSTRACT A34015

NAME OF SOFTWARE
  SYSTEM BY TOUCHE ROSS FOR AUDIT TECHNICAL ASSISTANCE

TYPE OF SOFTWARE
  FILE HANDLING

PURPOSE OF SOFTWARE
  EASY TO USE GENERAL PURPOSE REPORT GENERATOR DEVELOPED
  ORIGINALLY TO ASSIST WITH AUDITING COMPUTER SYSTEMS. STRATA
  INCLUDES POWERFUL UPDATING CALCULATING AND LOGICAL ABILITIES
  AND IS SUITABLE FOR GENERAL USE

CONFIGURATION AND OPERATING SYSTEM
  IBM 360 SERIES

  HAS RUN SUCCESSFULLY ON IBM 360/25, IBM 360/40
  AMOUNT OF PRIMARY STORAGE 33K-64K BYTES
  1 DISC DRIVE, 10K-100K BYTES STORAGE
  1 LINE PRINTER
  1 CARD READER
  RUN UNDER OPERATING SYSTEM DOS

  HAS RUN SUCCESSFULLY ON IBM 360/50, IBM 360/65
  AMOUNT OF PRIMARY STORAGE 65K-128K BYTES
  2 DISC DRIVES, 10K-100K BYTES STORAGE
  1 LINE PRINTER
  1 CARD READER
  RUN UNDER OPERATING SYSTEM OS-MFT

MODE OF USAGE
  BATCH

LANGUAGE
  BAL, COBOL

AVAILABILITY
  PROGRAM MAY BE AVAILABLE FOR USE OUTSIDE SUPPLIERS ORGANISATION.
  PROGRAM AVAILABLE AS A BUREAU SERVICE

NCC STAGE 1 SOFTWARE VERIFICATION ABSTRACT A34016

NAME OF SOFTWARE
  POLYFILE

TYPE OF SOFTWARE
  FILE HANDLING

PURPOSE OF SOFTWARE
  FILE MAINTENANCE CAPABILITIES: VARIABILITY OF FIELD LENGTHS AND
  NUMBER: AUTOMATIC HISTORY PROTECTION: NO REDUNDANT FIELDS:
  REPORTING FACILITIES: MULTI-FIELD SORTING AND SELECTION
  OPTIONS: AUTOMATIC TITLING FEATURES: OUTPUT FILE COMPATIBLE
  WITH IBM COBOL, PL/1, RPG, ETC.

CONFIGURATION AND OPERATING SYSTEM
  IBM 360 SERIES

  HAS RUN SUCCESSFULLY ON IBM 360/65
  AMOUNT OF PRIMARY STORAGE 65K-128K BYTES, OVERLAYS USED
  4 DISC DRIVES, 1.1M-10M BYTES STORAGE
  1 LINE PRINTER
  1 CARD READER
  RUN UNDER OPERATING SYSTEM IBM 360 O/S MFT2

MODE OF USAGE
  BATCH

LANGUAGE
  IBM 360 COBOL F-LEVEL

AVAILABILITY
  PROGRAM MAY BE AVAILABLE FOR USE OUTSIDE SUPPLIERS ORGANISATION.
  PROGRAM AVAILABLE AS A BUREAU SERVICE

SUPPLIERS COMMENT
  CURRENT APPLICATIONS OF THE PACKAGE INCLUDE A PROJECT CONTROL
  SYSTEM AND A COMPANY PERSONNEL RECORDS SYSTEM. MANY FUTURE
  APPLICATIONS ARE ENVISAGED AS THE PACKAGE PROVIDES A READILY
  ADAPTABLE SYSTEM USING SIMPLE PRE OR POST PROCESSING ROUTINES FOR
  THE PARTICULAR TASK IN HAND

      COPYRIGHT NCC 1972   PRINTED ON 19/04/72

NCC STAGE 1 SOFTWARE VERIFICATION ABSTRACT A34017

NAME OF SOFTWARE
    SALES ANALYSIS

TYPE OF SOFTWARE
    STATISTICAL APPLICATION

PURPOSE OF SOFTWARE
    STATISTICAL INFORMATION ON SALES AND PRODUCTION/CUSTOMER LEVELS
    FINANCIAL ACCOUNTING, BUDGETARY CONTROL, PRICE VARIANCES, ETC.

CONFIGURATION AND OPERATING SYSTEM
    ICL SYSTEM 4

    HAS RUN SUCCESSFULLY ON ICL SYSTEM 4/50
    AMOUNT OF PRIMARY STORAGE 64K-128K BYTES
    4 MAGNETIC TAPE DRIVES
    1 PAPER TAPE READER
    1 LINE PRINTER
    1 CARD READER
    RUN UNDER OPERATING SYSTEM ICL SYSTEM 4/50, 5J

MODE OF USAGE
    BATCH

LANGUAGE
    ICL SYSTEM 4 USERCODE

AVAILABILITY
    PROGRAM MAY BE AVAILABLE FOR USE OUTSIDE SUPPLIERS ORGANISATION.
    PROGRAM AVAILABLE AS A BUREAU SERVICE

        COPYRIGHT NCC 1972   PRINTED ON 19/04/72

NCC STAGE 1 SOFTWARE VERIFICATION ABSTRACT A34018

NAME OF SOFTWARE
  JOB EVALUATION AND WAGES DRIFT

TYPE OF SOFTWARE
  STATISTICAL APPLICATION (COMMERCIAL)

PURPOSE OF SOFTWARE
  TO ANALYSE THE PAY STRUCTURE OF A LABOUR FORCE AND ESTABLISH
  EFFECT OF PROPOSED CHANGES ON ALL EMPLOYEES AND EMPLOYER BY TRIAL
  MODELS

CONFIGURATION AND OPERATING SYSTEM
  ICL 1900

  HAS RUN SUCCESSFULLY ON ICL 1901, ICL 1902, ICL 1903, ICL 1904
  AMOUNT OF PRIMARY STORAGE 9K-16K WORDS STORAGE, OVERLAYS USED
  4 MAGNETIC TAPE DRIVES
  1 LINE PRINTER
  1 CARD READER
  RUN UNDER OPERATING SYSTEM EXECUTIVE

MODE OF USAGE
  BATCH

LANGUAGE
  COBOL

AVAILABILITY
  PROGRAM MAYBE AVAILABLE FOR USE OUTSIDE SUPPLIERS ORGANISATION.
  PROGRAM AVAILABLE AS A BUREAU SERVICE

SUPPLIERS COMMENT
  THE PACKAGE WILL CREATE A PROGRAM FOR PARTICULAR CONDITIONS BY
  INSERTION OF APPROPRIATE PARAMETERS. IT WILL ALSO RUN WITH DISC
  INSTEAD OF MAGNETIC TAPE. A PERSONNEL FILE IS CREATED AND
  MAINTAINED AS A BASIS FOR CALCULATION

NCC STAGE 1 SOFTWARE VERIFICATION ABSTRACT A34019

NAME OF SOFTWARE
    STRATEGIC FIXED DELIVERY ROUTE SCHEDULES AND DETOURS FOR
    TACTICAL IMPLEMENTATION

TYPE OF SOFTWARE
    OPERATIONAL RESEARCH APPLICATION

PURPOSE OF SOFTWARE
    GENERATION OF THE PATHS AND FREQUENCIES OF BASIC ROUTES
    FOR A GIVEN DELIVERY DEMAND PATTERN, FLEET COMPOSITION,
    AND CREW AVAILABILITY SO AS TO ACHIEVE A SPECIFIED LEVEL
    OF SERVICE. FOR ANY POTENTIAL ORDER, GIVES THE ROUTE TO
    BE DETOURED

CONFIGURATION AND OPERATING SYSTEM
    ICL 1900, IBM 360

    HAS RUN SUCCESSFULLY ON ICL 1904
    AMOUNT OF PRIMARY STORAGE 9K-16K WORDS
    1 MAGNETIC TAPE DRIVE
    1 LINE PRINTER
    1 CARD READER
    RUN UNDER OPERATING SYSTEM EXECUTIVE

    HAS RUN SUCCESSFULLY ON IBM 360/50
    AMOUNT OF PRIMARY STORAGE 65K-128K BYTES
    1 MAGNETIC TAPE DRIVE
    1 LINE PRINTER
    1 CARD READER
    RUN UNDER OPERATING SYSTEM OS UNDER HASP SPOOLING

MODE OF USAGE
    BATCH

LANGUAGE
    FORTRAN 2

AVAILABILITY
    PROGRAM MAY BE AVAILABLE FOR USE OUTSIDE SUPPLIERS
    ORGANISATION

SUPPLIERS COMMENT
    THIS PROGRAM IS COMPATIBLE WITH THE "ROADNET" DATABASE,
    WHICH PROVIDES ACCURATE TRAVEL TIMES FROM NATIONAL GRID
    REFERENCES AND SPEEDS ON SEVEN CLASSES OF ROAD (URBAN/RURAL).
    "TRANSIT" IS ALSO USED ITERATIVELY FOR EVALUATING PROPOSED
    ALTERATIONS TO FLEET COMPOSITIONS AND TO DEPOT LOCATIONS.

NCC STAGE 1 SOFTWARE VERIFICATION ABSTRACT A34020

NAME OF SOFTWARE
   DISK TAPE OPERATING SYSTEM AND SUPERVISORY CONTROL PROGRAM

TYPE OF SOFTWARE
   FILE HANDLING, UTILITY, OPERATING SYSTEM, REAL-TIME APPLICATION

PURPOSE OF SOFTWARE
   CONTROL OF REAL-TIME SAVINGS BANK COUNTER OPERATION.HANDLES
   COMMUNICATIONS WITH TERMINALS,ACCESSING OF CUSTOMER ACCOUNTS AND
   TELLER TOTALS, FILE SET-UP,MAINTENANCE AND RECOVERY PROGRAM
   LIBRARY CREATION AND MAINTENANCE DISC ALLOCATION ETC.

CONFIGURATION AND OPERATING SYSTEM
   BURROUGHS B500

   HAS RUN SUCCESSFULLY ON B502
   AMOUNT OF PRIMARY STORAGE 17K-32K CHARACTERS,OVERLAYS   USED
   3 DISC DRIVES,11M-100M CHARACTERS
   4 MAGNETIC TAPES
   1 LINE PRINTER
   1 CARD READER
   1 CARD PUNCH
   1 PAPER TAPE READER
   1 PAPER TAPE PUNCH
   1 TELETYPE
   DATA TRANSMISSION TERMINAL UNITS-2   .REMOTE TERMINALS-39

MODE OF USAGE
   BATCH, INTERACTIVE, REAL-TIME

LANGUAGE
   ADVANCED ASSEMBLER

AVAILABILITY
   PROGRAM MAY BE AVAILABLE FOR USE OUTSIDE SUPPLIERS ORGANISATION
   PROGRAM AVAILABLE AS A BUREAU SERVICE

SUPPLIERS COMMENT
   HANDLES ALL ASPECTS OF REAL TIME OPERATION EXCEPT ACTUAL
   UPDATING OF CUSTOMER ACCOUNT. SUITABLE ONLY FOR APPLICATION
   WHERE ON-LINE TRANSACTION UPDATES A SPECIFIC RECORD IN A
   SINGLE FILE,SUCH AS A SAVINGS BANK, BUILDING SOCIETY, ETC.

       COPYRIGHT NCC 1972   PRINTED ON 19/04/72

NCC STAGE 1 SOFTWARE VERIFICATION ABSTRACT A34021

NAME OF SOFTWARE
  SALARY PAYROLL SYSTEM

TYPE OF SOFTWARE
  PAYROLL

PURPOSE OF SOFTWARE
  TO PROCESS THE PAYMENT OF WEEKLY AND MONTHLY SALARIES

CONFIGURATION AND OPERATING SYSTEM
  ICL 1900, HONEYWELL H200 SERIES

  HAS RUN SUCCESSFULLY ON ICL 1902A
  AMOUNT OF PRIMARY STORAGE 9K-16K WORDS
  4 MAGNETIC TAPE DRIVES
  1 PAPER TAPE READER
  1 LINE PRINTER
  RUN UNDER OPERATING SYSTEM EXECUTIVE, SINGLE AND
  MULTI-PROGRAMMING

  HAS RUN SUCCESSFULLY ON HONEYWELL H200
  AMOUNT OF PRIMARY STORAGE 17K-32K CHARACTERS, OVERLAYS USED
  4 MAGNETIC TAPE DRIVES
  1 LINE PRINTER
  1 CARD READER
  RUN UNDER OPERATING SYSTEM STANDARD LOAD AND MONITOR

MODE OF USAGE
  BATCH

LANGUAGE
  COBOL WITH PLAN SUBROUTINES (1900), COBOL "D" WITH EASYCODER
  ROUTINES (H200)

AVAILABILITY
  PROGRAM IS AVAILABLE FOR USE OUTSIDE SUPPLIERS
  ORGANISATION. PROGRAM AVAILABLE AS A BUREAU SERVICE

SUPPLIERS COMMENT
  DIRECT CREDIT PAYMENTS VIA MAGNETIC TAPE TO THE INTER BANK
  COMPUTER BUREAU ARE AVAILABLE WITH EITHER VERSION: FULL END
  OF YEAR STATUORY RETURNS ARE PROVIDED: MAGNETIC TAPE ENCODED
  "KEYTAPE" INPUT IS AVAILABLE AS AN OPTION ON THE H200 VERSION:
  A COMPREHENSIVE USER MANUAL IS PROVIDED. DISC/MAGNETIC TAPE,
  CARD/PAPER TAPE INPUT, ARE OPTIONAL. PRICE £1500 BOTH VERSIONS.

NCC STAGE 1 SOFTWARE VERIFICATION ABSTRACT A34022

NAME OF SOFTWARE
  SHARE REGISTRATION

TYPE OF SOFTWARE
  ACCOUNTING APPLICATION

PURPOSE OF SOFTWARE
  UPDATE OF SHARE/DEBENTURE REGISTER, PRINTING OF DIVIDEND/INTEREST
  WARRANTS, TAX CERTIFICATES, SHARE REGISTER, ANNUAL RETURN.

CONFIGURATION AND OPERATING SYSTEM
  ICL 4100

  HAS RUN SUCCESSFULLY ON ICL 4120
  AMOUNT OF PRIMARY STORAGE 9K-16K WORDS
  3 MAGNETIC TAPE DRIVES
  1 PAPER TAPE READER
  1 LINE PRINTER
  RUN UNDER OPERATING SYSTEM 4100 MAGNETIC TAPE EXECUTIVE

MODE OF USAGE
  BATCH

LANGUAGE
  LANGUAGE H

AVAILABILITY
  PROGRAM MAY BE AVAILABLE FOR USE OUTSIDE SUPPLIERS ORGANISATION.
  PROGRAM AVAILABLE AS A BUREAU SERVICE

    COPYRIGHT NCC 1972   PRINTED ON 19/04/72

NCC STAGE 1 SOFTWARE VERIFICATION ABSTRACT A34023

NAME OF SOFTWARE
  LAUNDRY ACCOUNTING SYSTEM

TYPE OF SOFTWARE
  ACCOUNTING

PURPOSE OF SOFTWARE
  TO PROVIDE JOURNEY SHEETS, STATEMENTS, LEDGERS AND MANAGEMENT
  INFORMATION ETC. ON CUSTOMER ACCOUNTS

CONFIGURATION AND OPERATING SYSTEM
  ELLIOTT 900

  HAS RUN SUCCESSFULLY ON ELLIOTT 903
  AMOUNT OF PRIMARY STORAGE 4K-8K WORDS
  1 PAPER TAPE READER
  1 PAPER TAPE PUNCH
  3 TELETYPES
  NO OPERATING SYSTEM USED

MODE OF USAGE
  BATCH

LANGUAGE
  S.I.R.

AVAILABILITY
  PROGRAM MAY BE AVAILABLE FOR USE OUTSIDE SUPPLIERS
  ORGANISATION

SUPPLIERS COMMENT
  ALTHOUGH DESIGNED FOR THE LAUNDRY INDUSTRY, THE PROGRAMS CAN
  BE ADAPTED FOR ANY INDUSTRY THAT DEALS WITH CUSTOMER ACCOUNTING.
  IT IS OF PARTICULAR INTEREST TO INDUSTRIES MADE UP OF SMALL
  UNITS WHICH COULD NOT AFFORD A LARGE D.P. TYPE OF MACHINE, TO
  PROVIDE A COMMERCIAL SYSTEM ON A SCIENTIFIC COMPUTER.

NCC STAGE 1 SOFTWARE VERIFICATION ABSTRACT A34024

NAME OF SOFTWARE
   SALES LEDGER AND ANALYSIS

TYPE OF SOFTWARE
   ACCOUNTING

PURPOSE OF SOFTWARE
   SALES ACCOUNTING AND ANALYSIS

CONFIGURATION AND OPERATING SYSTEM
   BURROUGHS B500 SERIES, HONEYWELL 200 SERIES

   HAS RUN SUCCESSFULLY ON BURROUGHS B3500
   AMOUNT OF PRIMARY STORAGE 33K-64K BYTES, OVERLAYS USED
   1 DISC DRIVE, 1.1M-10M BYTES STORAGE
   3 MAGNETIC TAPE DRIVES
   1 PAPER TAPE READER
   1 LINE PRINTER
   1 CARD READER
   TC500, ASR33 TERMINALS
   RUN UNDER OPERATING SYSTEM MCP

   HAS RUN SUCCESSFULLY ON HONEYWELL H1200
   AMOUNT OF PRIMARY STORAGE 17K-32K CHARACTERS
   5 MAGNETIC TAPE DRIVES
   1 PAPER TAPE READER
   1 LINE PRINTER
   1 CARD READER
   RUN UNDER OPERATING SYSTEM MOD ONE

MODE OF USAGE
   BATCH

LANGUAGE
   COBOL

AVAILABILITY
   PROGRAM MAY BE AVAILABLE FOR USE OUTSIDE SUPPLIERS ORGANISATION.
   PROGRAM AVAILABLE AS A BUREAU SERVICE.

SUPPLIERS COMMENT
   HAS BEEN IN USE SINCE 1969 , 60 USERS.

NCC STAGE 1 SOFTWARE VERIFICATION ABSTRACT A34025

NAME OF SOFTWARE
  INVESTMENT MANAGEMENT SYSTEM

TYPE OF SOFTWARE
  ACCOUNTING

PURPOSE OF SOFTWARE
  ACCOUNTING AND REPORTING FOR LONDON STOCK EXCHANGE AND SOME
  FOREIGN INVESTMENTS - INCLUDING PORTFOLIO ANALYSIS AND INCOME
  FORECASTING AND ACCOUNTING

CONFIGURATION AND OPERATING SYSTEM
  HONEYWELL 200 SERIES, BURROUGHS 500 SERIES

  HAS RUN SUCCESSFULLY ON HONEYWELL 1200
  AMOUNT OF PRIMARY STORAGE 17K-32K CHARACTERS, OVERLAYS USED
  5 MAGNETIC TAPE DRIVES
  1 LINE PRINTER
  1 CARD READER
  RUN UNDER OPERATING SYSTEM MOD ONE

  HAS RUN SUCCESSFULLY ON BURROUGHS 3500
  AMOUNT OF PRIMARY STORAGE 65K-128K BYTES, OVERLAYS USED
  1 DISC DRIVE, 1.1M-10M BYTES STORAGE
  3 MAGNETIC TAPE DRIVES
  1 LINE PRINTER.
  1 CARD READER
  RUN UNDER OPERATING SYSTEM MCP

MODE OF USAGE
  BATCH

LANGUAGE
  COBOL

AVAILABILITY
  PROGRAM MAY BE AVAILABLE FOR USE OUTSIDE SUPPLIERS
  ORGANISATION. PROGRAM AVAILABLE AS A BUREAU SERVICE.

SUPPLIERS COMMENT
  HAS BEEN IN USE SINCE 1969, SIX USERS.

     COPYRIGHT NCC 1972   PRINTED ON 19/04/72

NCC STAGE 1 SOFTWARE VERIFICATION ABSTRACT A34026

NAME OF SOFTWARE
  INSTITUTIONAL INFORMATION SYSTEM

TYPE OF SOFTWARE
  ACCOUNTING

PURPOSE OF SOFTWARE
  HANDLES MEMBERSHIP RECORDS, SUBSCRIPTION ACCOUNTING, JOURNAL
  DISTRIBUTION AND TYPESETTING FOR MEMBERSHIP LISTS

CONFIGURATION AND OPERATING SYSTEM
  HONEYWELL 200 SERIES

  HAS RUN SUCCESSFULLY ON HONEYWELL 1200
  AMOUNT OF PRIMARY STORAGE 17K-32K CHARACTERS, OVERLAYS USED
  5 MAGNETIC TAPE DRIVES
  1 LINE PRINTER
  1 CARD READER
  RUN UNDER OPERATING SYSTEM MOD ONE

MODE OF USAGE
  BATCH

LANGUAGE
  COBOL

AVAILABILITY
  PROGRAM IS AVAILABLE FOR USE OUTSIDE SUPPLIERS ORGANISATION.
  PROGRAM AVAILABLE AS A BUREAU SERVICE.

SUPPLIERS COMMENT
  HAS BEEN IN USE FOR 3 YEARS WITH 17 USERS.

     COPYRIGHT NCC 1972   PRINTED ON 19/04/72

NCC STAGE 1 SOFTWARE VERIFICATION ABSTRACT A34027

NAME OF SOFTWARE
   ACCOUNTANTS TIME LEDGER

TYPE OF SOFTWARE
   ACCOUNTING

PURPOSE OF SOFTWARE
   PROVIDES AN ACCOUNTANTS TIMEKEEPING AND COSTING SYSTEM WITH
   MONTHLY WORK-IN-PROGRESS SUMMARIES, TIME ACCOUNT BALANCES, AND
   A SIMILAR NON-CHARGEABLE TIME SUMMARY

CONFIGURATION AND OPERATING SYSTEM
   HONEYWELL 200 SERIES

   HAS RUN SUCCESSFULLY ON HONEYWELL 1200
   AMOUNT OF PRIMARY STORAGE 17K-32K CHARACTERS
   5 MAGNETIC TAPE DRIVES
   1 LINE PRINTER
   1 CARD READER
   RUN UNDER OPERATING SYSTEM MOD ONE

MODE OF USAGE
   BATCH

LANGUAGE
   COBOL

AVAILABILITY
   PROGRAM MAY BE AVAILABLE FOR USE OUTSIDE SUPPLIERS ORGANISATION.
   PROGRAM AVAILABLE AS A BUREAU SERVICE

SUPPLIERS COMMENT
   HAS BEEN IN BUREAU USE FOR 5 YEARS, WITH 130 USERS

NCC STAGE 1 SOFTWARE VERIFICATION ABSTRACT A34028

NAME OF SOFTWARE
  QUANTITY SURVEYORS BILLS OF QUANTITY

TYPE OF SOFTWARE
  ENGINEERING APPLICATION

PURPOSE OF SOFTWARE
  TO MAINTAIN COST AND DIMENSION LIBRARIES AND PRODUCE BILLS OF
  QUANTITY

CONFIGURATION AND OPERATING SYSTEM
  HONEYWELL H200 SERIES

  HAS RUN SUCCESSFULLY ON HONEYWELL H1200
  AMOUNT OF PRIMARY STORAGE 17K-32K, OVERLAYS USED
  5 MAGNETIC TAPE DRIVES
  1 LINE PRINTER
  1 CARD READER
  1 PAPER TAPE READER
  1 PAPER TAPE PUNCH
  RUN UNDER OPERATING SYSTEM MOD ONE

MODE OF USAGE
  BATCH

LANGUAGE
  COBOL

AVAILABILITY
  PROGRAM IS AVAILABLE FOR USE OUTSIDE SUPPLIERS ORGANISATION.
  PROGRAM AVAILABLE AS A BUREAU SERVICE

SUPPLIERS COMMENT
  IN USE SINCE 1969, 6 USERS.

      COPYRIGHT NCC 1972   PRINTED ON 19/04/72

NCC STAGE 1 SOFTWARE VERIFICATION ABSTRACT A34029

NAME OF SOFTWARE
   UNIPAY SYSTEM - GENERAL PURPOSE PAYROLL SYSTEM

TYPE OF SOFTWARE
   PAYROLL

PURPOSE OF SOFTWARE
   TO VALIDATE PAYROLL INPUT DATA, MAINTAIN MASTER FILES, MAKE
   ALL NECESSARY CALCULATIONS TO NET PAY, PRINT PAYSLIPS, COST
   ANALYSES, PAYROLLS, CREDIT TRANSFERS/CHEQUES, PAYROLL
   TOTALS COIN ANALYSES AND CONTROL STATISTICS

CONFIGURATION AND OPERATING SYSTEM
   IBM 1400 , HONEYWELL 200 SERIES, ICL 1900
   ICL 1500, IBM 360 , ICL SYSTEM 4, IBM 370

   HAS RUN SUCCESSFULLY ON IBM 360/40
   AMOUNT OF PRIMARY STORAGE 33K-64K BYTES
   3 DISC DRIVES, 1.1M-10M BYTES STORAGE
   1 LINE PRINTER
   1 CARD READER
   1 CARD PUNCH
   RUN UNDER OPERATING SYSTEM DOS RELEASE 21

   HAS RUN SUCCESSFULLY ON ICL SYSTEM 4/50
   AMOUNT OF PRIMARY STORAGE 33K-64K BYTES
   2 DISC DRIVES, 1.1M-10M BYTES STORAGE
   4 MAGNETIC TAPE DRIVES
   1 LINE PRINTER
   1 CARD READER
   1 PAPER TAPE READER
   RUN UNDER OPERATING SYSTEM LEVEL J 1300

   HAS RUN SUCCESSFULLY ON ICL 1902A
   AMOUNT OF PRIMARY STORAGE 33K-64K WORDS
   6 MAGNETIC TAPE DRIVES
   1 LINE PRINTER
   1 CARD READER
   1 PAPER TAPE READER
   RUN UNDER OPERATING SYSTEM EXECUTIVE

MODE OF USAGE
   BATCH

LANGUAGE
   IBM 1400 AUTOCODE, HONEYWELL EASYCODER, ICL 1900 PLAN,
   ICL SYSTEM 4 ASSEMBLER, IBM 360 ASSEMBLER, ICL 1500 FAS

AVAILABILITY
   PROGRAM IS AVAILABLE FOR USE OUTSIDE SUPPLIERS
   ORGANISATION. PROGRAM AVAILABLE AS A BUREAU SERVICE

SUPPLIERS COMMENT

UNIPAY CONSISTS OF A SERIES OF MODULES WHICH ARE TAILORED
TO THE EXACT REQUIREMENTS OF EACH CLIENT ORGANISATION AND
COMPUTER CONFIGURATION. THIS PAYROLL IS BEING USED BY OVER
50 ORGANISATIONS IN THE U.K. (INCLUDING SEVERAL BUREAUX).
IT HAS ALSO RUN ON IBM 360/25,IBM 360/30,IBM 360/50,IBM 370/155,
ICL SYSTEM 4/70. MAINTENANCE AND UPDATE FACILITIES ARE
PROVIDED.

COPYRIGHT NCC 1972   PRINTED ON 19/04/72

NCC STAGE 1 SOFTWARE VERIFICATION ABSTRACT A34030

NAME OF SOFTWARE
   DEPOT LOCATION

TYPE OF SOFTWARE
   OPERATIONAL RESEARCH APPLICATION

PURPOSE OF SOFTWARE
   THE PROGRAM SELECTS THE SET OF DEPOTS GIVING MINIMUM COST WITHIN
   A TOTAL DISTRIBUTION SYSTEM. THE TOTAL COSTS ARE CALCULATED FROM
   THE SUM OF FIXED SITE COSTS AND VARIABLE DISTRIBUTION COSTS.

CONFIGURATION AND OPERATING SYSTEM
   UNIVAC 1100 SERIES

   HAS RUN SUCCESSFULLY ON UNIVAC 1108
   AMOUNT OF PRIMARY STORAGE 33K-64K WORDS
   1 LINE PRINTER
   1 CARD READER
   RUN UNDER OPERATING SYSTEM EXEC 8, LEVEL 25

MODE OF USAGE
   BATCH

LANGUAGE
   FORTRAN

AVAILABILITY
   PROGRAM MAY BE AVAILABLE FOR USE OUTSIDE SUPPLIERS ORGANISATION.
   PROGRAM AVAILABLE AS A BUREAU SERVICE

      COPYRIGHT NCC 1972   PRINTED ON 19/04/72

NCC STAGE 1 SOFTWARE VERIFICATION ABSTRACT A34036

NAME OF SOFTWARE
   UTILITY SUBROUTINE FOR USE WITH TAPE ENCODER INPUT SYSTEMS,
   ENCOSUB

TYPE OF SOFTWARE
   UTILITY

PURPOSE OF SOFTWARE
   PLAN SUBROUTINE FOR USE IN PLAN OR COBOL PROGRAMS,
   TO READ A NON-STANDARD FORMAT MAGNETIC TAPE ENCODER
   FILE, AND/OR A CARD FILE

CONFIGURATION AND OPERATING SYSTEM
   ICL 1900

   HAS RUN SUCCESSFULLY ON ICL 1901, 1902, 1903, 1904 AND 'A' SERIES,
   ICL 1902S
   AMOUNT OF PRIMARY STORAGE <4K WORDS
   1 MAGNETIC TAPE DRIVE
   1 CARD READER (OPTIONAL)
   RUN UNDER OPERATING SYSTEM EXECUTIVE

MODE OF USAGE
   BATCH

LANGUAGE
   PLAN

AVAILABILITY
   PROGRAM IS AVAILABLE FOR USE OUTSIDE SUPPLIERS
   ORGANISATION. PROGRAM AVAILABLE AS A BUREAU SERVICE

SUPPLIERS COMMENT
   THIS ROUTINE HAS BEEN DEVELOPED AND BEEN IN CONTINUOUS USE
   OVER A PERIOD OF 12 MONTHS AND REPRESENTS SOLUTIONS TO ALL
   THE PROBLEMS ENCOUNTERED IN THE IMPLEMENTATION OF ENCODER
   INPUT. IT HAS BEEN EASILY INCORPORATED INTO UPWARDS OF 15
   EXISTING PROGRAMS TO REPLACE CARD READING ROUTINES. THE
   CORE STORE REQUIREMENT IS LESS THAN 256 WORDS.
   THIS ROUTINE IS FOR USE WITH PLAN OR COBOL BASED PROGRAMS

      COPYRIGHT NCC 1972   PRINTED ON 19/04/72

NCC STAGE 1 SOFTWARE VERIFICATION ABSTRACT A34037

NAME OF SOFTWARE
  DATA FILTER A DATA VETTING PROGRAM GENERATOR

TYPE OF SOFTWARE
  FILE HANDLING

PURPOSE OF SOFTWARE
  TO MINIMISE THE COST OF PRODUCING AND MAINTAINING DATA VETTING
  PROGRAMS BY USING PARAMETERS TO DEFINE THE MAJOR PORTION OF THE
  PROGRAM, BY ALLOWING THE INCLUSION OF USER ROUTINES
  ECONOMIC AND BY INCLUDING MODULAR TESTING FACILITIES

CONFIGURATION AND OPERATING SYSTEM
  ICL SYSTEM 4, IBM 360 SERIES

  HAS RUN SUCCESSFULLY ON ICL 4/40, ICL 4/50
  AMOUNT OF PRIMARY STORAGE 17K-32K BYTES
  1 DISC DRIVE, <10K BYTES STORAGE
  1 LINE PRINTER
  1 CARD READER
  RUN UNDER OPERATING SYSTEM 4 1200

  HAS RUN SUCCESSFULLY ON IBM 360/40
  AMOUNT OF PRIMARY STORAGE 17K-32K BYTES
  1 DISC DRIVE, <10K BYTES STORAGE
  1 LINE PRINTER
  1 CARD READER
  RUN UNDER OPERATING SYSTEM OS

MODE OF USAGE
  BATCH

LANGUAGE
  SYSTEM 4 USERCODE, IBM BAL

AVAILABILITY
  PROGRAM MAY BE AVAILABLE FOR USE OUTSIDE SUPPLIERS ORGANISATION.
  PROGRAM AVAILABLE AS A BUREAU SERVICE

SUPPLIERS COMMENT
  THE PACKAGE WILL VET DATA FROM ANY MEDIUM, ANY CODE, FIXED OR
  VARIABLE FORMAT. IT IS POSSIBLE TO VET DATA WITHIN A FEW HOURS
  OF STARTING TO CODE. DEMONSTRATIONS GIVEN ON REQUEST

NCC STAGE 1 SOFTWARE VERIFICATION ABSTRACT A34038

NAME OF SOFTWARE
   TRANSPORT AND PLANT COSTING SYSTEM

TYPE OF SOFTWARE
   ACCOUNTING

PURPOSE OF SOFTWARE
   THE FIRST ASPECT IS THE CREATION AND/OR AMENDMENT OF THE
   VEHICLES AND PLANT REGISTER TO FORM AN HISTORICAL RECORD OF
   EACH VEHICLE. THE SECOND IS THE RECORDING OF ACCUMULATED
   RUNNING COSTS AND FINAL ASPECT IS CALCULATION OF WEEKLY
   ALLOCATIONS

CONFIGURATION AND OPERATING SYSTEM
   ICL 1900

   HAS RUN SUCCESSFULLY ON ICL 1901A
   AMOUNT OF PRIMARY STORAGE 4K-8K WORDS, OVERLAYS USED
   4 MAGNETIC TAPE DRIVES
   1 LINE PRINTER
   1 PAPER TAPE READER
   RUN UNDER OPERATING SYSTEM EXECUTIVE

MODE OF USAGE
   BATCH

LANGUAGE
   PLAN AND COBOL

AVAILABILITY
   PROGRAM MAY BE AVAILABLE FOR USE OUTSIDE SUPPLIERS
   ORGANISATION. PROGRAM AVAILABLE ON A BUREAU SERVICE

NCC STAGE 1 SOFTWARE VERIFICATION ABSTRACT A34039

NAME OF SOFTWARE
  DATA CLASSIFICATION SYSTEM

TYPE OF SOFTWARE
  STATISTICAL APPLICATION (COMMERCIAL), FILE HANDLING

PURPOSE OF SOFTWARE
  TO OPERATE ON COMPUTER FILES, IN PARTICULAR THOSE
  REPRESENTING SURVEY-TYPE DATA, AND PRODUCE STATISTICAL
  TABLES - COMPREHENSIVE CELL DERIVATION IS A KEY FEATURE.
  NORMAL RECORD-PROCESSING DATA RETRIEVAL ALSO INCLUDED.

CONFIGURATION AND OPERATING SYSTEM
  ICL 1900

  HAS RUN SUCCESSFULLY ON ICL 1904, ICL 1904E, ICL 1904A
  AMOUNT OF PRIMARY STORAGE 17K-32K WORDS
  3 MAGNETIC TAPE DRIVES
  1 LINE PRINTER
  1 CARD READER
  RUN UNDER OPERATING SYSTEM 1900 EXECUTIVE

MODE OF USAGE
  BATCH

LANGUAGE
  PLAN

AVAILABILITY
  PROGRAM MAY BE AVAILABLE FOR USE OUTSIDE SUPPLIERS
  ORGANISATION.

SUPPLIERS COMMENT
  THE SYSTEM TAKES MAXIMUM ADVANTAGE OF THE COMMON
  CHARACTERISTICS OF TABLE GENERATION BY THE INCLUSION OF A
  DICTIONARY CONCEPT WHICH PERMITS ONCE-ONLY DEFINITIONS OF
  FILE LAYOUT, HEADINGS, SELECTION CONDITIONS, LEVELS AND ARRAYS.
  THEREAFTER REFERENCE TO SUCH ITEMS IS MADE BY NAME.

NCC STAGE 1 SOFTWARE VERIFICATION ABSTRACT A34040

NAME OF SOFTWARE
    SALES LEDGER ACCOUNTING ANALYSIS AND CREDIT CONTROL PACKAGE

TYPE OF SOFTWARE
    SALES ANALYSIS, ACCOUNTING

PURPOSE OF SOFTWARE
    A SYSTEM TO PROVIDE AN ACCURATE AND CONTROLLED SALES LEDGER,
    STATEMENTS CONTAINING CURRENT MONTHS TRANSACTIONS TOGETHER WITH
    OPEN ITEM OR BROUGHT FORWARD BALANCES AND MONTHS OVERDUE
    A FINANCIAL ANALYSIS OF SALES AND COST ANALYSES OVER
    FOUR STRUCTURES.

CONFIGURATION AND OPERATING SYSTEM
    IBM 360, ICL 1900

    HAS RUN SUCCESSFULLY ON IBM 360/30, IBM 360/50
    AMOUNT OF PRIMARY STORAGE 33K-64K BYTES
    4 MAGNETIC TAPE DRIVES
    1 LINE PRINTER
    1 CARD READER
    1 PAPER TAPE READER
    RUN UNDER OPERATING SYSTEM OS

    HAS RUN SUCCESSFULLY ON ICL 1902A
    AMOUNT OF PRIMARY STORAGE 17K-32K WORDS
    4 MAGNETIC TAPE DRIVES
    1 LINE PRINTER
    1 CARD READER
    1 PAPER TAPE READER
    RUN UNDER OPERATING SYSTEM EXECUTIVE

MODE OF USAGE
    BATCH

LANGUAGE
    COBOL

AVAILABILITY
    PROGRAM AVAILABLE ON A BUREAU SERVICE

SUPPLIERS COMMENT
    SEE ALSO PURCHASE LEDGER PACKAGE PROVIDING SIMILAR FACILITIES FOR
    PURCHASE LEDGER AND ANALYSIS

        COPYRIGHT NCC 1972   PRINTED ON 19/04/72

NCC STAGE 1 SOFTWARE VERIFICATION ABSTRACT A34041

NAME OF SOFTWARE
  ICL 1900 TESTING SOFTWARE

TYPE OF SOFTWARE
  PROGRAM MODULE LINKAGE AND TESTING

PURPOSE OF SOFTWARE
  PROVIDES THE LINKAGE AND TESTING ROUTINES FOR MODULAR PROGRAMS.
  ENABLES TESTING OF MODULES SEPARATELY OR IN ANY COMBINATION.
  CALLS TO MODULES MAY BE BYPASSED AND DATA SET UP AND DISPLAYED
  AS REQUIRED

CONFIGURATION AND OPERATING SYSTEM
  ICL 1900 SERIES

  HAS RUN SUCCESSFULLY ON ICL 1905
  AMOUNT OF PRIMARY STORAGE 4K-8K WORDS
  1 LINE PRINTER
  1 CARD READER
  RUN UNDER OPERATING SYSTEM ICL 1900 EXECUTIVE

  HAS RUN SUCCESSFULLY ON ICL 1902
  AMOUNT OF PRIMARY STORAGE 4K-8K WORDS
  1 LINE PRINTER
  1 PAPER TAPE READER
  RUN UNDER OPERATING SYSTEM ICL 1900 EXECUTIVE

MODE OF USAGE
  BATCH

LANGUAGE
  PLAN

AVAILABILITY
  PROGRAM MAY BE AVAILABLE FOR USE OUTSIDE SUPPLIERS ORGANISATION.
  PROGRAM AVAILABLE AS A BUREAU SERVICE

SUPPLIERS COMMENT
  THE SOFTWARE IS USED ON ALL 1900 PROGRAM DEVELOPMENT BY SUPPLIER
  AND SEVERAL CLIENTS. IT ENABLES MODULES TO BE TESTED IN
  ISOLATION OR IN FAMILIES WHILE OTHER MODULES ARE STILL UNDER
  DEVELOPMENT. ALL LOGICAL PATHS MAY BE TESTED WITHIN A PROGRAM
  IN FEWER COMPUTER SUBMISSIONS, SINCE ON FAILURE IN A TEST CORE
  IS PRINTED AND THE RUN CONTINUED WITH NEXT TEST

NCC STAGE 1 SOFTWARE VERIFICATION ABSTRACT A34042

NAME OF SOFTWARE
  MANAGEMENT INFORMATION DATA PROCESSING SYSTEM

TYPE OF SOFTWARE
  FILE HANDLING, PERT, CRITICAL PATH

PURPOSE OF SOFTWARE
  EMPRENT PROVIDES AN EXTREMELY FLEXIBLE SYSTEM FOR PERT
  TIME/COST/RESOURCE ANALYSIS, COMBINED WITH A COMPREHENSIVE
  REPORT GENERATION SYSTEM. THE USER IS ALLOWED TO DEFINE
  IN DETAIL THE REPORTS HE WISHES TO RECEIVE

CONFIGURATION AND OPERATING SYSTEM
  ICL 4100

  HAS RUN SUCCESSFULLY ON ICL 4130
  AMOUNT OF PRIMARY STORAGE 33K-64K WORDS
  6 MAGNETIC TAPE DRIVES
  1 LINE PRINTER
  2 PAPER TAPE READERS
  1 PAPER TAPE PUNCH
  1 GRAPH PLOTTER
  NO OPERATING SYSTEM USED

MODE OF USAGE
  BATCH

LANGUAGE
  NEAT

AVAILABILITY
  PROGRAM AVAILABLE ON A BUREAU SERVICE

SUPPLIERS COMMENT
  FURTHER APPLICATIONS INCLUDE PRODUCTION OF DEVELOPMENT COST
  PLANS, PRODUCTION OF AIRCRAFT WIRING SCHEDULES, DOCUMENTATION
  CONTROL

      COPYRIGHT NCC 1972   PRINTED ON 19/04/72

NCC STAGE 1 SOFTWARE VERIFICATION ABSTRACT A34043

NAME OF SOFTWARE
  ROADNET

TYPE OF SOFTWARE
  OPERATIONAL RESEARCH APPLICATION

PURPOSE OF SOFTWARE
  GIVEN A LIST OF MAP REFERENCES, ALLOWING DIFFERENT SPEEDS
  FOR DIFFERENT CLASSES OF ROAD AND FOR URBAN AND RURAL
  ENVIRONMENTS, ROADNET PRODUCES A MATRIX OF INTER-MAP
  -REFERENCE MINIMUM TRAVEL-TIMES,FOR USE BY THE TRANSIT
  PACKAGE

CONFIGURATION AND OPERATING SYSTEM
  ICL 1900

  HAS RUN SUCCESSFULLY ON ICL 1902A
  AMOUNT OF PRIMARY STORAGE 17K-32K WORDS
  2 DISC DRIVES, 101K-1M WORDS STORAGE
  1 MAGNETIC TAPE DRIVE
  1 LINE PRINTER
  1 CARD READER
  RUN UNDER OPERATING SYSTEM EXECUTIVE

  HAS RUN SUCCESSFULLY ON IBM 360/50
  AMOUNT OF PRIMARY STORAGE 65K-128K BYTES
  1 DISC DRIVE,101K-1M BYTES STORAGE
  1 MAGNETIC TAPE DRIVE
  1 LINE PRINTER
  1 CARD READER
  RUN UNDER OPERATING SYSTEM O/S UNDER HASP SPOOLING

MODE OF USAGE
  BATCH

LANGUAGE
  COBOL

AVAILABILITY
  PROGRAM MAY BE AVAILABLE FOR USE OUTSIDE SUPPLIERS
  ORGANISATION. PROGRAM IS AVAILABLE ON BUREAU SERVICE

    COPYRIGHT NCC 1972   PRINTED ON 19/04/72

NCC STAGE 1 SOFTWARE VERIFICATION ABSTRACT A34044

NAME OF SOFTWARE
    COMPUTER PROGRAM TO TRANSLATE ICL 4100 ALGOL INTO ICL 1900
    ALGOL

TYPE OF SOFTWARE
    EDITOR FOR CHANGING LANGUAGE DIALECT

PURPOSE OF SOFTWARE
    TAKES ICL 4100 ALGOL PROGRAM (ON PAPER TAPE) EDITS IT AND
    PRODUCES ICL 1900 ALGOL PROGRAM ON CARDS/PAPER TAPE/LINE PRINTER.
    HAS ALSO BEEN USED FOR ICL 803 ALGOL (TO 4100 THEN 1900
    ALGOL)

CONFIGURATION AND OPERATING SYSTEM
    ICL 1900

    HAS RUN SUCCESSFULLY ON ICL 1907
    AMOUNT OF PRIMARY STORAGE 17K-32K WORDS
    1 LINE PRINTER
    1 CARD PUNCH
    1 PAPER TAPE READER
    1 PAPER TAPE PUNCH
    CARD OR PAPER TAPE ARE ALTERNATIVE OUTPUTS
    RUN UNDER MANUAL EXECUTIVE

    HAS RUN SUCCESSFULLY ON ICL 1904A
    AMOUNT OF PRIMARY STORAGE 17K-32K WORDS
    1 LINE PRINTER
    1 PAPER TAPE READER
    1 PAPER TAPE PUNCH
    RUN UNDER OPERATING SYSTEM GEORGE 3

MODE OF USAGE
    BATCH

LANGUAGE
    ICL 1900 ALGOL

AVAILABILITY
    PROGRAM MAY BE AVAILABLE FOR USE OUTSIDE SUPPLIERS
    ORGANISATION

SUPPLIERS COMMENT
    DOCUMENTATION AVAILABLE AS R.A.E. TECHNICAL REPORT: EDALG - A
    COMPUTER PROGRAM TO TRANSLATE ELLIOTT 4100 ALGOL INTO ICL 1900
    ALGOL BY M. J. MARTIN, M.SC., ARCS.

NCC STAGE 1 SOFTWARE VERIFICATION ABSTRACT A34045

NAME OF SOFTWARE
  ODHAMS (WATFORD) PAYROLL

TYPE OF SOFTWARE
  PAYROLL, ACCOUNTING

PURPOSE OF SOFTWARE
  TO PROVIDE A GROSS TO NET PAYROLL SYSTEM INCLUDING THE
  PRODUCTION OF N.H.I. QUARTERLY RETURNS, END OF TAX YEAR AND
  PENSION RETURNS PLUS PAYROLL ACCOUNTING AND LABOUR COSTING
  INFORMATION

CONFIGURATION AND OPERATING SYSTEM
  IBM 360

  HAS RUN SUCCESSFULLY ON IBM 360/30
  AMOUNT OF PRIMARY STORAGE 33K-64K BYTES, OVERLAYS USED
  2 DISC DRIVES, 1.1M-10M BYTES STORAGE
  4 MAGNETIC TAPE DRIVES
  1 LINE PRINTER
  1 CARD READER
  RUN UNDER OPERATING SYSTEM DOS

MODE OF USAGE
  BATCH

LANGUAGE
  COBOL, 360 BAL

AVAILABILITY
  PROGRAM MAY BE AVAILABLE FOR USE OUTSIDE
  SUPPLIERS ORGANISATION

      COPYRIGHT NCC 1972   PRINTED ON 19/04/72

NCC STAGE 1 SOFTWARE VERIFICATION ABSTRACT A34046

NAME OF SOFTWARE
  DIETARY ANALYSIS BY INGREDIENTS

TYPE OF SOFTWARE
  SCIENTIFIC APPLICATION

PURPOSE OF SOFTWARE
  THE PROGRAM ANALYSES A DIET BREAKING DOWN EACH DISH BY
  INGREDIENTS INTO PROTEIN, FAT, CARBOHYDRATES AND CALORIE CONTENT
  PER OUNCE OR 100 GM. IT PRODUCES A SUBTOTAL FOR EACH DISH AS
  WELL AS TOTALS AVERAGE PORTION SIZE FOR EACH 'COVER' INCLUDED

CONFIGURATION AND OPERATING SYSTEM
  ICL 1900 , IBM 1620

  HAS RUN SUCCESSFULLY ON ICL 1903A
  AMOUNT OF PRIMARY STORAGE 17K-32K WORDS
  1 DISC DRIVE, 10K-100K WORDS STORAGE
  1 LINE PRINTER
  1 CARD READER
  RUN UNDER OPERATING SYSTEM GEORGE 2 AND GEORGE 3

  HAS RUN SUCCESSFULLY ON IBM 1620 MODEL 1
  AMOUNT OF PRIMARY STORAGE 33K-64K CHARACTERS
  1 DISC DRIVE, 10K-100K CHARACTERS STORAGE
  1 LINE PRINTER
  1 CARD READER
  NO OPERATING SYSTEM USED

MODE OF USAGE
  BATCH

LANGUAGE
  FORTRAN IV, FORTRAN 2D

AVAILABILITY
  PROGRAM AVAILABLE ON A BUREAU SERVICE

SUPPLIERS COMMENT
  AT THE END OF EACH MENU A GRAND TOTAL IS PRODUCED OF CONSTITUENTS
  AND CONSTITUENT RATIOS ARE CALCULATED ONE TO ANOTHER AND CAN BE
  USED TO EVALUATE THE BALANCE OF THE DIET. A NUMBER OF DIETS CAN BE
  ANALYSED CONSECUTIVELY; INDIVIDUAL AND ACCUMULATED DEVIATIONS ARE
  SHOWN IN TABULAR AND GRAPHIC FORM
  CONSECUTIVE ANALYSIS OF A NUMBER OF DIETS ON ICL 1900
  ONLY

NCC STAGE 1 SOFTWARE VERIFICATION ABSTRACT A34047

NAME OF SOFTWARE
    DIETARY ANALYSIS BY STANDARD RECIPES

TYPE OF SOFTWARE
    SCIENTIFIC APPLICATION
    STORES REQUISITIONS

PURPOSE OF SOFTWARE
    ANALYSES AND COSTS A DIET USING INDIVIDUAL STANDARD RECIPES.
    THE PROGRAM PRINTS A STORES REQUISITION LIST AND NUTRITIONAL
    ANALYSES. THESE CAN THEN BE COMPARED WITH SPECIFIED STANDARDS .
    READ IN TO THE PROGRAM

CONFIGURATION AND OPERATING SYSTEM
    ICL 1900

    HAS RUN SUCCESSFULLY ON ICL 1903A
    AMOUNT OF PRIMARY STORAGE 17K-32K WORDS
    1 DISC DRIVE, 10K-100K WORDS STORAGE
    1 MAGNETIC TAPE DRIVE
    1 LINE PRINTER
    1 CARD READER
    RUN UNDER OPERATING SYSTEM GEORGE 2 AND GEORGE 3

MODE OF USAGE
    BATCH

LANGUAGE
    FORTRAN IV

AVAILABILITY
    PROGRAM AVAILABLE ON A BUREAU SERVICE

SUPPLIERS COMMENT
    A NUMBER OF DIETS CAN ANALYSED CONSECUTIVELY; INDIVIDUAL
    AND ACCUMULATED DEVIATIONS ARE SHOWN IN TABULAR AND GRAPHIC
    FORM.

        COPYRIGHT NCC 1972   PRINTED ON 19/04/72

NCC STAGE 1 SOFTWARE VERIFICATION ABSTRACT A34048

NAME OF SOFTWARE
  MENU COSTING

TYPE OF SOFTWARE
  STORES REQUISITIONS

PURPOSE OF SOFTWARE
  PRODUCES A COSTED LISTING OF VARYING NUMBERS OF INDIVIDUAL
  DISHES WITH OR WITHOUT NUTRITIONAL CONSTITUENTS. A STORES
  REQUISITION LIST IS ALSO GENERATED GIVING QUANTITIES OF FOODS
  REQUIRED AND COST OF STORES

CONFIGURATION AND OPERATING SYSTEM
  ICL 1900

  HAS RUN SUCCESSFULLY ON ICL 1903A
  AMOUNT OF PRIMARY STORAGE 17K-32K WORDS
  1 DISC DRIVE, 10K-100K WORDS STORAGE
  1 MAGNETIC TAPE DRIVE
  1 LINE PRINTER
  1 CARD READER
  RUN UNDER OPERATING SYSTEM GEORGE 2 AND GEORGE 3

MODE OF USAGE
  BATCH

LANGUAGE
  FORTRAN IV

AVAILABILITY
  PROGRAM AVAILABLE ON A BUREAU SERVICE

      COPYRIGHT NCC 1972   PRINTED ON 19/04/72

NCC STAGE 1 SOFTWARE VERIFICATION ABSTRACT A34049

NAME OF SOFTWARE
   RANDOM MENU GENERATION

TYPE OF SOFTWARE
   STORES REQUISITIONS

PURPOSE OF SOFTWARE
   THIS PROGRAM GENERATES A MENU WITHIN ALL OR ANY OF THE
   FOLLOWING SPECIFIED LIMITS: (1) FOOD GROUPS, E.G. SOUP, FISH,
   ETC. (2) MIN-MAX NUTRITIONAL REQUIREMENTS, PROTEIN, FAT,
   CARBOHYDRATE, CALORIES (3) MIN-MAX COST (4) COLOUR AND TEXTURE
   BALANCE

CONFIGURATION AND OPERATING SYSTEM
   ICL 1900

   HAS RUN SUCCESSFULLY ON ICL 1903A
   AMOUNT OF PRIMARY STORAGE 17K-32K WORDS
   1 DISC DRIVE, 10K-100K STORAGE
   1 MAGNETIC TAPE DRIVE
   1 LINE PRINTER
   1 CARD READER
   RUN OPERATING SYSTEM GEORGE 2 AND GEORGE 3

MODE OF USAGE
   BATCH

LANGUAGE
   FORTRAN IV

AVAILABILITY
   PROGRAM AVAILABLE ON A BUREAU SERVICE

SUPPLIERS COMMENT
   SELECTED DISHES ARE PRINTED FOLLOWED BY A STORES REQUISITION
   SHEET FOR USE IN STOCK CONTROL.INDIVIDUAL AND ACCUMULATED
   DEVIATIONS FROM STANDARDS WITHIN GIVEN MINIMUM AND MAXIMUM
   REQUIREMENTS CAN BE SHOWN IN TABULAR AND OR GRAPHIC FORM

NCC STAGE 1 SOFTWARE VERIFICATION ABSTRACT A34050

NAME OF SOFTWARE
  I.C.D.P. PAYROLL PACKAGE

TYPE OF SOFTWARE
  PAYROLL

PURPOSE OF SOFTWARE
  TO PROCESS PAYROLL UP TO GROSS, GROSS TO NETT: TO MAINTAIN
  PAYROLL MASTER FILE: TO PRODUCE PAYSLIPS, COIN ANALYSIS, N.H.I.
  ANALYSIS AND END-OF-YEAR TAX FIGURES, ETC.

CONFIGURATION AND OPERATING SYSTEM
  HONEYWELL 200 SERIES

  HAS RUN SUCCESSFULLY ON HONEYWELL 120, HONEYWELL 200
  AMOUNT OF PRIMARY STORAGE 17K-32K CHARACTERS
  4 MAGNETIC TAPE DRIVES
  1 LINE PRINTER
  1 CARD READER
  RUN UNDER OPERATING SYSTEM MOD 1 TR (HONEYWELL)

MODE OF USAGE
  BATCH

LANGUAGE
  HONEYWELL EASYCODER AND COBOL

AVAILABILITY
  PROGRAM MAY BE AVAILABLE FOR USE OUTSIDE SUPPLIERS
  ORGANISATION. PROGRAM AVAILABLE ON A BUREAU SERVICE

SUPPLIERS COMMENT
  THIS PACKAGE IS BEING USED BY SEVERAL OF OUR CLIENTS VERY
  SATISFACTORILY. CONTINUAL REFINEMENTS ARE BEING MADE

NCC STAGE 1 SOFTWARE VERIFICATION ABSTRACT A34051

NAME OF SOFTWARE
  I.C.D.P. SALES LEDGER PACKAGE

TYPE OF SOFTWARE
  INVOICING PROCEDURE

PURPOSE OF SOFTWARE
  PROCESSES DAYBOOK,OPEN OR CLOSED ENDED LEDGER/STATEMENT,
  DEBTORS AGED BALANCES REPORT AND ANALYSES FROM SALES
  INVOICE DATA

CONFIGURATION AND OPERATING SYSTEM
  HONEYWELL 200 SERIES

  HAS RUN SUCCESSFULLY ON HONEYWELL 120, HONEYWELL 200
  AMOUNT OF PRIMARY STORAGE 17K-32K CHARACTERS
  4 MAGNETIC TAPE DRIVES
  1 LINE PRINTER
  1 CARD READER
  RUN UNDER OPERATING SYSTEM MOD 1 TR (HONEYWELL)

MODE OF USAGE
  BATCH

LANGUAGE
  HONEYWELL EASYCODER AND COBOL

AVAILABILITY
  PROGRAM MAY BE AVAILABLE FOR USE OUTSIDE SUPPLIERS
  ORGANISATION. PROGRAM AVAILABLE ON A BUREAU SERVICE

SUPPLIERS COMMENT
  THIS PACKAGE IS BEING USED BY SEVERAL OF OUR BUREAU CLIENTS
  TO THEIR SATISFACTION AND ALSO BY ONE CUSTOMER ON HIS
  OWN MACHINE

      COPYRIGHT NCC 1972   PRINTED ON 19/04/72

NCC STAGE 1 SOFTWARE VERIFICATION ABSTRACT A34052

NAME OF SOFTWARE
  I.C.D.P. PURCHASE LEDGER PACKAGE

TYPE OF SOFTWARE
  INVOICING PROCEDURE

PURPOSE OF SOFTWARE
  TO PROCESS DAYBOOK, REMITTANCE ADVICES/LEDGER, CHEQUES/CREDIT
  TRANSFERS, BANK LISTS, ANALYSES FROM PURCHASE INVOICE DATA

CONFIGURATION AND OPERATING SYSTEM
  HONEYWELL 200 SERIES

  HAS RUN SUCCESSFULLY ON HONEYWELL 120, HONEYWELL 200
  AMOUNT OF PRIMARY STORAGE 17K-32K CHARACTERS
  4 MAGNETIC TAPE DRIVES
  1 LINE PRINTER
  1 CARD READER
  RUN UNDER OPERATING SYSTEM MOD 1 TR (HONEYWELL)

MODE OF USAGE
  BATCH

LANGUAGE
  HONEYWELL COBOL

AVAILABILITY
  PROGRAM MAY BE AVAILABLE FOR USE OUTSIDE SUPPLIERS
  ORGANISATION. PROGRAM AVAILABLE ON A BUREAU SERVICE

SUPPLIERS COMMENT
  THIS PACKAGE HAS BEEN FULLY TESTED OVER SEVERAL YEARS AND IS
  BEING USED BY SEVERAL CLIENTS ON OUR OWN MACHINE

NCC STAGE 1 SOFTWARE VERIFICATION ABSTRACT A34053

NAME OF SOFTWARE
  DETAILING REINFORCED CONCRETE

TYPE OF SOFTWARE
  ENGINEERING APPLICATION

PURPOSE OF SOFTWARE
  TO ANALYSE BUILDING AND BRIDGE STRUCTURES.THE DESIGN AND
  DETAIL OF REINFORCEMENT. RESULTS CONSIST OF MOMENTS, SHEARS,
  DEFLECTIONS, ETC. FROM ANALYSIS, CALCULATIONS SHEET, BAR
  SCHEDULES, WEIGHT, SUMMARIES, FIXING DIAGRAMS; QUANTITIES
  FROM DESIGN

CONFIGURATION AND OPERATING SYSTEM
  IBM 360,SIGMA, CDC 6600

  HAS RUN SUCCESSFULLY ON IBM 360/40
  AMOUNT OF PRIMARY STORAGE 65K-128K BYTES
  1 DISC DRIVE, <10K BYTES STORAGE
  1 MAGNETIC TAPE DRIVE
  1 LINE PRINTER
  1 CARD READER
  RUN UNDER OPERATING SYSTEM OS

  HAS RUN SUCCESSFULLY ON CDC 6600 (SIA CONFIGURATION)
  AMOUNT OF PRIMARY STORAGE 65K-128K WORDS
  1 DISC DRIVE,>100M CHARACTERS
  6 MAGNETIC TAPE DRIVES
  2 LINE PRINTERS
  2 CARD READERS
  1 CARD READER
  1 CARD PUNCH
  1 GRAPH PLOTTER
  6 VDU'S
  RUN UNDER OPERATING SYSTEM SCOPE

MODE OF USAGE
  BATCH

LANGUAGE
  FORTRAN AND ASSEMBLER

AVAILABILITY
  PROGRAM MAY BE AVAILABLE FOR USE OUTSIDE SUPPLIERS
  ORGANISATION. PROGRAM AVAILABLE ON A BUREAU SERVICE

SUPPLIERS COMMENT
  THESE PROGRAMS HAVE BEEN AVAILABLE FOR A NUMBER OF YEARS.THE
  PROGRAMS ARE DESIGNED TO CARRY OUT CONSIDERABLE VALIDATION
  OF USERS DATA

NCC STAGE 1 SOFTWARE VERIFICATION ABSTRACT A34054

NAME OF SOFTWARE
    GENERAL PURPOSE STRUCTURAL ANALYSIS PROGRAM

TYPE OF SOFTWARE
    ENGINEERING APPLICATION

PURPOSE OF SOFTWARE
    FOR STRUCTURAL ANALYSIS OF FRAME PROBLEMS.SIX TYPES OF FRAME
    CAN BE CONSIDERED;CONTINUOUS BEAM, PLANE TRUSS, PLANE FRAME,
    GRID, SPACE TRUSS, SPACE FRAME. SPECIAL FACILITIES ARE JOINT
    MEMBER LOAD, TRANSFORMED AXES, LOAD COMBINATIONS

CONFIGURATION AND OPERATING SYSTEM
    CDC 6600, UNIVAC 1108, IBM 360

    HAS RUN SUCCESSFULLY ON IBM 360/40
    AMOUNT OF PRIMARY STORAGE 65K-128K BYTES
    2 DISC DRIVES, 10K-100K BYTES STORAGE
    2 MAGNETIC TAPE DRIVES
    1 LINE PRINTER
    1 CARD READER
    RUN UNDER OPERATING SYSTEM OS

    HAS RUN SUCCESSFULLY ON CDC 6600
    AMOUNT OF PRIMARY STORAGE 65K-128K WORDS
    2 DISC DRIVES, 10K-100K CHARACTERS STORAGE
    2 MAGNETIC TAPE DRIVES
    1 LINE PRINTER
    1 CARD READER
    RUN UNDER OPERATING SYSTEM SCOPE

MODE OF USAGE
    BATCH

LANGUAGE
    FORTRAN

AVAILABILITY
    PROGRAM MAY BE AVAILABLE FOR USE OUTSIDE SUPPLIERS
    ORGANISATION. PROGRAM AVAILABLE ON A BUREAU SERVICE

SUPPLIERS COMMENT
    TWO VERSIONS OF THE PROGRAM ARE AVAILABLE: LEAP 1 FOR
    MEDIUM FRAMES: LEAP 2 FOR LARGE FRAMES. PROGRAMS HAVE BEEN
    IN REGULAR PRODUCTION USE FOR FOUR YEARS

        COPYRIGHT NCC 1972   PRINTED ON 19/04/72

NCC STAGE 1 SOFTWARE VERIFICATION ABSTRACT A34055

NAME OF SOFTWARE
   OPTIMISED REINFORCEMENT BAR CUTTING

TYPE OF SOFTWARE
   ENGINEERING APPLICATION

PURPOSE OF SOFTWARE
   USED BY REINFORCEMENT SUPPLIERS TO SORT BAR ORDERED AT
   RANDOM INTO TYPES AND SIZE BY ORDERS. PRODUCES A CUTTING
   SCHEDULE THAT INSTRUCTS THE OPERATOR HOW TO CUT BARS FROM
   STOCK LENGTHS WITH MINIMUM LOSS OF MATERIAL. NORMAL JOB
   PRODUCES ONE PER CENT SCRAP

CONFIGURATION AND OPERATING SYSTEM
   IBM 360

   HAS RUN SUCCESSFULLY ON IBM 360/50
   AMOUNT OF PRIMARY STORAGE 65K-128K BYTES
   1 DISC DRIVE, <10K BYTES STORAGE
   1 MAGNETIC TAPE DRIVE
   1 LINE PRINTER
   1 CARD READER
   RUN UNDER OPERATING SYSTEM OS

MODE OF USAGE
   BATCH, INTERACTIVE

LANGUAGE
   FORTRAN AND ASSEMBLER

AVAILABILITY
   PROGRAM MAY BE AVAILABLE FOR USE OUTSIDE SUPPLIERS
   ORGANISATION. PROGRAM AVAILABLE ON A BUREAU SERVICE

SUPPLIERS COMMENT
   PROGRAM IS BUILT IN MODULES SO THAT MODIFICATIONS TO MEET
   PARTICULAR SUPPLIERS NEEDS CAN BE EASILY ADDED. MOST
   SUPPLIERS WANT DOCUMENTATION TO MEET THEIR PARTICULAR
   METHODS.USED BY LARGE FACTORIES WITH SATELLITE
   ESTABLISHMENTS FOR REMOTE BATCH WORK.

NCC STAGE 1 SOFTWARE VERIFICATION ABSTRACT A34056

NAME OF SOFTWARE
  MANAGEMENT JOB COST CONTROL PROGRAM

TYPE OF SOFTWARE
  MANAGEMENT INFORMATION SYSTEM,PROFESSIONAL JOB COSTING

PURPOSE OF SOFTWARE
  PRIME OBJECT IS TO PRESENT MANAGEMENT WITH COST INFORMATION
  RAPIDLY SO THAT IT IS NOT TOO LATE TO ACT. IT PROVIDES
  MANAGEMENT SUMMARIES, CONTRACT COST REPORT, COST CODE
  ANALYSIS, STAFF TIME ANALYSIS, BUDGET REPORTS, MERGE
  FACILITY, OVERHEAD DETERMINATION

CONFIGURATION AND OPERATING SYSTEM
  IBM 360

  HAS RUN SUCCESSFULLY ON IBM 360/50, IBM 360/65, IBM 360/75,
  IBM 360/85
  AMOUNT OF PRIMARY STORAGE 65K-128K BYTES
  1 DISC DRIVE, <10K BYTES STORAGE
  2 MAGNETIC TAPE DRIVES
  1 LINE PRINTER
  1 CARD READER
  RUN UNDER OPERATING SYSTEM OS OR DOS

MODE OF USAGE
  BATCH, INTERACTIVE

LANGUAGE
  FORTRAN AND ASSEMBLER

AVAILABILITY
  PROGRAM MAY BE AVAILABLE FOR USE OUTSIDE SUPPLIERS
  ORGANISATION. PROGRAM AVAILABLE ON A BUREAU SERVICE

SUPPLIERS COMMENT
  MANUALS AND FLOW CHARTS AVAILABLE.
  PROGRAM HAS BEEN IN OPERATION FOR MANY YEARS.
  MODULAR PROGRAM SO THAT ADDITIONS CAN BE MADE EASILY.
  USERS ARE ARCHITECTS, ACCOUNTANTS, LOCAL AUTHORITIES,
  ENGINEERS
  USED BY FACTORIES WITH SATELLITE ESTABLISHMENTS

NCC STAGE 1 SOFTWARE VERIFICATION ABSTRACT A34057

NAME OF SOFTWARE
  TOWER DESIGN PROGRAMS

TYPE OF SOFTWARE
  ENGINEERING APPLICATION

PURPOSE OF SOFTWARE
  PROGRAMS ANALYSE SELF SUPPORTING TOWERS, DESIGNS THE
  MEMBERS AND BOLTS. CALCULATES MATERIAL SCHEDULE AND TOWER
  WEIGHTS: DESIGNS FOUNDATIONS: PRODUCES QUANTITIES:
  COMPUTES SAGS AND TENSIONS FOR THE CABLES

CONFIGURATION AND OPERATING SYSTEM
  IBM 360, CDC 6600

  HAS RUN SUCCESSFULLY ON IBM 360/65
  AMOUNT OF PRIMARY STORAGE 65K-128K BYTES
  1 DISC DRIVE, <10K BYTES STORAGE
  1 MAGNETIC TAPE DRIVE
  1 LINE PRINTER
  1 CARD READER
  RUN UNDER OPERATING SYSTEM OS

MODE OF USAGE
  BATCH, INTERACTIVE

LANGUAGE
  FORTRAN

AVAILABILITY
  PROGRAM MAY BE AVAILABLE FOR USE OUTSIDE SUPPLIERS
  ORGANISATION. PROGRAM AVAILABLE ON A BUREAU SERVICE

SUPPLIERS COMMENT
  PROGRAMS PRODUCED FOR A MAJOR TOWER SUPPLIER AS A COMPLETE
  DESIGN SUITE. PROGRAMS AVAILABLE TO OTHERS. USER SUBJECT
  TO CERTAIN AGREEMENTS
  USED BY FACTORIES WITH SATELLITE ESTABLISHMENTS

     COPYRIGHT NCC 1972   PRINTED ON 19/04/72

NCC STAGE 1 SOFTWARE VERIFICATION ABSTRACT A34058

NAME OF SOFTWARE
   BILLS OF QUANTITIES AND THEIR RE-ANALYSIS BY COMPUTER

TYPE OF SOFTWARE
   ENGINEERING APPLICATION

PURPOSE OF SOFTWARE
   TO PRODUCE BILLS OF QUANTITIES BY MEANS OF PROCESSING CODED
   TAKING OFF DIMENSIONS. CODES ARE BASED ON VARIOUS STANDARD
   LIBRARIES AVAILABLE TO THE BUILDING INDUSTRY

CONFIGURATION AND OPERATING SYSTEM
   ICL 803

   HAS RUN SUCCESSFULLY ON ICL 803B
   AMOUNT OF PRIMARY STORAGE 4K-8K WORDS, OVERLAYS USED
   3 MAGNETIC TAPE DRIVES
   1 PAPER TAPE READER
   1 PAPER TAPE PUNCH
   1 TELETYPE
   NO OPERATING SYSTEM USED

MODE OF USAGE
   BATCH

LANGUAGE
   803 MACHINE CODE

AVAILABILITY
   PROGRAM AVAILABLE ON A BUREAU SERVICE

SUPPLIERS COMMENT
   THE PROGRAMS ARE AVAILABLE FOR USE ON A BUREAU BASIS FROM
   OLDACRES COMPUTERS LTD. FULL TRAINING AND DOCUMENTATION ARE
   PROVIDED TO USERS. THE SUITE OF PROGRAMS HAS BEEN OPERATIONAL
   SINCE 1964 AND HAS BEEN IN CONTINUOUS USE EVER SINCE

NCC STAGE 1 SOFTWARE VERIFICATION ABSTRACT A34059

NAME OF SOFTWARE
  CASH PULL

TYPE OF SOFTWARE
  FILE HANDLING

PURPOSE OF SOFTWARE
  TO EXTRACT ANY NUMBER OF SPECIFIED TRANSACTIONS FROM A CARD FILE.
  RECORDS ARE INDENTIFIED BY THEIR POSITION WITHIN THE FILE AND NOT
  BY ANY IDENTIFICATION PUNCHED IN THE CARD. THUS DUPLICATE RECORDS
  MAY BE HELD WITHOUT HAND PULLING

CONFIGURATION AND OPERATING SYSTEM
  IBM 360

  HAS RUN SUCCESSFULLY ON IBM 360/20, SUB MODEL 4
  AMOUNT OF PRIMARY STORAGE 4K-8K BYTES
  MULTI-FUNCTION CARD MACHINE
  RUN UNDER OPERATING SYSTEM CPS

MODE OF USAGE
  BATCH

LANGUAGE
  BASIC ASSEMBLER

AVAILABILITY
  PROGRAM MAY BE AVAILABLE FOR USE OUTSIDE SUPPLIERS ORGANISATION.
  PROGRAM AVAILABLE ON A BUREAU SERVICE

    COPYRIGHT NCC 1972   PRINTED ON 19/04/72

NCC STAGE 1 SOFTWARE VERIFICATION ABSTRACT A34060

NAME OF SOFTWARE
   PROGRAM FOR THE ANALYSIS OF PLANE SHEAR WALLS CONTAINING
   TWO ROWS OF OPENINGS

TYPE OF SOFTWARE
   ENGINEERING APPLICATION

PURPOSE OF SOFTWARE
   TO ANALYSE A PLANE SHEAR WALL CONTAINING TWO ROWS OF
   OPENINGS SUBJECT TO A UNIFORMLY DISTRIBUTED LOAD

CONFIGURATION AND OPERATING SYSTEM
   ICL 1900

   HAS RUN SUCCESSFULLY ON ICL 1909
   AMOUNT OF PRIMARY STORAGE 9K-16K WORDS
   1 PAPER TAPE READER
   1 PAPER TAPE PUNCH
   RUN UNDER OPERATING SYSTEM EXECUTIVE

   HAS RUN SUCCESSFULLY ON ICL 1904
   AMOUNT OF PRIMARY STORAGE 9K-16K WORDS
   1 LINE PRINTER
   1 PAPER TAPE READER
   RUN UNDER OPERATING SYSTEM EXECUTIVE

MODE OF USAGE
   BATCH

LANGUAGE
   EXTENDED MERCURY AUTOCODE

AVAILABILITY
   PROGRAM AVAILABLE ON A BUREAU SERVICE

SUPPLIERS COMMENT
   THE PROGRAM ANALYSES A WALL BY THE STIFFNESS METHOD BUT
   ALLOWS FOR THE FINITE LATERAL DIMENSIONS OF THE MEMBERS.
   THE METHOD INCLUDES DEFORMATION DUE TO BENDING SHEAR AND
   AXIAL SHORTENING. ALL VARIABLES FOR EACH STOREY MUST BE
   SIMILAR EXCEPT STOREY AND OPENING HEIGHT AND THICKNESS

      COPYRIGHT NCC 1972   PRINTED ON 19/04/72

NCC STAGE 1 SOFTWARE VERIFICATION ABSTRACT A34061

NAME OF SOFTWARE
    PROGRAM FOR THE ANALYSIS OF PLANE SHEAR WALLS CONTAINING
    ONE ROW OF OPENINGS

TYPE OF SOFTWARE
    ENGINEERING APPLICATION

PURPOSE OF SOFTWARE
    TO ANALYSE A PLANE SHEAR WALL CONTAINING ONE ROW OF
    OPENINGS SUBJECT TO A UNIFORMLY DISTRIBUTED LOAD

CONFIGURATION AND OPERATING SYSTEM
    ICL 1900

    HAS RUN SUCCESSFULLY ON ICL 1909
    AMOUNT OF PRIMARY STORAGE 9K-16K WORDS
    1 PAPER TAPE READER
    1 PAPER TAPE PUNCH
    RUN UNDER OPERATING SYSTEM EXECUTIVE

    HAS RUN SUCCESSFULLY ON ICL 1904
    AMOUNT OF PRIMARY STORAGE 9K-16K WORDS
    1 LINE PRINTER
    1 PAPER TAPE READER
    RUN UNDER OPERATING SYSTEM EXECUTIVE

MODE OF USAGE
    BATCH

LANGUAGE
    EXTENDED MERCURY AUTOCODE

AVAILABILITY
    PROGRAM AVAILABLE ON A BUREAU SERVICE

SUPPLIERS COMMENT
    THE PROGRAM ANALYSES A WALL BY THE STIFFNESS METHOD BUT
    ALLOWS FOR THE FINITE LATERAL DIMENSIONS OF THE MEMBERS.
    THE METHOD INCLUDES DEFORMATION DUE TO BENDING,SHEAR,AND
    AXIAL SHORTENING. ALL VARIABLES FOR EACH STOREY MUST BE
    SIMILAR EXCEPT STOREY AND OPENING HEIGHT AND THICKNESS

    COPYRIGHT NCC 1972   PRINTED ON 19/04/72

NCC STAGE 1 SOFTWARE VERIFICATION ABSTRACT A34062

NAME OF SOFTWARE
   ASSEMBLER U30

TYPE OF SOFTWARE
   COMPILER

PURPOSE OF SOFTWARE
   TO TRANSLATE MNEMONIC LANGUAGE INTO MACHINE CODE AND ALLOCATE
   ABSOLUTE ADDRESSES AND PUNCH OBJECT PROGRAM ONTO PAPER TAPE. ALSO
   TO PERMIT INSERTION OF AMENDMENTS OR CHANGE IN RELATIVISERS IN
   EXISTING CODE SEGMENTS

CONFIGURATION AND OPERATING SYSTEM
   PHILIPS DATA

   HAS RUN SUCCESSFULLY ON PHILIPS 5000N
   AMOUNT OF PRIMARY STORAGE 4K-8K BYTES
   1 PAPER TAPE READER
   1 PAPER TAPE PUNCH
   NO OPERATING SYSTEM USED

MODE OF USAGE
   BATCH

AVAILABILITY
   PROGRAM MAY BE AVAILABLE FOR USE OUTSIDE SUPPLIERS ORGANISATION

SUPPLIERS COMMENT
   PROGRAM SIZE IS RESTRICTED ON A MACHINE WITH ONLY 4 BLOCKS

   COPYRIGHT NCC 1972   PRINTED ON 19/04/72

NCC STAGE 1 SOFTWARE VERIFICATION ABSTRACT A34063

NAME OF SOFTWARE
   MULTIPLE REGRESSION ANALYSIS WITH ELEMENT ANALYSIS,MRAEA

TYPE OF SOFTWARE
   STATISTICAL APPLICATION

PURPOSE OF SOFTWARE
   TO CALCULATE MULTIPLE REGRESSIONS AND THE CORRESPONDING
   ELEMENTS.ALSO PRELIMINARY ARITHMETIC,DATA SUMMARY,SUMS OF
   SQUARES AND PRODUCTS MATRIX,CORRELATION MATRIX,INVERSE MATRIX

CONFIGURATION AND OPERATING SYSTEM
   ELLIOTT 900

   HAS RUN SUCCESSFULLY ON ELLIOTT 903B
   AMOUNT OF PRIMARY STORAGE 4K-8K WORDS
   1 PAPER TAPE READER
   1 PAPER TAPE PUNCH
   NO OPERATING SYSTEM USED

   HAS RUN SUCCESSFULLY ON ELLIOTT 903C
   AMOUNT OF PRIMARY STORAGE 4K-8K WORDS
   1 PAPER TAPE READER
   1 PAPER TAPE PUNCH
   1 TELETYPE
   NO OPERATING SYSTEM USED

MODE OF USAGE
   INTERACTIVE

LANGUAGE
   ELLIOTT 903 SIR (SYMBOLIC INPUT ROUTINE)

AVAILABILITY
   PROGRAM MAY BE AVAILABLE FOR USE OUTSIDE SUPPLIERS
   ORGANISATION

SUPPLIERS COMMENT
   PROGRAM USED SUCCESSFULLY SINCE DECEMBER 1967 BY APPROXIMATELY
   20 PEOPLE IN 9 ESTABLISHMENTS.ISSUED AS BINARY TAPE ONLY BUT
   DETAILED USER GUIDE SUPPLIED.CHARGE £275.REDUCTION FOR
   RESEARCH ASSOCIATIONS.NO CHARGE TO MEMBRS OF BGIRA.MAY
   BE USED BY ARRANGEMENT AT BGIRA.FORTRAN VERSION AVAILABLE FOR
   16K 903.NEEDS MODIFICATIONS FOR OTHER COMPUTERS.CHARGE £50

NCC STAGE 1 SOFTWARE VERIFICATION ABSTRACT A34064

NAME OF SOFTWARE
  MULTIBILL 2; SUBSYSTEM 1, STANDARD LIBRARY OF ITEM DESCRIPTIONS.
  SUBSYSTEM 2 EPC BILLING

TYPE OF SOFTWARE
  QUANTITY SURVEYING

PURPOSE OF SOFTWARE
  SUBSYSTEM 1: A METHOD OF STORING INFORMATION RELATING TO A
  SERIES OF BUILDINGS AND OUTPUTTING SELECTIVE PRINTOUTS, BILLS OF
  QUANTITIES, ETC. SUBSYSTEM 2: A MEANS OF GATHERING AND
  INPUTTING THE INFORMATION TO SUBSYSTEM 1

CONFIGURATION AND OPERATING SYSTEM
  IBM 360

  HAS RUN SUCCESSFULLY ON IBM 360/40, IBM 360/50
  AMOUNT OF PRIMARY STORAGE 33K-64K BYTES
  1 DISC DRIVE, 101K-1M BYTES STORAGE
  4 MAGNETIC TAPE DRIVES
  1 LINE PRINTER
  1 CARD READER
  1 PAPER TAPE READER
  RUN UNDER OPERATING SYSTEM IBM DOS 24

MODE OF USAGE
  BATCH

LANGUAGE
  PART OF THE SUITE IN COBOL AND PART IN ASSEMBLER

AVAILABILITY
  PROGRAM MAY BE AVAILABLE FOR OUTSIDE SUPPLIERS
  ORGANISATION. PROGRAM AVAILABLE ON A BUREAU SERVICE

SUPPLIERS COMMENT
  ALL PROGRAMS FOR BOTH SUBSYSTEMS HAVE BEEN TESTED AND ACCEPTED.
  SUBSYSTEM 1 - SLID IS NOW WORKING AND SUBSYSTEM 2 - EPC BILLING
  WILL BE IN USE SUMMER 1971

NCC STAGE 1 SOFTWARE VERIFICATION ABSTRACT A34065

NAME OF SOFTWARE
  ECONOMIC DATA SERVICES STOCK CONTROL PACKAGE

TYPE OF SOFTWARE
  STOCK CONTROL

PURPOSE OF SOFTWARE
  PROVIDES STOCK RECORDS, MOVEMENTS AND DEMAND ANALYSES FROM
  INVOICE DATA. INPUT EITHER AS BY-PRODUCT TAPE FROM FRIDEN OR
  BISMECH MACHINES OR NORMAL ICL CODED CARDS OR PAPER TAPE

CONFIGURATION AND OPERATING SYSTEM
  ICL 1900

  HAS RUN SUCCESSFULLY ON ICL 1901
  AMOUNT OF PRIMARY STORAGE 9K-16K WORDS
  4 MAGNETIC TAPE DRIVES
  1 LINE PRINTER
  1 PAPER TAPE READER
  RUN UNDER OPERATING SYSTEM ICL EXECUTIVE

MODE OF USAGE
  BATCH

LANGUAGE
  COBOL

AVAILABILITY
  PROGRAM MAY BE AVAILABLE FOR USE OUTSIDE SUPPLIERS ORGANISATION.
  PROGRAM AVAILABLE ON A BUREAU SERVICE

NCC STAGE 1 SOFTWARE VERIFICATION ABSTRACT A34066

NAME OF SOFTWARE
  ECONOMIC DATA SERVICES SALES LEDGER PACKAGE

TYPE OF SOFTWARE
  ACCOUNTING

PURPOSE OF SOFTWARE
  INPUT: CARDS, PAPER TAPE OR BISMECH OR FRIDEN BY-PRODUCT
  PAPER TAPE FROM INVOICING MACHINES. OUTPUT: SALES LEDGER,
  STATEMENTS, INVOICE REGISTER, CASH BOOK, DEBT-AGEING
  SALES ANALYSES, PROFITABILITY BY PRODUCT, SALESMAN

CONFIGURATION AND OPERATING SYSTEM
  ICL 1900

  HAS RUN SUCCESSFULLY ON ICL 1901
  AMOUNT OF PRIMARY STORAGE 9K-16K WORDS
  4 MAGNETIC TAPE DRIVES
  1 LINE PRINTER
  1 PAPER TAPE READER
  RUN UNDER OPERATING SYSTEM ICL EXECUTIVE

MODE OF USAGE
  BATCH

LANGUAGE
  COBOL

AVAILABILITY
  PROGRAM MAY BE AVAILABLE FOR USE OUTSIDE SUPPLIERS
  ORGANISATION. PROGRAM AVAILABLE ON A BUREAU SERVICE

      COPYRIGHT NCC 1972   PRINTED ON 19/04/72

NCC STAGE 1 SOFTWARE VERIFICATION ABSTRACT A34067

NAME OF SOFTWARE
   ECONOMIC DATA SERVICES EXPLOSION PROGRAM

TYPE OF SOFTWARE
   PRODUCTION CONTROL

PURPOSE OF SOFTWARE
   SUMMARISES PIECE-PART REQUIREMENTS BY 9 TIME-PERIODS USING FINAL
   ASSEMBLY QUANTITIES AND DUE-DATES

CONFIGURATION AND OPERATING SYSTEM
   ICL 1900

   HAS RUN SUCCESSFULLY ON ICL 1901
   AMOUNT OF PRIMARY STORAGE 9K-16K WORDS
   4 MAGNETIC TAPE DRIVES
   1 LINE PRINTER
   1 PAPER TAPE READER
   RUN UNDER OPERATING SYSTEM ICL EXECUTIVE

MODE OF USAGE
   BATCH

LANGUAGE
   COBOL

AVAILABILITY
   PROGRAM MAY BE AVAILABLE FOR USE OUTSIDE SUPPLIERS ORGANISATION.
   PROGRAM AVAILABLE ON A BUREAU SERVICE

      COPYRIGHT NCC 1972   PRINTED ON 19/04/72

NCC STAGE 1 SOFTWARE VERIFICATION ABSTRACT A34068

NAME OF SOFTWARE
  PRECEDENCE DIAGRAM ANALYSIS PROGRAM PDA

TYPE OF SOFTWARE
  PERT, CRITICAL PATH

PURPOSE OF SOFTWARE
  PROGRAM USED FOR ANALYSIS OF PRECEDENCE NETWORK DIAGRAM
  CRITICAL PATH PROGRAMME

CONFIGURATION AND OPERATING SYSTEM
  CDC 6000, HONEYWELL 200/G, HONEYWELL 600/G

  HAS RUN SUCCESSFULLY ON CDC 6600
  AMOUNT OF PRIMARY STORAGE 65K-128K WORDS
  2 DISC DRIVES,>100M CHARACTERS STORAGE
  1 LINE PRINTER
  1 CARD READER
  RUN UNDER OPERATING SYSTEM SCOPE 3.2

  HAS RUN SUCCESSFULLY ON HONEYWELL 265/G
  AMOUNT OF PRIMARY STORAGE 9K-16K WORDS
  1 DISC DRIVE, 11M-100M CHARACTERS STORAGE
  1 TELETYPE
  RUN UNDER REMOTE ACCESS TIME-SHARING SYSTEM

  HAS RUN SUCCESSFULLY ON HONEYWELL 615/G
  AMOUNT OF PRIMARY STORAGE 65K-128K WORDS
  1 DISC DRIVE, >100M CHARACTERS STORAGE
  1 TELETYPE
  RUN UNDER GECOS 3 TIME-SHARING SYSTEM

MODE OF USAGE
  BATCH, INTERACTIVE

LANGUAGE
  FORTRAN IV (CDC), BASIC (GE)

AVAILABILITY
  PROGRAM MAY BE AVAILABLE FOR USE OUTSIDE SUPPLIERS
  ORGANISATION. PROGRAM AVAILABLE ON A BUREAU SERVICE

SUPPLIERS COMMENT
  PROGRAM FOR CDC 6600 WILL HANDLE UP TO 5,000 ACTIVITIES
  AND PRODUCES OUTPUTS IN BOTH BAR-CHART AND ACTIVITY LIST
  FORMATS - ALSO ACCEPTS ALTERNATIVE INPUT OF ARROW DIAGRAM
  DATA. OPTIONAL CALENDAR DATE FACILITY. FINISH-START,
  START-START AND FINISH-FINISH RELATIONSHIPS MAY BE SPECIFIED
  WITH DELAYS. GE PROGRAMS LIMITED TO 150 ACTIVITIES
  PRECEDENCE DATA

NCC STAGE 1 SOFTWARE VERIFICATION ABSTRACT A34069

NAME OF SOFTWARE
   CBH SCHEDULE PROGRAM SYSTEM SPS

TYPE OF SOFTWARE
   MANAGEMENT INFORMATION, FILE HANDLING, UTILITY

PURPOSE OF SOFTWARE
   A MODULAR PROGRAM PACKAGE USED SELECTIVELY FOR GENERATING
   STRUCTURING, EDITING, REFORMATTING AND PRINTING OUT OF
   INFORMATION CONTAINED IN A DATA BASE CONSISTING OF A SET OF
   RELATED ARCHITECTURAL PROJECT FILES

CONFIGURATION AND OPERATING SYSTEM
   CDC 6000

   HAS RUN SUCCESSFULLY ON CDC 6600
   AMOUNT OF PRIMARY STORAGE 129K-256K WORDS
   1 DISC DRIVE, >100M CHARACTERS STORAGE
   1 MAGNETIC TAPE DRIVE
   1 LINE PRINTER
   1 CARD READER
   1 CARD PUNCH
   1 PAPER TAPE READER
   1 PAPER TAPE PUNCH
   1 VDU
   RUN UNDER OPERATING SYSTEM SCOPE 3.2

MODE OF USAGE
   BATCH

LANGUAGE
   CDC FORTRAN IV AND COMPASS ASSEMBLY LANGUAGE SUBROUTINES

AVAILABILITY
   PROGRAM MAY BE AVAILABLE FOR USE OUTSIDE SUPPLIERS ORGANISATION.
   PROGRAM AVAILABLE ON A BUREAU SERVICE

SUPPLIERS COMMENT
   PROGRAM - APPROXIMATELY 3,500 SOURCE CARDS - APPROXIMATELY 1000
   CARDS IN BINARY OBJECT DECK. OBJECT DECK RESIDES IN 5 HALF TRACKS
   ON DISC (165,000 CHARACTERS). PROGRAM TYPICALLY USES 57K WORDS
   OF CENTRAL MEMORY FOR RUN. DATA MAY BE INPUT FROM CARDS, PAPER
   TAPE, MAGNETIC TAPE OR DISC. OUTPUTS MAY BE STORED ON DISC AND
   INSPECTED ON VDU PRIOR TO PRINTING

NCC STAGE 1 SOFTWARE VERIFICATION ABSTRACT A34070

NAME OF SOFTWARE
  CBH GENERAL SCHEDULE PROGRAM GSP

TYPE OF SOFTWARE
  MANAGEMENT INFORMATION SYSTEM

PURPOSE OF SOFTWARE
  A PROGRAM ALLOWING CERTAIN FORMS OF ARCHITECTURAL PROJECT
  INFORMATION TO BE INPUT BY MEANS OF A DEFINED LANGUAGE AND
  ALLOWING ANALYSES AND OUTPUTS OF SELECTED SETS OF THE
  INFORMATION TO BE PRODUCED

CONFIGURATION AND OPERATING SYSTEM
  CDC 6000

  HAS RUN SUCCESSFULLY ON CDC 6600
  AMOUNT OF PRIMARY STORAGE 129K-256K WORDS
  1 DISC DRIVE,> 100M CHARACTERS STORAGE
  1 LINE PRINTER
  1 CARD READER
  1 CARD PUNCH
  RUN UNDER OPERATING SYSTEM SCOPE 3.2

MODE OF USAGE
  BATCH

LANGUAGE
  CDC FORTRAN IV, AND SOME COMPASS ASSEMBLER SUBROUTINES

AVAILABILITY
  PROGRAM MAY BE AVAILABLE FOR USE OUTSIDE SUPPLIERS ORGANISATION.
  PROGRAM AVAILABLE ON A BUREAU SERVICE

SUPPLIERS COMMENT
  THE INFORMATION INPUT LANGUAGE PROVIDED ALLOWS CONSIDERABLE
  REDUCTION OF DATA WHICH IS EXPANDED BY THE PROGRAM AFTER INPUT.
  TYPICAL USES ARE FOR ARCHITECTURAL SCHEDULES OF FINISHES, DOORS,
  WINDOWS, ETC.

NCC STAGE 1 SOFTWARE VERIFICATION ABSTRACT A34071

NAME OF SOFTWARE
   BUSINESS SIMULATION EXERCISE - DYNAMIC RESTAURANT MODELS SERIES 1
   AND SERIES 2

TYPE OF SOFTWARE
   EDUCATIONAL

PURPOSE OF SOFTWARE
   THE EFFECT OF ONE TEAM'S DECISION IS MODIFIED BY THE OTHER
   COMPETITORS. SERIES 1: TEAM INPUT: SELLING PRICE, SERVICE,
   ADVERTISING, ESTABLISHMENT OF MARKET IMAGE. CONTROLLER INPUT:
   COSTS, OVERALL MARKET STABILITY, LABOUR MOBILITY, CREDIT AND
   MARKET SENSITIVITY TO PRICE, SERVICE, ADVERTISING, IMAGE, ETC.
   SERIES 2: AS FOR SERIES 1 WITH ADDITIONAL FACILITIES FOR DECOR,
   GROUP TRADING, MERGERS OR TAKEOVERS OF COMPETING TEAMS

CONFIGURATION AND OPERATING SYSTEM
   ICL 1900

   HAS RUN SUCCESSFULLY ON ICL 1903A
   AMOUNT OF PRIMARY STORAGE 9K-16K WORDS
   2 MAGNETIC TAPE DRIVES
   1 LINE PRINTER
   1 CARD READER
   RUN UNDER OPERATING SYSTEMS GEORGE 2 AND GEORGE 3

MODE OF USAGE
   BATCH

LANGUAGE
   FORTRAN IV

AVAILABILITY
   PROGRAM AVAILABLE ON A BUREAU SERVICE

SUPPLIERS COMMENT
   MODIFIED VERSION OF SERIES 1 USED FOR THE POSTAL SECTION
   OF THE NATIONAL CATERING BUSINESS GAME 1971-72

NCC STAGE 1 SOFTWARE VERIFICATION ABSTRACT A34073

NAME OF SOFTWARE
  SIRA FORECASTING SUITE

TYPE OF SOFTWARE
  OPERATIONAL RESEARCH APPLICATION

PURPOSE OF SOFTWARE
  MONITORS ACTUAL PRODUCT DEMAND AND DEVIATIONS FROM SALES TARGETS.
  PRODUCES STATISTICALLY CORRECTED FORECASTS AND EXCEPTION
  REPORTS FOR PRODUCTS OUT OF CONTROL

CONFIGURATION AND OPERATING SYSTEM
  ICL 4100

  HAS RUN SUCCESSFULLY ON ICL 4120
  AMOUNT OF PRIMARY STORAGE 9K-16K WORDS
  4 MAGNETIC TAPE DRIVES
  1 LINE PRINTER
  1 PAPER TAPE READER
  RUN UNDER OPERATING SYSTEM NICE

MODE OF USAGE
  BATCH

LANGUAGE
  ALGOL

AVAILABILITY
  PROGRAM MAY BE AVAILABLE FOR USE OUTSIDE SUPPLIERS ORGANISATION.
  PROGRAM AVAILABLE ON A BUREAU SERVICE

    COPYRIGHT NCC 1972   PRINTED ON 19/04/72

NCC STAGE 1 SOFTWARE VERIFICATION ABSTRACT A34074

NAME OF SOFTWARE
  SIRA REGRESSION PACKAGE

TYPE OF SOFTWARE
  STATISTICAL APPLICATION

PURPOSE OF SOFTWARE
  PRODUCES A LINEAR LEAST SQUARES REGRESSION EQUATION EITHER BY
  AUTOMATIC SELECTION OF SIGNIFICANT VARIABLES OR ON ALL VARIABLES

CONFIGURATION AND OPERATING SYSTEM
  ICL 4100

  HAS RUN SUCCESSFULLY ON ICL 4120
  AMOUNT OF PRIMARY STORAGE 9K-16K WORDS
  2 MAGNETIC TAPE DRIVES
  1 LINE PRINTER
  1 PAPER TAPE READER
  RUN UNDER OPERATING SYSTEM NICE

MODE OF USAGE
  BATCH

LANGUAGE
  ALGOL

AVAILABILITY
  PROGRAM MAY BE AVAILABLE FOR USE OUTSIDE SUPPLIERS ORGANISATION.
  PROGRAM AVAILABLE ON A BUREAU SERVICE

NCC STAGE 1 SOFTWARE VERIFICATION ABSTRACT A34075

NAME OF SOFTWARE
    FILETAB REPORT GENERATOR PROGRAM - TABN

TYPE OF SOFTWARE
    PARAMETERISED REPORT GENERATOR AND FILE HANDLER

PURPOSE OF SOFTWARE
    PREPARATION OF REPORTS,DATA RETRIEVAL AND ENQUIRY ANSWERING
    SYSTEM,FILE MAINTENANCE. THE SYSTEM INCLUDES A SORT,LOOK-UP TABLES
    AND DECISION TABLE SELECTION AND EDITING.

CONFIGURATION AND OPERATING SYSTEM
    ICL1900

    HAS RUN SUCCESSFULLY ON ICL 1901
    AMOUNT OF PRIMARY STORAGE 9K-16K WORDS
    1 DISC DRIVE <10K WORDS STORAGE
    1 MAGNETIC TAPE DRIVE
    1 LINE PRINTER
    1 CARD READER
    DISC (PREFERRED) BUT TAPE ALTERNATIVE
    RUN UNDER OPERATING SYSTEM EXECUTIVE

    HAS RUN SUCCESSFULLY ON ICL 1905F
    AMOUNT OF PRIMARY STORAGE 33K-64K WORDS
    4 DISC DRIVES,11M-100M WORDS STORAGE
    6 MAGNETIC TAPE DRIVES
    1 LINE PRINTER
    1 CARD READER
    1 PAPER TAPE READER
    1 CARD PUNCH
    1 PAPER TAPE PUNCH
    8 TELETYPES
    1 7901 COMMUNICATIONS PROCESSOR
    RUN UNDER OPERATING SYSTEM GEORGE 2 MK 8,GEORGE 3 MK 6.2

MODE OF USAGE
    BATCH

LANGUAGE
    PLAN

AVAILABILITY
    PROGRAM MAY BE AVAILABLE FOR USE OUTSIDE SUPPLIERS
    ORGANISATION. PROGRAM AVAILABLE AS A BUREAU SERVICE

SUPPLIERS COMMENT
    THE SOFTWARE HAS BEEN USED ON OVER 50 INSTALLATIONS WITHIN
    THE RANGE ICL 1901 TO ICL 1905F.

NCC STAGE 1 SOFTWARE VERIFICATION ABSTRACT A34077

NAME OF SOFTWARE
  INPUT VALIDATE, OUTPUT AND REPORT SUBROUTINE, I.V.O.R.

TYPE OF SOFTWARE
  NON-MATHEMATICAL SUBROUTINE/ALGORITHM

PURPOSE OF SOFTWARE
  A GENERAL PURPOSE SUBROUTINE WHICH PERFORMS MOST OF THE TASKS FOR
  VALIDATION PROGRAMS THE SUBROUTINE VALIDATES EACH FIELD FOR
  CORRECT FORMAT PERFORMS NECESSARY CONVERSIONS AND FORMS AN OUTPUT
  RECORD AND ERROR REPORT LINES

CONFIGURATION AND OPERATING SYSTEM
  ICL 1900 SERIES IBM 360 SERIES

  HAS RUN SUCCESSFULLY ON ICL 1905, ICL 1901A, IBM 360/30
  AMOUNT OF STORAGE<4K WORDS
  RUN UNDER OPERATING SYSTEM ICL 1900 EXECUTIVE

  HAS RUN SUCCESSFULLY ON ICL 1901A
  AMOUNT OF STORAGE<4K WORDS
  RUN UNDER OPERATING SYSTEM ICL 1900 EXECUTIVE

  HAS RUN SUCCESSFULLY ON IBM 360/30
  AMOUNT OF STORAGE 4K-8K BYTES
  RUN UNDER OPERATING SYSTEM DOS

MODE OF USAGE
  BATCH

LANGUAGE
  ICL 1900 PLAN IBM 360 ASSEMBLER

AVAILABILITY
  PROGRAM MAY BE AVAILABLE FOR USE OUTSIDE SUPPLIERS ORGANISATION.
  PROGRAM AVAILABLE AS A BUREAU SERVICE

SUPPLIERS COMMENT
  THE SUBROUTINE MAY BE CALLED FROM COBOL, PLAN OR ASSEMBLER.
  VALIDATION PROGRAMS BECOME EASIER TO WRITE AND AMEND AND CORE
  USAGE IS VERY EFFICIENT ESPECIALLY IN COBOL PROGRAMS. USER HAS
  ONLY TO SPECIFY THE DATA TYPE FOR EACH FIELD AND THE FORM OF THE
  OUTPUT RECORD - THE SUBROUTINE VALIDATES CONVERTS AND EDITS.

NCC STAGE 1 SOFTWARE VERIFICATION ABSTRACT A34078

NAME OF SOFTWARE
   THE 1900 LUST PACKAGE LISTING UPDATING SORTING AND TOTALLING

TYPE OF SOFTWARE
   FILE HANDLING

PURPOSE OF SOFTWARE
   L.U.S.T. IS A HIGH - LEVEL PROGRAM GENERATOR ENABLING LISTING
   UPDATING SORTING AND TOTALLING PROGRAMS TO BE WRITTEN VERY QUICKLY
   THE LANGUAGE IS EASY TO LEARN AND USE AND NON-ESSENTIAL CODING
   IS OBVIATED

CONFIGURATION AND OPERATING SYSTEM
   REPRESENTATIVE CONFIGURATIONS
   ICL1900

   HAS RUN SUCCESSFULLY ON ICL 1906F
   AMOUNT OF STORAGE 17K-32K WORDS
   1 DISC DRIVE,10K-100K WORDS STORAGE
   4 MAGNETIC TAPE DRIVES
   1 LINE PRINTER
   1 CARD READER
   RUN UNDER OPERATING SYSTEM GEORGE 3

   HAS RUN SUCCESSFULLY ON ICL 1902A
   AMOUNT OF PRIMARY STORAGE 9K-16K WORDS, OVERLAYS USED
   1 DISC DEVICE, 10K-100K WORDS STORAGE
   1 LINE PRINTER
   1 PAPER TAPE READER
   RUN UNDER OPERATING SYSTEM ICL 1900 EXECUTIVE

   HAS RUN SUCCESSFULLY ON ICL 1905
   AMOUNT OF STORAGE 17K-32K WORDS
   1 MAGNETIC TAPE DRIVE
   1 LINE PRINTER
   1 CARD READER
   RUN UNDER OPERATING SYSTEM ICL 1900 EXECUTIVE

MODE OF USAGE
   BATCH

LANGUAGE
   PLAN

AVAILABILITY
   PROGRAM MAY BE AVAILABLE FOR USE OUTSIDE SUPPLIERS
   ORGANISATION.   PROGRAM AVAILABLE AS A BUREAU SERVICE

SUPPLIERS COMMENT
   L.U.S.T. WAS DESIGNED TO SAVE DEVELOPMENT TIME AND COSTS ON
   PROGRAMS.SIMPLE PROGRAMS MAY BE DEVELOPED AND IMPLEMENTED WITHIN
   A FEW HOURS BY ANALYST OR PROGRAMMER YET THE LANGUAGE ALSO CATERS
   FOR COMPLEX PROCESSING.L.U.S.T. ALLOWS MANY PARAMETERS (E.G. FILE

NAMES,FILE DEVICES) TO BE SPECIFIED AT RUNTIME

        COPYRIGHT NCC 1972   PRINTED ON 19/04/72

NCC STAGE 1 SOFTWARE VERIFICATION ABSTRACT A34079

NAME OF SOFTWARE
  DATA FIELD CHECKING ROUTINE

TYPE OF SOFTWARE
  DATA CHECKING SUBROUTINE

PURPOSE OF SOFTWARE
  ENABLES DATA FIELDS READ BY A PL/1 PROGRAM TO BE CHECKED FOR
  VALID TYPE OF DATA WITHOUT RISK OF PROGRAM INTERRUPTS AND WITHOUT
  COMPLEX PL/1 CODING

CONFIGURATION AND OPERATING SYSTEM
  IBM 360

  HAS RUN SUCCESSFULLY ON IBM 360/30
  AMOUNT OF PRIMARY STORAGE <4K BYTES
  1 DISC DRIVE,10K-100K BYTES STORAGE
  1 LINE PRINTER
  1 CARD READER
  RUN UNDER OPERATING SYSTEM DOS RELEASE 24

MODE OF USAGE
  BATCH

LANGUAGE
  ASSEMBLER

AVAILABILITY
  PROGRAM MAY BE AVAILABLE FOR USE OUTSIDE SUPPLIERS ORGANISATION

SUPPLIERS COMMENT
  THIS SUBROUTINE OCCUPIES LESS THAN 900 BYTES OF STORAGE AND IS FOR
  USE WITH PL/1 PROGRAMS WHICH CHECK INPUT DATA. IT PROVIDES A
  SIMPLE AND FLEXIBLE METHOD OF CHECKING THAT FIELDS CONTAIN DATA
  OF THE CORRECT TYPE AND FORMAT-EACH CHARACTER IN THE FIELD AND
  ALSO THE FIELD AS A WHOLE ARE CHECKED BY ONE CALL OF THE
  SUBROUTINE

    COPYRIGHT NCC 1972   PRINTED ON 19/04/72

NCC STAGE 1 SOFTWARE VERIFICATION ABSTRACT A34080

NAME OF SOFTWARE
  WORKSHOP ANALYSIS AND SCHEDULING PROCEDURE,WASP

TYPE OF SOFTWARE
  PRODUCTION CONTROL

PURPOSE OF SOFTWARE
  WASP PRODUCES A COMPREHENSIVE PRODUCTION SCHEDULE BY
  INCORPORATING CRITICAL PATH TECHNIQUES & A DEPENDABLE PRIORITY
  SYSTEM.THE PROGRAM PROVIDES A TOTAL COMMUNICATION SYSTEM
  WITH ADVANCE WARNING OF BOTTLENECKS AND OVERLOADS.

CONFIGURATION AND OPERATING SYSTEM
  IBM 360,ICL 1900,CDC 6600,UNIVAC 1100

  HAS RUN SUCCESSFULLY ON IBM 360/65,IBM 360/75
  AMOUNT OF PRIMARY STORAGE 65K-128K BYTES
  4 DISC DRIVES,101K-1M BYTES STORAGE
  1 LINE PRINTER
  1 CARD READER
  1 CARD PUNCH
  FILES MAY BE ON TAPE OR DISC
  RUN UNDER OPERATING SYSTEM MFT II R7

  HAS RUN SUCCESSFULLY ON ICL 1902A
  AMOUNT PRIMARY STORAGE 17K-32K WORDS
  4 DISC DRIVES,101K-1M WORDS STORAGE
  1 LINE PRINTER
  1 CARD READER
  1 CARD PUNCH
  FILES MAY BE ON TAPE OR DISC
  RUN UNDER OPERATING SYSTEM EXECUTIVE

  HAS RUN SUCCESSFULLY ON UNIVAC 1108
  AMOUNT OF PRIMARY STORAGE 65K-128K BYTES
  4 DISC DRIVES,101K-1M BYTES STORAGE
  1 LINE PRINTER
  1 CARD READER
  1 CARD PUNCH
  FILES MAY BE ON TAPE OR DISC
  RUN UNDER OPERATING SYSTEM EXEC 8

  HAS RUN SUCCESSFULLY ON CDC 6600
  AMOUNT OF PRIMARY STORAGE 17K-32K WORDS
  4 DISC DRIVES,101K-1M WORDS STORAGE
  1 LINE PRINTER
  1 CARD READER
  1 CARD PUNCH
  FILES MAY BE ON TAPE OR DISC
  RUN UNDER OPERATING SYSTEM SCOPE

MODE OF USAGE
  BATCH

NCC STAGE 1 SOFTWARE VERIFICATION ABSTRACT A34081

NAME OF SOFTWARE
  FLOOR DESIGN

TYPE OF SOFTWARE
  ENGINEERING APPLICATION

PURPOSE OF SOFTWARE
  PRODUCES STRESSES AND DEFLECTIONS AND REQUIRED SIZE FOR EACH
  BEAM IN A SYSTEM OF SIMPLY SUPPORTED STEEL BEAMS.DESIGN
  CRITERIA MAY BE CHANGED AT WILL.LOADING MAY BE POINT,LINE,
  OR SUPER; DEAD AND LIVE LOADS ARE TREATED SEPARATELY.

CONFIGURATION AND OPERATING SYSTEM
  ICL 1900

  HAS RUN SUCCESSFULLY ON ICL 1904E
  AMOUNT OF PRIMARY STORAGE 17K-32K WORDS,OVERLAYS USED
  2 DISC DRIVES,101K-1M WORDS STORAGE
  2 MAGNETIC TAPE DRIVES
  1 LINE PRINTER
  1 CARD READER
  RUN UNDER OPERATING SYSTEM GEORGE 2 MK 8C

MODE OF USAGE
  BATCH

LANGUAGE
  ALGOL,FORTRAN IV,PLAN

AVAILABILITY
  PROGRAM AVAILABLE AS A BUREAU SERVICE

SUPPLIERS COMMENT
  THE SYSTEM COMPRISES A SUITE OF 7 PROGRAMS WHICH ARE RUN
  SERIALLY USING A COMMON DISC AREA DATA STORAGE

     COPYRIGHT NCC 1972   PRINTED ON 19/04/72

NCC STAGE 1 SOFTWARE VERIFICATION ABSTRACT A34082

NAME OF SOFTWARE
  SECTION CONSTANTS FOR JOISTS

TYPE OF SOFTWARE
  ENGINEERING APPLICATION

PURPOSE OF SOFTWARE
  PRODUCES THE SECTIONAL PROPERTIES FOR ANY JOIST SHAPE. IT IS OF
  USE FOR NEW OR PROPOSED SHAPES BEFORE THE FIGURES HAVE BEEN
  PUBLISHED OR TO PRODUCE THEM FOR PUBLICATION - PROPERTIES
  INCLUDE THOSE FOR THE TEE AND STANDARD CASTELLA

CONFIGURATION AND OPERATING SYSTEM
  ICL 1900

  HAS RUN SUCCESSFULLY ON ICL 1904E
  AMOUNT OF PRIMARY STORAGE 4K-8K WORDS
  1 MAGNETIC TAPE DRIVE
  1 LINE PRINTER
  1 CARD READER
  RUN UNDER OPERATING SYSTEM GEORGE 2 MK 8C

MODE OF USAGE
  BATCH

LANGUAGE
  ALGOL

AVAILABILITY
  PROGRAM AVAILABLE AS A BUREAU SERVICE.

    COPYRIGHT NCC 1972   PRINTED ON 19/04/72

NCC STAGE 1 SOFTWARE VERIFICATION ABSTRACT A34083

NAME OF SOFTWARE
   SECTION CONSTANTS FOR BUILT UP COLUMNS

TYPE OF SOFTWARE
   ENGINEERING APPLICATION

PURPOSE OF SOFTWARE
   GIVES THE AREA, INERTIA, MODULUS, RADIUS OF GYRATION ON BOTH AXES
   FOR A COLUMN FORMED FROM 3 PLATES (EQUAL FLANGES)

CONFIGURATION AND OPERATING SYSTEM
   ICL 1900

   HAS RUN SUCCESSFULLY ON ICL 1904E
   AMOUNT OF PRIMARY STORAGE 4K-8K WORDS
   1 MAGNETIC TAPE DRIVE
   1 LINE PRINTER
   1 CARD READER
   RUN UNDER OPERATING SYSTEM GEORGE 2 MK 8C

MODE OF USAGE
   BATCH

LANGUAGE
   ALGOL

AVAILABILITY
   PROGRAM AVAILABLE AS A BUREAU SERVICE.

SUPPLIERS COMMENT
   A SERIES OF RESULTS ARE FORMED COMMENCING WITH A MAXIMUM OVERALL
   DEPTH, MAXIMUM FLANGE THICKNESS AND MAXIMUM WIDTH, AND A CONSTANT
   WEB THICKNESS. EACH OF THE FIRST 3 DIMENSIONS MAY BE INCREMENTED
   TO PRODUCE A LARGE PERMUTATION OF SIZES

NCC STAGE 1 SOFTWARE VERIFICATION ABSTRACT A34084

NAME OF SOFTWARE
  BENDING MOMENTS FOR ROLLING LOAD OVER SIMPLY SUPPORTED SPAN

TYPE OF SOFTWARE
  ENGINEERING APPLICATION

PURPOSE OF SOFTWARE
  THE MAXIMUM BENDING MOMENT THAT OCCURS AT SPECIFIED POINTS ON
  THE SPAN IS PRINTED, AS AN ARBITRARY TRAIN OF WHEELS ROLLS OVER
  THE SPAN. MAXIMUM NO. OF WHEELS IN TRAIN IS 49

CONFIGURATION AND OPERATING SYSTEM
  ICL 1900

  HAS RUN SUCCESSFULLY ON ICL 1904E
  AMOUNT OF PRIMARY STORAGE 4K-8K WORDS
  1 MAGNETIC TAPE DRIVE
  1 LINE PRINTER
  1 CARD READER
  RUN UNDER OPERATING SYSTEM GEORGE 2 MK 8C

MODE OF USAGE
  BATCH

LANGUAGE
  ALGOL

AVAILABILITY
  PROGRAM AVAILABLE AS A BUREAU SERVICE.

  COPYRIGHT NCC 1972   PRINTED ON 19/04/72

NCC STAGE 1 SOFTWARE VERIFICATION ABSTRACT A34085

NAME OF SOFTWARE
    PROPERTIES OF CRANE GIRDERS

TYPE OF SOFTWARE
    ENGINEERING APPLICATION

PURPOSE OF SOFTWARE
    THE SECTIONAL PROPERTIES REQUIRED FOR DESIGN OF CRANE GIRDERS
    ARE PRODUCED FROM A STATEMENT OF THE SIZE OF THE PIECES MAKING
    UP THE CROSS SECTION

CONFIGURATION AND OPERATING SYSTEM
    ICL 1900

    HAS RUN SUCCESSFULLY ON ICL 1904E
    AMOUNT OF PRIMARY STORAGE 4K-8K WORDS
    1 MAGNETIC TAPE DRIVE
    1 LINE PRINTER
    1 CARD READER
    RUN UNDER OPERATING SYSTEM GEORGE 2 MK 8C

MODE OF USAGE
    BATCH

LANGUAGE
    ALGOL

AVAILABILITY
    PROGRAM AVAILABLE AS A BUREAU SERVICE.

NCC STAGE 1 SOFTWARE VERIFICATION ABSTRACT A34086

NAME OF SOFTWARE
  BS449 TABLE 7 AXIAL COLUMN STRESS

TYPE OF SOFTWARE
  ENGINEERING APPLICATION

PURPOSE OF SOFTWARE
  PRODUCES A TABLE OF PERMISSIBLE AXIAL STRESSES ON COLUMNS
  AGAINST THE RATIO L/R TO APPENDIX B, BS449 1965. IT IS USEFUL
  WHEN CONSIDERING NEW STEEL SPECIFICATIONS

CONFIGURATION AND OPERATING SYSTEM
  ICL 1900

  HAS RUN SUCCESSFULLY ON ICL 1904E
  AMOUNT OF PRIMARY STORAGE <4K WORDS
  1 MAGNETIC TAPE DRIVE
  1 LINE PRINTER
  1 CARD READER
  RUN UNDER OPERATING SYSTEM GEORGE 2 MK 8C

MODE OF USAGE
  BATCH

LANGUAGE
  ALGOL

AVAILABILITY
  PROGRAM AVAILABLE AS A BUREAU SERVICE.

    COPYRIGHT NCC 1972   PRINTED ON 19/04/72

NCC STAGE 1 SOFTWARE VERIFICATION ABSTRACT A34087

NAME OF SOFTWARE
  FRAME ANALYSIS FLEXIBILITY METHOD

TYPE OF SOFTWARE
  ENGINEERING APPLICATION

PURPOSE OF SOFTWARE
  THIS PROGRAM IS INTENDED FOR USE ON SMALL STRUCTURES WITH
  TAPERED MEMBERS OR PIN JOINTS WHICH DO NOT OCCUR AT A
  FOUNDATION. IT IS BASICALLY A SERIES OF MATRIX MANIPULATIONS
  CONNECTING WITH AN INPUT OF BENDING MOMENTS CASE BY CASE

CONFIGURATION AND OPERATING SYSTEM
  ICL 1900

  HAS RUN SUCCESSFULLY ON ICL 1904E
  AMOUNT OF PRIMARY STORAGE 9K-16K WORDS, OVERLAYS USED
  2 MAGNETIC TAPE DRIVES
  1 LINE PRINTER
  1 CARD READER
  RUN UNDER OPERATING SYSTEM GEORGE 2 MK 8C

MODE OF USAGE
  BATCH

LANGUAGE
  ALGOL,PLAN

AVAILABILITY
  PROGRAM AVAILABLE AS A BUREAU SERVICE

    COPYRIGHT NCC 1972   PRINTED ON 19/04/72

NCC STAGE 1 SOFTWARE VERIFICATION ABSTRACT A34088

NAME OF SOFTWARE
  COLUMN DESIGN

TYPE OF SOFTWARE
  ENGINEERING APPLICATION

PURPOSE OF SOFTWARE
  DESIGN OF COLUMN IS TO BS449 INCLUDING THE CRITERIA FOR
  STRUCTURAL CONCRETE CASTING,IF REQUIRED.A SLAB BASE IS ALSO
  DESIGNED.

CONFIGURATION AND OPERATING SYSTEM
  ICL 1900

  HAS RUN SUCCESSFULLY ON ICL 1904E
  AMOUNT OF PRIMARY STORAGE 9K-16K WORDS
  2 MAGNETIC TAPE DRIVES
  1 LINE PRINTER
  1 CARD READER
  RUN UNDER OPERATING SYSTEM GEORGE 2 MK 8C

MODE OF USAGE
  BATCH

LANGUAGE
  ALGOL,PLAN

AVAILABILITY
  PROGRAM AVAILABLE AS A BUREAU SERVICE

SUPPLIERS COMMENT
  RESULTS INCLUDE THE SIZE CHOSEN,WEIGHT OF STEEL,WEIGHT OF
  CONCRETE,DESIGN LOAD AND STRESS RATIOS FOR AXIAL LOADS AND
  BENDING ON EACH AXIS AT THE TOP AND BOTTOM OF EACH STOREY.
  DATA REQUIRED IS MAXIMUM AND MINIMUM LOADS,ACTUAL AND
  EFFECTIVE LENGTHS,MINIMUM SIZE AND OPTIONALLY THE WIND
  LOADING. ANY NO. OF JOINT ARRANGEMENTS IN THE SAME RUN IS
  ACCEPTABLE.

NCC STAGE 1 SOFTWARE VERIFICATION ABSTRACT A34089

NAME OF SOFTWARE
  SECTION CONSTANTS FOR ROLLED STEEL ANGLES

TYPE OF SOFTWARE
  ENGINEERING APPLICATION

PURPOSE OF SOFTWARE
  PRODUCES THE SECTIONAL PROPERTIES ON 4 AXES FROM A
  STATEMENT OF THE LEG LENGTH AND TOE AND ROOT RADII.

CONFIGURATION AND OPERATING SYSTEM
  ICL 1900

  HAS RUN SUCCESSFULLY ON ICL 1904E
  AMOUNT OF PRIMARY STORAGE 4K-8K WORDS
  1 MAGNETIC TAPE DRIVE
  1 LINE PRINTER
  1 CARD READER
  RUN UNDER OPERATING SYSTEM GEORGE 2 MK 8C

MODE OF USAGE
  BATCH

LANGUAGE
  ALGOL

AVAILABILITY
  PROGRAM AVAILABLE AS A BUREAU SERVICE.

NCC STAGE 1 SOFTWARE VERIFICATION ABSTRACT A34090

NAME OF SOFTWARE
  SECTION CONSTANTS FOR ROLLED STEEL CHANNELS

TYPE OF SOFTWARE
  ENGINEERING APPLICATION

PURPOSE OF SOFTWARE
  PRODUCES THE SECTIONAL PROPERTIES FOR ANY CHANNEL SHAPE. IT IS
  OF USE FOR ANY NEW OR PROPOSED SHAPE, BEFORE THE FIGURES HAVE
  BEEN PUBLISHED OR TO PRODUCE THEM FOR PUBLICATION, THE
  PROPERTIES INCLUDE THOSE FOR THE STANDARD CASTELLA

CONFIGURATION AND OPERATING SYSTEM
  ICL 1900

  HAS RUN SUCCESSFULLY ON ICL 1904E
  AMOUNT OF PRIMARY STORAGE 4K-8K WORDS
  1 MAGNETIC TAPE DRIVE
  1 LINE PRINTER
  1 CARD READER
  RUN UNDER OPERATING SYSTEM GEORGE 2 MK 8C

MODE OF USAGE
  BATCH

LANGUAGE
  ALGOL

AVAILABILITY
  PROGRAM AVAILABLE AS A BUREAU SERVICE.

      COPYRIGHT NCC 1972   PRINTED ON 19/04/72

NCC STAGE 1 SOFTWARE VERIFICATION ABSTRACT A34091

NAME OF SOFTWARE
  SECTION CONSTANS FOR BULB FLATS COMBINED WITH PLATE

TYPE OF SOFTWARE
  ENGINEERING APPLICATION

PURPOSE OF SOFTWARE
  A PERMUTATION OF PROPERTIES ARE PRODUCED FOR A BULB FLAT OF
  KNOWN PROPERTIES IN COMBINATION WITH VARIOUS PLATE SIZES

CONFIGURATION AND OPERATING SYSTEM
  ICL 1900

  HAS RUN SUCCESSFULLY ON ICL 1904E
  AMOUNT OF PRIMARY STORAGE 4K-8K WORDS
  1 MAGNETIC TAPE DRIVE
  1 LINE PRINTER
  1 CARD READER
  RUN UNDER OPERATING SYSTEM GEORGE 2 MK 8C

MODE OF USAGE
  BATCH

LANGUAGE
  ALGOL

AVAILABILITY
  PROGRAM AVAILABLE AS A BUREAU SERVICE.

    COPYRIGHT NCC 1972   PRINTED ON 19/04/72

NCC STAGE 1 SOFTWARE VERIFICATION ABSTRACT A34092

NAME OF SOFTWARE
   SECTION CONSTANTS FOR BULB FLATS

TYPE OF SOFTWARE
   ENGINEERING APPLICATION

PURPOSE OF SOFTWARE
   PRODUCES THE SECTION CONSTANTS FOR ANY BULB FLAT SHAPE

CONFIGURATION AND OPERATING SYSTEM
   ICL 1900

   HAS RUN SUCCESSFULLY ON ICL 1904E
   AMOUNT OF PRIMARY STORAGE 4K-8K WORDS
   1 MAGNETIC TAPE DRIVE
   1 LINE PRINTER
   1 CARD READER
   RUN UNDER OPERATING SYSTEM GEORGE 2 MK 8C

MODE OF USAGE
   BATCH

LANGUAGE
   ALGOL

AVAILABILITY
   PROGRAM AVAILABLE AS A BUREAU SERVICE.

   COPYRIGHT NCC 1972   PRINTED ON 19/04/72

NCC STAGE 1 SOFTWARE VERIFICATION ABSTRACT A34093

NAME OF SOFTWARE
   PLASTIC CONSTANTS FOR JOISTS

TYPE OF SOFTWARE
   ENGINEERING APPLICATION

PURPOSE OF SOFTWARE
   THE PLASTIC MOMENT OF RESISTANCE IS PRODUCED FOR ANY JOIST SHAPE

CONFIGURATION AND OPERATING SYSTEM
   ICL 1900

   HAS RUN SUCCESSFULLY ON ICL 1904E
   AMOUNT OF PRIMARY STORAGE 4K-8K WORDS
   1 MAGNETIC TAPE DRIVE
   1 LINE PRINTER
   1 CARD READER
   RUN UNDER OPERATING SYSTEM GEORGE 2 MK 8C

MODE OF USAGE
   BATCH

LANGUAGE
   ALGOL

AVAILABILITY
   PROGRAM AVAILABLE AS A BUREAU SERVICE.

NCC STAGE 1 SOFTWARE VERIFICATION ABSTRACT A34094

NAME OF SOFTWARE
   MAXIMUM END REACTION FOR ROLLING LOADS OVER ADJACENT SPANS

TYPE OF SOFTWARE
   ENGINEERING APPLICATION

PURPOSE OF SOFTWARE
   THE MAXIMUM END SHEAR ON EACH GIRDER AND THE MAXIMUM END
   REACTION ON EACH COLUMN IS PRODUCED FOR A CRANE GANTRY MADE
   UP OF A SERIES OF UNEQUAL LENGTH SPANS AND ROLLING TRAIN
   OF WHEELS.MAXIMUM NO. OF WHEELS IN TRAIN IS 50.THE GIRDERS
   ARE ASSUMED SIMPLY SUPPORTED.

CONFIGURATION AND OPERATING SYSTEM
   ICL 1900

   HAS RUN SUCCESSFULLY ON ICL 1904E
   AMOUNT OF PRIMARY STORAGE. <4K WORDS
   1 MAGNETIC TAPE DRIVE
   1 LINE PRINTER
   1 CARD READER
   RUN UNDER OPERATING SYSTEM GEORGE 2 MK 8C

MODE OF USAGE
   BATCH

LANGUAGE
   ALGOL

AVAILABILITY
   PROGRAM MAY BE AVAILABLE FOR USE OUTSIDE SUPPLIERS
   ORGANISATION. PROGRAM AVAILABLE AS A BUREAU SERVICE

NCC STAGE 1 SOFTWARE VERIFICATION ABSTRACT A34095

NAME OF SOFTWARE
   ACTUARIAL AND FINANCIAL COLUMN MANIPULATION LANGUAGE, ACT

TYPE OF SOFTWARE
   STATISTICAL APPLICATION

PURPOSE OF SOFTWARE
   COLUMN MANIPULATION LANGUAGE, PRINCIPALLY FOR FINANCIAL AND
   ACTUARIAL APPLICATIONS. SPECIAL COMPOUND INTEREST, ACTUARIAL AND
   I/O ROUTINES AND A DATA LIBRARY OF ACTUARIAL FUNCTIONS ARE
   INCLUDED. PROVISION FOR USER SUBROUTINES

CONFIGURATION AND OPERATING SYSTEM
   IBM 360, ICL 1900, CDC 6000 SERIES, UNIVAC 1108, IBM 7094

   HAS RUN SUCCESSFULLY ON IBM 360/65
   AMOUNT OF PRIMARY STORAGE 65K-128K BYTES
   1 DISC DRIVE, 10K-100K BYTES STORAGE
   1 MAGNETIC TAPE DRIVE
   1 LINE PRINTER
   1 CARD READER
   1 CARD PUNCH
   RUN UNDER OPERATING SYSTEM OS

   HAS RUN SUCCESSFULLY ON ICL 1905E
   AMOUNT OF PRIMARY STORAGE 17K-32K WORDS
   1 DISC DRIVE, 10K-100K WORDS STORAGE
   1 MAGNETIC TAPE DRIVE
   1 LINE PRINTER
   1 CARD READER
   1 CARD PUNCH
   RUN UNDER OPERATING SYSTEM GEORGE 2

MODE OF USAGE
   BATCH, INTERACTIVE

LANGUAGE
   FORTRAN IV

AVAILABILITY
   PROGRAM MAY BE AVAILABLE FOR USE OUTSIDE SUPPLIERS ORGANISATION.
   PROGRAM AVAILABLE ON A BUREAU SERVICE

SUPPLIERS COMMENT
   AVAILABLE ON ITT DATA SERVICES REACTIVE TERMINAL SYSTEM AS
   APPLICATION PACKAGE

      COPYRIGHT NCC 1972   PRINTED ON 19/04/72

NCC STAGE 1 SOFTWARE VERIFICATION ABSTRACT A34096

NAME OF SOFTWARE
   INCOMPLETE RECORDS PACKAGE - PK35

TYPE OF SOFTWARE
   ACCOUNTING

PURPOSE OF SOFTWARE
   PRODUCTION OF PROFIT AND LOSS ACCOUNTS AND BALANCE SHEETS FROM
   SOURCE DOCUMENTS. INTERIM OR FINAL ACCOUNTS MAY ALSO BE PRODUCED.
   COMPARATIVE FIGURES ARE INCLUDED

CONFIGURATION AND OPERATING SYSTEM
   IBM 360

   HAS RUN SUCCESSFULLY ON IBM 360/30, IBM 360/40
   AMOUNT OF PRIMARY STORAGE 33K-64K BYTES
   3 DISC DRIVES, 1.1M-10M BYTES STORAGE
   2 MAGNETIC DRIVES
   1 LINE PRINTER
   1 CARD READER
   RUN UNDER OPERATING SYSTEM DOS 23

MODE OF USAGE
   BATCH

LANGUAGE
   COBOL

AVAILABILITY
   PROGRAM MAY BE AVAILABLE FOR USE OUTSIDE SUPPLIERS ORGANISATION.
   PROGRAM AVAILABLE ON A BUREAU SERVICE

SUPPLIERS COMMENT
   SYSTEM WORKS BY SIMPLE CODING OF OPENING BALANCES, TRANSACTIONS
   DURING YEAR, FROM SOURCE DOCUMENTS AND ACCRUALS AT YEAR END.
   EASY TO UNDERSTAND BY ACCOUNTANT. FLEXIBLE CHOICE OF USER
   CODING AND NARRATIVE. VERSATILE ON AMENDMENTS. ADDITIONS AND
   DELETIONS AFTER INITIAL SET OF ACCOUNTS. NO SPECIAL EQUIPMENT
   OR TRAINING REQUIRED. INPUT BY CARD OR PAPER TAPE

NCC STAGE 1 SOFTWARE VERIFICATION ABSTRACT A34097

NAME OF SOFTWARE
  MEMBERSHIP DIRECTORY PACKAGE - PK05

TYPE OF SOFTWARE
  FILE HANDLING, MEMBERSHIP RECORDS

PURPOSE OF SOFTWARE
  COMPLETE MEMBERSHIP RECORDING WITH SELECTIVITY CODING FACILITY
  COVERING NAME ADDRESS, ETC.

CONFIGURATION AND OPERATING SYSTEM
  IBM 360

  HAS RUN SUCCESSFULLY ON IBM 360/30, IBM 360/40
  AMOUNT OF PRIMARY STORAGE 33K-64K BYTES
  4 DISC DRIVES, 1.1M-10M BYTES STORAGE
  4 MAGNETIC TAPE DRIVES
  1 LINE PRINTER
  1 CARD READER
  RUN UNDER OPERATING SYSTEM DOS 23

MODE OF USAGE
  BATCH

LANGUAGE
  COBOL

AVAILABILITY
  PROGRAM MAY BE AVAILABLE FOR USE OUTSIDE SUPPLIERS ORGANISATION.
  PROGRAM AVAILABLE ON A BUREAU SERVICE

SUPPLIERS COMMENT
  SELECTIVITY OF MEMBERSHIP BY GRADE, AREA, GROUP, INTEREST, ETC.
  SUBSCRIPTION DAY BOOK OPTION. INPUT BY CARD OR PAPER TAPE.
  MAILING SERVICE BY ARRANGEMENT. INDUSTRIAL VERSION AVAILABLE AS
  BUREAU SERVICE

NCC STAGE 1 SOFTWARE VERIFICATION ABSTRACT A34098

NAME OF SOFTWARE
   SALES LEDGER PACKAGE - PK17

TYPE OF SOFTWARE
   ACCOUNTING

PURPOSE OF SOFTWARE
   LEDGER MAINTENANCE, MANAGEMENT REPORTING INCORPORATING DEBTOR
   CONTROL AND SALES ANALYSIS OPTION, ALSO STATEMENT PRODUCTION

CONFIGURATION AND OPERATING SYSTEM
   IBM 360

   HAS RUN SUCCESSFULLY ON IBM 360/30, IBM 360/40
   AMOUNT OF PRIMARY STORAGE 33K-64K BYTES
   2 DISC DRIVES, 1.1M-1.0M BYTES STORAGE
   3 MAGNETIC TAPE DRIVES
   1 LINE PRINTER
   1 CARD READER
   RUN UNDER OPERATING SYSTEM DOS 23

MODE OF USAGE
   BATCH

LANGUAGE
   COBOL

AVAILABILITY
   PROGRAM MAY BE AVAILABLE FOR USE OUTSIDE SUPPLIERS ORGANISATION.
   PROGRAM AVAILABLE ON A BUREAU SERVICE

SUPPLIERS'COMMENT
   FLEXIBILITY GIVEN BY USING BASIC PROGRAM STRUCTURE WITH USER
   PROGRAM MODULES. POSTING SUMMARY ENABLES USER TO INTERFACE
   PACKAGE WITH REST OF HIS ACCOUNTING SYSTEM. CHOICE OF OPEN ITEM
   OR BALANCE FORWARD SYSTEM. CASH CAN BE ALLOCATED AGAINST SPECIAL
   INVOICES AND IS SELF RECONCILING. CREDIT CONTROL WITH AGED
   ANALYSIS IN DETAIL OR SUMMARY FORM

      COPYRIGHT NCC 1972   PRINTED ON 19/04/72

NCC STAGE 1 SOFTWARE VERIFICATION ABSTRACT A34099

NAME OF SOFTWARE
  BUDGETARY CONTROL PACKAGE - PK17

TYPE OF SOFTWARE
  ACCOUNTING

PURPOSE OF SOFTWARE
  THE PACKAGE PROVIDES FOR THE ANALYSIS OF A COMPANY'S EXPENDITURE
  AT TWO LEVELS, DETAILED AND SUMMARY ON A REGULAR BASIS

CONFIGURATION AND OPERATING SYSTEM
  IBM 360

  HAS RUN SUCCESSFULLY ON IBM 360/30, IBM 360/40
  AMOUNT OF PRIMARY STORAGE 33K-64K BYTES
  3 DISC DRIVES, 1.1M-10M BYTES STORAGE
  3 MAGNETIC TAPE DRIVES
  1 LINE PRINTER
  1 CARD READER
  RUN UNDER OPERATING SYSTEM DOS 23

MODE OF USAGE
  BATCH

LANGUAGE
  COBOL

AVAILABILITY
  PROGRAM MAY BE AVAILABLE FOR USE OUTSIDE SUPPLIERS ORGANISATION.
  PROGRAM AVAILABLE ON A BUREAU SERVICE

SUPPLIERS COMMENT
  PACKAGE INCLUDES RECORDING AND ANALYSIS OF CAPITAL EXPENDITURE,
  BREAKDOWN BY LEVELS OF MANAGERIAL RESPONSIBILITY, NOMINAL LEDGER
  CONTROL, DEPARTMENTAL ACTIVITY MEASUREMENT, INDIRECT STORES
  COSTING UNBUDGETED EXPENDITURE LISTING, BUDGET FORECAST SYSTEM,
  ADJUSTMENT OF BUDGET TO DEPARTMENTAL ACTIVITY, UP TO 13 FINANCIAL
  PERIODS COVERED.

     COPYRIGHT NCC 1972   PRINTED ON 19/04/72

NCC STAGE 1 SOFTWARE VERIFICATION ABSTRACT A34100

NAME OF SOFTWARE
   PURCHASE LEDGER PACKAGE - PK34

TYPE OF SOFTWARE
   ACCOUNTING

PURPOSE OF SOFTWARE
   PURCHASE LEDGER MAINTENANCE, PRODUCING DETAILED REPORTS OF
   OUTSTANDING BALANCES, ANALYSIS OF LEDGER, COMMITMENT REPORTS AND
   PRODUCTION OF PAYMENT DOCUMENTS

CONFIGURATION AND OPERATING SYSTEM
   IBM 360

   HAS RUN SUCCESSFULLY ON IBM 360/30, IBM 360/40
   AMOUNT OF PRIMARY STORAGE 33K-64K BYTES
   3 DISC DRIVES, 1.1M-10M BYTES STORAGE
   2 MAGNETIC TAPE DRIVES
   1 LINE PRINTER
   1 CARD READER
   RUN UNDER OPERATING SYSTEM DOS 23

MODE OF USAGE
   BATCH

LANGUAGE
   COBOL

AVAILABILITY
   PROGRAM MAY BE AVAILABLE FOR USE OUTSIDE SUPPLIERS ORGANISATION.
   PROGRAM AVAILABLE ON A BUREAU SERVICE

SUPPLIERS COMMENT
   SYSTEM CAN BE TAILORED TO SUIT INDIVIDUAL REQUIREMENTS, INPUT
   BATCHED AND CHECKED FOR VALIDITY. PAYMENT CARD PRODUCTION FOR
   INDIVIDUAL ITEM CONTROL. DETAILED COMMITMENT AND OUTSTANDING
   REPORT PRODUCTION. USER DICTATES PAYMENTS TO BE MADE AND SYSTEM
   PRODUCES PAYMENT DOCUMENTS WITH REMITTANCE ADVICES. INPUT BY
   CARD OR PAPER TAPE

NCC STAGE 1 SOFTWARE VERIFICATION ABSTRACT A34101

NAME OF SOFTWARE
   INDEPENDENT MODULE DEVELOPMENT, IMD

TYPE OF SOFTWARE
   UTILITY

PURPOSE OF SOFTWARE
   TEST HARNESS WHICH IS USED TO TEST MODULES INDEPENDENTLY IN
   MODULAR PROGRAMS. IMD PROVIDES FACILITIES TO FORMAT TEST DATA
   AND ACCEPT MODULE OUTPUT. MODULES CAN BE REPETITIVELY TESTED IN
   ONE TEST RUN AND A SPECIFIED NUMBER OF ERRORS HANDLED

CONFIGURATION AND OPERATING SYSTEM
   IBM 360, ICL SYSTEM 4

   HAS RUN SUCCESSFULLY ON IBM 360/30
   AMOUNT OF PRIMARY STORAGE 17K-32K BYTES
   1 DISC DRIVE, 10K-100K BYTES STORAGE
   1 LINE PRINTER
   1 CARD READER
   RUN UNDER OPERATING SYSTEM DOS

   HAS RUN SUCCESSFULLY ON ICL SYSTEM 4/40
   AMOUNT OF PRIMARY STORAGE 17K-32K BYTES
   1 DISC DRIVE, 10K-100K BYTES STORAGE
   1 LINE PRINTER
   1 CARD READER
   RUN UNDER OPERATING SYSTEM J

MODE OF USAGE
   BATCH

LANGUAGE
   BAL/USERCODE

AVAILABILITY
   PROGRAM MAY BE AVAILABLE FOR USE OUTSIDE SUPPLIERS ORGANISATION.
   PROGRAM AVAILABLE ON A BUREAU SERVICE

SUPPLIERS COMMENT
   IMD IS A WELL-ESTABLISHED SYSTEM WITH 36 USERS TO DATE AMONG 360
   DOS, 360 OS AND ICL SYSTEM 4 RANGES

      COPYRIGHT NCC 1972   PRINTED ON 19/04/72

NCC STAGE 1 SOFTWARE VERIFICATION ABSTRACT A34102

NAME OF SOFTWARE
  RECORD VALIDATION LANGUAGE

TYPE OF SOFTWARE
  UTILITY

PURPOSE OF SOFTWARE
  THIS PACKAGE IS A SPECIAL PURPOSE COMPILER TO GENERATE PROGRAMS
  TO VALIDATE RECORDS OF UP TO 100 BYTES. INPUT AND OUTPUT MAY BE
  FROM CARD OR MAGNETIC STORAGE. USUAL VALIDATION REQUIREMENTS ARE
  INCLUDED

CONFIGURATION AND OPERATING SYSTEM
  IBM 360

  HAS RUN SUCCESSFULLY ON IBM 360/25
  AMOUNT OF PRIMARY STORAGE 9K-16K BYTES
  1 DISC DRIVE, <10K BYTES STORAGE
  1 LINE PRINTER
  1 CARD READER
  RUN UNDER OPERATING SYSTEM DOS

MODE OF USAGE
  BATCH

LANGUAGE
  ASSEMBLER

AVAILABILITY
  PROGRAM MAY BE AVAILABLE FOR USE OUTSIDE SUPPLIERS ORGANISATION

SUPPLIERS COMMENT
  COMPREHENSIVE VALIDATION OF THE INPUT TO COMPUTER SYSTEMS IS
  ESSENTIAL FOR THE PRODUCTION OF ACCURATE INFORMATION. THIS SYSTEM
  ALLOWS PROGRAMMERS AND SYSTEMS ANALYSTS TO WRITE VALIDATION
  PROGRAMS QUICKLY AND CHEAPLY, OFTEN PRODUCING MORE COMPREHENSIVE
  CHECKS THAN WOULD OTHERWISE BE ECONOMICALLY JUSTIFIABLE

NCC STAGE 1 SOFTWARE VERIFICATION ABSTRACT A34103

NAME OF SOFTWARE
  JOB COSTING/PAYROLL SYSTEM

TYPE OF SOFTWARE
  PROJECT COSTING/PAYROLL

PURPOSE OF SOFTWARE
  THE PACKAGE INCORPORATES A MONTHLY PAYROLL SYSTEM INCLUDING
  PAYSLIP PREPARATION AND CREDIT TRANSFER TRANSACTIONS TOGETHER
  WITH A JOB COSTING SYSTEM GIVING DETAILED REPORTS ON EMPLOYEE
  ACTIVITY, PROJECT COSTS, ETC.

CONFIGURATION AND OPERATING SYSTEM
  IBM 360

  HAS RUN SUCCESSFULLY ON IBM 360/30
  AMOUNT OF PRIMARY STORAGE 33K-64K BYTES, OVERLAYS USED
  5 DISC DRIVES, 11M-100M BYTES STORAGE
  2 MAGNETIC TAPE DRIVES
  1 LINE PRINTER
  1 CARD READER
  1 CARD PUNCH
  RUN UNDER OPERATING SYSTEM DOS

MODE OF USAGE
  BATCH

LANGUAGE
  COBOL, ASSEMBLER

AVAILABILITY
  PROGRAM MAY BE AVAILABLE FOR USE OUTSIDE SUPPLIERS ORGANISATION.
  PROGRAM AVAILABLE ON A BUREAU SERVICE

SUPPLIERS COMMENT
  PACKAGE OF INTEREST TO LOCAL AUTHORITY ENGINEERING SERVICE
  DEPARTMENTS OR TO LARGE FIRMS OF BUILDING ARCHITECTS. THE SYSTEM
  IS IN CURRENT USE AND AVAILABLE FOR DEMONSTRATION

NCC STAGE 1 SOFTWARE VERIFICATION ABSTRACT A34104

NAME OF SOFTWARE
  L.A. PROJECT CONTROL SYSTEM

TYPE OF SOFTWARE
  COMPUTER SYSTEM DEVELOPMENT CONTROL,PROJECT CONTROL

PURPOSE OF SOFTWARE
  THE SYSTEM PROVIDES ACCURATE MONITORING AND CONTROL OF SYSTEMS
  AND PROGRAMMING PROJECTS. MULTI-LEVEL MANAGEMENT REPORTS
  SHOW THE EXACT STATUS OF PROJECTS AND PROVIDE AN ANALYSIS
  OF DEPARTMENTAL EFFORT AND COSTS AT ACTIVITY LEVEL.

CONFIGURATION AND OPERATING SYSTEM
  IBM 360,ICL 1900

  HAS RUN SUCCESSFULLY ON ICL 1902
  AMOUNT OF PRIMARY STORAGE 17K-32K WORDS
  1 DISC DRIVE,10K-100K WORDS STORAGE
  2 MAGNETIC TAPE DRIVES
  1 LINE PRINTER
  1 CARD READER
  1 PAPER TAPE READER
  CARD OR PAPER TAPE INPUT
  MAGNETIC TAPE/DISC ARE ALTERNATIVES
  RUN UNDER OPERATING SYSTEM EXECUTIVE

  HAS RUN SUCCESSFULLY ON IBM 360/30
  AMOUNT OF PRIMARY STORAGE 33K-64K BYTES
  1 DISC DRIVE,10K-100K BYTES STORAGE
  1 LINE PRINTER
  1 CARD READER
  RUN UNDER OPERATING SYSTEM 360 DOS

MODE OF USAGE
  BATCH

LANGUAGE
  IBM COBOL, ICL COBOL

AVAILABILITY
  PROGRAM MAY BE AVAILABLE FOR USE OUTSIDE SUPPLIERS
  ORGANISATION. PROGRAM AVAILABLE AS A BUREAU SERVICE.

SUPPLIERS COMMENT
  THIS SYSTEM IS EFFECTIVE BECAUSE IT IS SIMPLE TO ADMINISTER,
  THE MAIN DOCUMENT INPUT IS TIME SHEET DATA. OF THE SEVEN
  REPORTS AVAILABLE FROM THE SYSTEM THE MAIN THREE ARE:-
  WEEKLY PROGRESS FOR JUNIOR MANAGEMENT
  PROJECT SUMMARIES FOR MIDDLE MANAGEMENT
  PERIOD ANALYSIS FOR SENIOR MANAGEMENT
  DELIVERY TIME FOR SYSTEM 2-3 WEEKS

NCC STAGE 1 SOFTWARE VERIFICATION ABSTRACT A34105

NAME OF SOFTWARE
  JOB COST CONTROL SYSTEM FOR THE PROFESSIONAL DESIGN OFFICE
  PARTICULARLY ENGINEERS, ARCHITECTS OR MANAGEMENT CONSULTANTS

TYPE OF SOFTWARE
  ACCOUNTING

PURPOSE OF SOFTWARE
  AN AID TO MANAGEMENT OF PROFESSIONAL OFFICES. THE COST OF
  DESIGN-LABOUR FOR EACH PROJECT IS COMPARED WITH THE KNOWN
  FEE. THE SYSTEM MONITORS PROGRESS AND PRODUCTIVITY;
  IMPROVES FORECASTING AND ESTIMATING TECHNIQUES.

CONFIGURATION AND OPERATING SYSTEM
  IBM 1130

  HAS RUN SUCCESSFULLY ON IBM 1130
  AMOUNT OF PRIMARY STORAGE 9K-16K WORDS
  2 DISC DRIVES,10K-100K WORDS STORAGE
  1 LINE PRINTER
  1 CARD READER
  RUN UNDER OPERATING SYSTEM DMS

MODE OF USAGE
  BATCH

LANGUAGE
  R.P.G. VERSION 8

AVAILABILITY
  PROGRAM MAY BE AVAILABLE FOR USE OUTSIDE SUPPLIERS
  ORGANISATION. PROGRAM AVAILABLE AS A BUREAU SERVICE

SUPPLIERS COMMENT
  THE SYSTEM AFFORDS THE OPPORTUNITY TO RE-ASSESS ANNUALLY THE
  COSTS FOR EACH JOB AND THE PROFITABILITY IN THE LIGHT OF THE
  CURRENT ECONOMIC CLIMATE.
  IT IS SUITABLE FOR ANY TYPE OF PROFESSIONAL OFFICE
  (E.G. ARCHITECTS, ENGINEERS, OR MANAGEMENT CONSULTANTS)

NCC STAGE 1 SOFTWARE VERIFICATION ABSTRACT A34106

NAME OF SOFTWARE
   JOB COST CONTROL FOR THE PROFESSIONAL ENGINEERS DESIGN
   OFFICE, PARTICULARLY FOR CIVIL AND STRUCTURAL ENGINEERS.

TYPE OF SOFTWARE
   ACCOUNTING

PURPOSE OF SOFTWARE
   AN AID TO MANAGEMENT OF PROFESSIONAL OFFICES. FOR EACH
   PROJECT, COST OF DESIGN-LABOUR & O'HEADS IS COMPARED WITH A
   PREDICTED COST. PROJECTS ARE GROUPED TO PROFIT CENTRES & THE
   SYSTEM BREAKS DOWN COSTS & FEES WITHIN THESE PROFIT CENTRES

CONFIGURATION AND OPERATING SYSTEMS
   IBM 360

   HAS RUN SUCCESSFULLY ON IBM 360/50
   AMOUNT OF PRIMARY STORAGE 65K-128K BYTES
   2 MAGNETIC TAPE DRIVES
   2 LINE PRINTERS
   1 CARD READER
   RUN UNDER OPERATING SYSTEM O.S.

MODE OF USAGE
   BATCH

LANGUAGE
   COBOL

AVAILABILITY
   PROGRAM MAY BE AVAILABLE FOR USE OUTSIDE SUPPLIERS
   ORGANISATION. PROGRAM AVAILABLE AS A BUREAU SERVICE.

SUPPLIERS COMMENT
   THIS SYSTEM PROVIDES FOR EACH PROJECT TO BE CONTROLLED IN
   16 SUB-STAGES & ACCUMULATES EXPENSES FOR TELEPHONE, PRINTING,
   TRAVEL, SUBSISTENCE WHICH MAY BE FULLY RECOVERABLE OR BASED
   ON TARGETS. THIS SYSTEM IS PARTICULARLY USEFUL FOR CIVIL OR
   STRUCTURAL ENGINEERS.

NCC STAGE 1 SOFTWARE VERIFICATION ABSTRACT A34107

NAME OF SOFTWARE
  SMITHS INDUSTRIES BREAKDOWN AND NETTING ROUTINES

TYPE OF SOFTWARE
  PRODUCTION CONTROL

PURPOSE OF SOFTWARE
  CALCULATES SCHEDULES OF PRODUCTION REQUIRMENTS/COMPONENT ORDERS
  VIA MULTI-LEVEL ASSEMBLY STRUCTURE. MAINTAINS FILES OF BILLS OF
  MATERIALS AND OTHER STATIC DATA. SELECTIVE CALCULATION OF
  OF IMPACT OF DEMAND CHANGES. SUITS NET OR GROSS BREAKDOWN.

CONFIGURATION AND OPERATING SYSTEM
  ICL 1900

  HAS RUN SUCCESSFULLY ON ICL 1904E
  AMOUNT OF PRIMARY STORAGE 9K-16K WORDS
  5 MAGNETIC TAPE DRIVES
  1 LINE PRINTER
  1 CARD READER
  RUN UNDER OPERATING SYSTEM EXECUTIVE

MODE OF USAGE
  BATCH

LANGUAGE
  1900 COBOL & PLAN SUB-ROUTINES

AVAILABILITY
  PROGRAM MAY BE AVAILABLE FOR USE OUTSIDE SUPPLIERS
  ORGANISATION. PROGRAM AVAILABLE AS A BUREAU SERVICE

SUPPLIERS COMMENT
  BREAKDOWN TAKES ACCOUNT OF 1. EXTERNAL DEMANDS AT ALL ASSEMBLY
  LEVELS 2. STOCK/WORK IN PROGRESS AT ALL LEVELS 3. STAGE BY
  STAGE LEAD TIMES AND SLACK TIMES 4. BATCHING/ECONOMIC
  ORDER QUANTITIES.5. SCRAP ALLOWANCES 6. CALENDAR ANOMALIES. CAN
  LINK WITH EXISTING STOCK RECORDING, SHOP LOADING, PURCHASE
  CONTROL.COMPREHENSIVE ERROR PROTECTION. IMPLEMENTED FOR
  70000 CODES AT 12 LEVELS.

NCC STAGE 1 SOFTWARE VERIFICATION ABSTRACT A34108

NAME OF SOFTWARE
  S.I. GROUP INVOICE PACKAGE

TYPE OF SOFTWARE
  STOCK CONTROL/ACCOUNTING/INVOICING PROCEDURE

PURPOSE OF SOFTWARE
  MODULAR; USER'S CHOICE TAILORS SUITE. MODULES TO-PRODUCE INVOICE,
  CREDIT, DESPATCH DOCUMENTATION; APPLY DISCOUNTS, PURCHASE TAX
  AND OTHER CHARGES; MAINTAIN CURRENT STOCK DATA; MAINTAIN CURRENT,
  OVERDUE AND FORWARD ORDER DATA; UPDATE SALES ANALYSIS/LEDGER

CONFIGURATION AND OPERATING SYSTEM
  ICL 1900

  HAS RUN SUCCESSFULLY ON ICL 1904E
  AMOUNT OF PRIMARY STORAGE 9K-16K WORDS
  2 DISC DRIVES 1.1M-10M CHARACTERS STORAGE
  4 MAGNETIC TAPE DRIVES
  1 LINE PRINTER
  1 PAPER TAPE READER
  RUN UNDER OPERATING SYSTEM EXECUTIVE

MODE OF USAGE
  BATCH

LANGUAGE
  1900 COBOL AND PLAN SUBROUTINES

AVAILABILITY
  PROGRAM MAY BE AVAILABLE FOR USE OUTSIDE SUPPLIERS
  ORGANISATION. PROGRAM AVAILABLE AS A BUREAU SERVICE

SUPPLIERS COMMENT
  INPUT FROM REAL-TIME DATA CAPTURE AND STOCK RECORDING AVAILABLE.
  CUSTOMER/PRODUCT PERFORMANCE MONITORING. MODULES INTEGRATE
  ORDER ADMINISTRATION, STOCK CONTROL, STOCK FORECASTING,
  INVOICING,INPUT TO SALES ANALYSIS AND SALES LEDGER. ALTERNATIVE
  FUNCTION MODULES ALLOW SUITE TAILORED TO USER REQUIREMENT

NCC STAGE 1 SOFTWARE VERIFICATION ABSTRACT A34109

NAME OF SOFTWARE
   SMITHS INDUSTRIES STOCK EVALUATION

TYPE OF SOFTWARE
   STOCK CONTROL/ACCOUNTING

PURPOSE OF SOFTWARE
   CALCULATES STANDARD COST. EVALUATES STOCK LEVELS BY SITE AND
   PRODUCT GROUP. ANALYSES ANNUAL, SEMI-ANNUAL STOCK TURNOVER.
   ANALYSES STOCK VALUE AND TURNOVER VALUE WITHIN RANGES.CAN
   CALCULATE SELLING PRICE FROM STANDARD COST AND PRODUCE PRICE
   LIST.

CONFIGURATION AND OPERATING SYSTEM
   ICL 1900

   HAS RUN SUCCESSFULLY ON ICL 1904E
   AMOUNT OF PRIMARY STORAGE 9K-16K WORDS
   4 MAGNETIC TAPE DRIVES
   1 LINE PRINTER
   1 CARD READER
   RUN UNDER OPERATING SYSTEM EXECUTIVE

MODE OF USAGE
   BATCH

LANGUAGE
   1900 COBOL & PLAN SUBROUTINES

AVAILABILITY
   PROGRAM MAY BE AVAILABLE FOR USE OUTSIDE SUPPLIERS
   ORGANISATION. PROGRAM AVAILABLE AS A BUREAU SERVICE

SUPPLIERS COMMENT
   INPUT FROM PUNCHED CARD AND/OR EXISTING MAGNETIC TAPE FILES.
   IMPLEMENTED AT TWO MEDIUM SIZED COMPANIES.

   COPYRIGHT NCC 1972   PRINTED ON 19/04/72

NCC STAGE 1 SOFTWARE VERIFICATION ABSTRACT A34110

NAME OF SOFTWARE
  PROCESSING TAPE AND DISC FILES IN COBOL USING PLAN SUBROUTINES

TYPE OF SOFTWARE
  FILE HANDLING

PURPOSE OF SOFTWARE
  TO ALLOW COBOL PROGRAMS TO:- (AMONG OTHER THINGS)
  (1) PROCESS MAGNETIC TAPES OF GIVEN PROPERTIES
  BY USING EXEC. PROPERTY CODE SYSTEM
  (2) SELECT TAPE OR DISC BY RUN TIME PARAMETERS

CONFIGURATION AND OPERATING SYSTEM
  ICL 1900

  HAS RUN SUCCESSFULLY ON ICL 1901,
  AMOUNT OF PRIMARY STORAGE < 4K WORDS
  CAN USE UP TO 14 TAPES AND/OR DISC FILES
   RUN UNDER OPERATING SYSTEM GEORGE 1

  HAS RUN SUCCESSFULLY ON ICL 1904
  AMOUNT OF PRIMARY STORAGE < 4K WORDS
  CAN PROCESS UP TO 14 TAPE AND/OR DISC FILES
  RUN UNDER OPERATING SYSTEM GEORGE 2

MODE OF USAGE
  BATCH

LANGUAGE
  PLAN

AVAILABILITY
  PROGRAM MAY BE AVAILABLE FOR USE OUTSIDE SUPPLIERS ORGANISATION

SUPPLIERS COMMENT
  THE ROUTINES ALLOW A COBOL USER TO SPECIFY TAPE OR DISC AT
  RUN TIME, TO SELECT TAPES OF GIVEN PROPERTY CODES, TO WRITE
  SENTINELS,RECOGNISE AND PROCESS SENTINELS, NORMAL READ/WRITE,
  CLOSE REEL/BLOCK EARLY, OPEN AT END OF TAPE/DISC FILE TO
  APPEND DATA,SPECIFY TAPE GENERATION AND REEL NUMBER,CLOSE
  TAPE FILES IN 3 MODES

NCC STAGE 1 SOFTWARE VERIFICATION ABSTRACT A34111

NAME OF SOFTWARE
    SMITHS INDUSTRIES GROUP SALES LEDGER

TYPE OF SOFTWARE
    ACCOUNTING

PURPOSE OF SOFTWARE
    MAINTAINS OPEN ITEM OR BALANCE FORWARD LEDGER FILE BY CUSTOMER.
    LEDGER MAY BE SECTIONALISED.SECTION RECONILITIONS BY
    TRANSACTION CODE. UP TO 30 DIFFERENT TRANSACTION TYPES. PRINTS
    STATEMENTS, TURNOVER ANALYSIS, 2 DEBT ANALYSES, CONTROL REPORTS.

CONFIGURATION AND OPERATING SYSTEM
    ICL 1900

    HAS RUN SUCCESSFULLY ON ICL 1904E
    AMOUNT OF PRIMARY STORAGE 9K-16K WORDS
    2 DISC DRIVES, 10K-100K CHARACTERS STORAGE
    5 MAGNETIC TAPE DRIVES
    1 LINE PRINTER
    1 CARD READER
    1 PAPER TAPE READER
    RUN UNDER OPERATING SYSTEM EXECUTIVE

MODE OF USAGE
    BATCH

LANGUAGE
    1900 COBOL & PLAN SUB-ROUTINES

AVAILABILITY
    PROGRAM MAY BE AVAILABLE FOR USE OUTSIDE SUPPLIERS
    ORGANISATION. PROGRAM AVAILABLE AS A BUREAU SERVICE

SUPPLIERS COMMENT
    PROVIDES UNIT FILE CARDS FOR CUSTOMER RECORDS-CAN BE USED AS
    TURN ROUND DOCUMENT FOR STATIC DATA UPDATE. INPUT PUNCHED CARD,
    PAPER TAPE, MAGNETIC TAPE.

NCC STAGE 1 SOFTWARE VERIFICATION ABSTRACT A34112

NAME OF SOFTWARE
  SMITHS INDUSTRIES MODULAR BONUS AND WEEKLY PAYROLL

TYPE OF SOFTWARE
  PAYROLL

PURPOSE OF SOFTWARE
  PERFORMS STATUTORY AND INTERNAL ROUTINES FOR PAYING PIECE-WORKERS
  AND DAY WORKERS. BONUS CALCULATED FROM PARAMETERS UNDER PAYROLL
  DEPARTMENT CONTROL.OFF-LINE VISIBLE RECORDS PRODUCED. ANALYSES
  COST, ESTABLISHMENT, DEDUCTION, EFFICIENCY, COINAGE, ETC.

CONFIGURATION AND OPERATING SYSTEM
  ICL 1900

  HAS RUN SUCCESSFULLY ON ICL 1904E
  AMOUNT OF PRIMARY STORAGE 17K-32K WORDS
  2 DISC DRIVES, 1.1M-10M CHARACTERS STORAGE
  4 MAGNETIC TAPE DRIVES
  1 LINE PRINTER
  1 PAPER TAPE READER
  RUN UNDER OPERATING SYSTEM EXECUTIVE

MODE OF USAGE
  BATCH

LANGUAGE
  1900 COBOL & PLAN SUB-ROUTINES

AVAILABILITY
  PROGRAM MAY BE AVAILABLE FOR USE OUTSIDE SUPPLIERS
  ORGANISATION. PROGRAM AVAILABLE AS A BUREAU SERVICE

SUPPLIERS COMMENT
  ALLOWS 11 FIXED, 4 REDUCING DEDUCTIONS, 99 INSURANCE RATES.
  PERSONNEL CLASSIFICATION FOR PERSONNEL INVENTORY ANALYSIS.
  SUCCESSFULLY IMPLEMENTED FOR 6 SITES AND 10,000 EMPLOYEES

NCC STAGE 1 SOFTWARE VERIFICATION ABSTRACT A34113

NAME OF SOFTWARE
  SMITHS INDUSTRIES SALES ANALYSIS

TYPE OF SOFTWARE
  ACCOUNTING

PURPOSE OF SOFTWARE
  MONTHLY ANALYSIS OF SALES BY BRANCH, PRODUCT GROUP, CUSTOMER,
  CATEGORY AREA, TERRITORY, WITH COMPARISON OF ACTUAL VERSUS
  BUDGETED SALES. PERIODIC ANALYSES BY PRODUCT AND/OR PRICE
  CATEGORY FACILITY FOR AD HOC ENQUIRIES. PRODUCT PROFITABILITY
  REPORTS

CONFIGURATION AND OPERATING SYSTEM
  ICL 1900

  HAS RUN SUCCESSFULLY ON ICL 1904E
  AMOUNT OF PRIMARY STORAGE 9K-16K WORDS
  2 DISC DRIVES 101K-1M CHARACTERS STORAGE
  5 MAGNETIC TAPE DRIVES
  1 LINE PRINTER
  1 CARD READER
  RUN UNDER OPERATING SYSTEM EXECUTIVE

MODE OF USAGE
  BATCH

LANGUAGE
  1900 COBOL & PLAN SUB-ROUTINES

AVAILABILITY
  PROGRAM MAY BE AVAILABLE FOR USE OUTSIDE SUPPLIERS
  ORGANISATION. PROGRAM AVAILABLE AS A BUREAU SERVICE

SUPPLIERS COMMENT
  INPUT VIA CARD, PAPER TAPE OR MAGNETIC TAPE

      COPYRIGHT NCC 1972   PRINTED ON 19/04/72

NCC STAGE 1 SOFTWARE VERIFICATION ABSTRACT A34114

NAME OF SOFTWARE
  SMITHS INDUSTRIES PENSION PAYROLL

TYPE OF SOFTWARE
  PENSIONS PAYROLL

PURPOSE OF SOFTWARE
  PERFORMS STATUTORY AND INTERNAL ROUTINES FOR PAYING
  PENSIONERS. ANALYSES PAYMENTS BY FUND AND OTHER SOURCES.
  PROVIDES UNIT CARDS FOR STATIC DATA ON PENSIONERS,PROVIDES
  ALL INFORMATION NEEDED FOR SCHEME EVALUATION

CONFIGURATION AND OPERATING SYSTEM
  ICL 1900

  HAS RUN SUCCESSFULLY ON ICL 1904E
  AMOUNT OF PRIMARY STORAGE 9K-16K WORDS
  1 DISC DRIVE,<10K CHARACTERS STORAGE
  4 MAGNETIC TAPE DRIVES
  1 LINE PRINTER
  1 CARD READER
  RUN UNDER OPERATING SYSTEM EXECUTIVE

MODE OF USAGE
  BATCH

LANGUAGE
  1900 COBOL & PLAN SUB-ROUTINES

AVAILABILITY
  PROGRAM MAY BE AVAILABLE FOR USE OUTSIDE SUPPLIERS
  ORGANISATION. PROGRAM AVAILABLE AS A BUREAU SERVICE

SUPPLIERS COMMENT
  THE SYSTEM HAS BEEN DESIGNED TO ALLOW PERIODIC EVALUATION
  OF THE PENSION SCHEME. THE SYSTEM IS CURRENTLY BEING EXTENDED
  TO PERFORM THIS EVALUATION BY COMPUTER.
  PAYMENT SYSTEM SUCCESSFULLY RUN OVER TWO YEARS. HAS BEEN
  SOLD BOTH AS A PACKAGE AND AS A BUREAU SERVICE.

NCC STAGE 1 SOFTWARE VERIFICATION ABSTRACT A34115

NAME OF SOFTWARE
  ROYAL MODULE TESTER

TYPE OF SOFTWARE
  PROGRAM TESTING

PURPOSE OF SOFTWARE
  TESTS MODULES WRITTEN IN IBM 360 COBOL OR ASSEMBLER HANDLES
  PROGRAM CHECKS. HANDLES CALL TO OTHER MODULES BY RESOLVING OR
  SIMULATING THEM. SUPPORTS MULTIPLE TEST SHOTS.

CONFIGURATION AND OPERATING SYSTEM
  IBM 360

  HAS RUN SUCCESSFULLY ON IBM 360/50 MODEL H50
  AMOUNT OF PRIMARY STORAGE 33K-64K BYTES
  1 DISC DRIVE, 10K-100K BYTES STORAGE
  1 LINE PRINTER
  1 CARD READER
  RUN UNDER OPERATING SYSTEM IBM 360 OS

MODE OF USAGE
  BATCH

LANGUAGE
  360 ASSEMBLER

AVAILABILITY
  PROGRAM MAY BE AVAILABLE FOR USE OUTSIDE SUPPLIERS ORGANISATION.

SUPPLIERS COMMENT
  CAN BE RUN ON MODEL F30 UPWARDS (I.E. 64K BYTES UPWARDS)

     COPYRIGHT NCC 1972   PRINTED ON 19/04/72

NCC STAGE 1 SOFTWARE VERIFICATION ABSTRACT A34116

NAME OF SOFTWARE
  SMITHS INDUSTRIES SALES ANALYSIS 2

TYPE OF SOFTWARE
  STATISTICAL APPLICATION (COMMERCIAL), ACCOUNTING

PURPOSE OF SOFTWARE
  MAINTAINS FILE OF PRODUCT COSTS. PRINTS UP TO 4 ANALYSES, PLUS
  CONTROL REPORTS OF INVOICES/CREDITS ANALYSES BY PRODUCT GROUP,
  CUSTOMER, OUTLET, BRANCH, TERRITORY, DISCOUNTS. CALCULATES GROSS
  PROFIT. PROVIDES PERIOD COMPARISONS

CONFIGURATION AND OPERATING SYSTEM
  ICL 1900

  HAS RUN SUCCESSFULLY ON ICL 1904E
  AMOUNT OF PRIMARY STORAGE 9K-16K WORDS
  1 DISC DRIVE, <10K CHARACTERS STORAGE
  5 MAGNETIC TAPE DRIVES
  1 LINE PRINTER
  1 CARD READER
  1 PAPER TAPE READER
  RUN UNDER OPERATING SYSTEM EXECUTIVE

MODE OF USAGE
  BATCH

LANGUAGE
  1900 COBOL PLUS PLAN SUBROUTINES

AVAILABILITY
  PROGRAM MAY BE AVAILABLE FOR USE OUTSIDE SUPPLIERS ORGANISATION.
  PROGRAM AVAILABLE ON A BUREAU SERVICE

SUPPLIERS COMMENT
  PAPER TAPE INPUT OF TRANSACTIONS. CARD OR PAPER TAPE INPUT OF
  STATIC DATA AMENDMENTS. FACILITY FOR AD HOC ENQUIRIES OF CURRENT
  AND HISTORIC DATA

NCC STAGE 1 SOFTWARE VERIFICATION ABSTRACT A34117

NAME OF SOFTWARE
   SMITHS INDUSTRIES GENERAL CARD BATCH VALIDATION

TYPE OF SOFTWARE
   UTILITY

PURPOSE OF SOFTWARE
   READS DATA INPUT ON CARDS AND VALIDATES ACCORDING TO PARAMETERS
   INPUT ON CARDS. DATA CARDS IN ERROR OUTPUT TO ERROR TAPE FILE
   IN CARD IMAGE OR EDITED FORMAT. VALID DATA OUTPUT TO MAGNETIC
   TAPE AS CARD IMAGE OR SELECTED PART SPECIFIED BY USER

CONFIGURATION AND OPERATING SYSTEM
   ICL 1900 SERIES

   HAS RUN SUCCESSFULLY ON ICL 1904E
   AMOUNT OF PRIMARY STORAGE 4K-8K WORDS
   2 DISC DRIVES, <10K
   2 MAGNETIC TAPE DRIVES
   1 LINE PRINTER
   1 CARD READER
   RUN UNDER OPERATING SYSTEM EXECUTIVE

MODE OF USAGE
   BATCH

LANGUAGE
   ICL PLAN

AVAILABILITY
   PROGRAM MAY BE AVAILABLE FOR USE OUTSIDE SUPPLIERS ORGANISATION.
   PROGRAM AVAILABLE ON A BUREAU SERVICE

SUPPLIERS COMMENT
   FACILITIES TO EDIT OUTPUT FIELDS BEFORE OUTPUT TO MAGNETIC. TAPE
   AND TO ACCEPT VALIDATION CRITERIA TO USER SPECIFICATION. ERROR
   TAPE AND MAIN OUTPUT FILE NAMED BY PARAMETER. CONTROLS ON BATCH
   TOTALS REJECTING AND/OR REPORTING CONTROL FAILURE TO USER
   SPECIFICATION. REPORTS COUNTS BATCHES READ, CARDS
   ACCEPTED/REJECTED/WRITTEN TO FILE,CARDS BY CARD TYPE WITHIN BATCH

   COPYRIGHT NCC 1972   PRINTED ON 19/04/72

NCC STAGE 1 SOFTWARE VERIFICATION ABSTRACT A34118

NAME OF SOFTWARE
  SMITHS INDUSTRIES SIMULATED OFF-LINE PRINT PROGRAM

TYPE OF SOFTWARE
  UTILITY

PURPOSE OF SOFTWARE
  PRINTS MAGNETIC TAPE OF CORRECT FORMAT. BY PARAMETERS
  FROM CARD OR PAPER TAPE PRINTS NOMINATED MAGNETIC TAPE OR
  SERIAL EXCHANGEABLE DISC STORE FILE ON UP TO FIVE SELECTIVE
  PRINT CHARACTERS AND NINE LINES OF PAPER ALIGNMENT PATTERN.
  FACILITIES FOR RESTART AND MULTI-REEL FILES

CONFIGURATION AND OPERATING SYSTEM
  ICL 1900

  HAS RUN SUCCESSFULLY ON ICL 1904E
  AMOUNT OF PRIMARY STORAGE <4K WORDS
  2 MAGNETIC TAPE DRIVES
  1 CARD READER
  1 PAPER TAPE READER
  1 LINE PRINTER
  RUN UNDER OPERATING SYSTEM EXECUTIVE

MODE OF USAGE
  BATCH

LANGUAGE
  ICL PLAN

AVAILABILITY
  PROGRAM MAY BE AVAILABLE FOR USE OUTSIDE SUPPLIERS
  ORGANISATION. PROGRAM AVAILABLE ON A BUREAU SERVICE

SUPPLIERS COMMENT
  PRINTING DOUBLE-BUFFERED. INPUT FILES TO BE IN STANDARD
  ICL SOFTWARE FORMAT. BLOCK SIZE UP TO 512 WORDS.
  RECORDS 3 TO 32 WORDS LONG

NCC STAGE 1 SOFTWARE VERIFICATION ABSTRACT A34119

NAME OF SOFTWARE
  PROFESSIONAL AND TECHNICAL OFFICES COST ACCOUNTING PACKAGE

TYPE OF SOFTWARE
  ACCOUNTING
  PROJECT COSTING & BUDGETING

PURPOSE OF SOFTWARE
  PROJECT ACCOUNTS SUB-DIVIDED BY WORK STAGES. BUDGETS ARE
  APPORTIONED BY STAGE.COSTS COLLECTED VIA TIME SHEETS & EXPENSE
  FORMS:COMPARED WITH PROGRESS VALUES CALCULATED FROM
  PROGRESS REPORTS AND BUDGETS.HIERARCHY REPORTS,OVERHEADS
  ALLOCATIONS,RECOVERABLES,OPTIONS,ETC.

CONFIGURATION AND OPERATING SYSTEM
  IBM 360

  HAS RUN SUCCESSFULLY ON IBM 360/30,IBM 360/40
  AMOUNT OF PRIMARY STORAGE 33K-64K BYTES
  2 DISC DRIVES,1.1M-10M BYTES STORAGE
  2 MAGNETIC TAPE DRIVES
  1 LINE PRINTER
  1 CARD READER
  RUN UNDER OPERATING SYSTEM DOS + GRASP

MODE OF USAGE
  BATCH

LANGUAGE
  COBOL

AVAILABILITY
  PROGRAM MAY BE AVAILABLE FOR USE OUTSIDE SUPPLIERS
  ORGANISATION.PROGRAM AVAILABLE AS A BUREAU SERVICE

SUPPLIERS COMMENT
  COMPUTER DEPTS,ARCHITECTS,CONSULTING ENGINEERS, & ACCOUNTANTS
  ARE CURRENT USERS,FLEXIBILITY THROUGH USER OPTIONS.CHOICE OF
  REPORTS,OVERHEAD ALLOCATION METHODS,CODING TECHNIQUES,SUMMARY
  TOTALS,MULTIPLE STAFF RATES.REPORTS CAN BE ARRANGED TO HANDLE
  ENTIRE BOOKKEEPING. INPUT FORMS ARE CUSTOMISED AND CAN BE
  MADE TO REPLACE PETTY CASH BOOK,PRINT REQUISITIONS ETC

NCC STAGE 1 SOFTWARE VERIFICATION ABSTRACT A34120

NAME OF SOFTWARE
  DIRECT MAIL LABELLING PACKAGE

TYPE OF SOFTWARE
  FILE HANDLING

PURPOSE OF SOFTWARE
  TO MAINTAIN NAMES AND ADDRESSES ON FILE ALLOWING FULL ABILITY TO
  DELETE DUPLICATES AND TO PRINT OUT NEAR-DUPLICATES. ALSO TO
  PRINT THE FILE IN ANY SEQUENCE IN FORMAT SUITABLE FOR INPUT TO
  AUTOMATIC ADDRESSING MACHINES, E.G. CHESHIRE MAILING MACHINE.

CONFIGURATION AND OPERATING SYSTEM
  HONEYWELL 200 SERIES

  HAS RUN SUCCESSFULLY ON HONEYWELL 120
  AMOUNT OF PRIMARY STORAGE 9K-16K CHARACTERS
  4 MAGNETIC TAPE DRIVES
  1 LINE PRINTER
  1 CARD READER
  RUN UNDER OPERATING SYSTEM MOD 1 TR

  HAS RUN SUCCESSFULLY ON HONEYWELL 200
  AMOUNT OF PRIMARY STORAGE 17K-32K CHARACTERS
  5 MAGNETIC TAPE DRIVES
  1 LINE PRINTER
  1 CARD READER
  1 PAPER TAPE READER
  RUN UNDER OPERATING SYSTEM MOD 1 TR

MODE OF USAGE
  BATCH

LANGUAGE
  EASYCODER

AVAILABILITY
  PROGRAM AVAILABLE ON A BUREAU SERVICE

SUPPLIERS COMMENT
  THE PACKAGE CATERS FOR ABC AND MDF REQUIREMENTS, AND TOWN AND
  COUNTY SORTING TO GPO REQUIREMENTS

    COPYRIGHT NCC 1972   PRINTED ON 19/04/72

NCC STAGE 1 SOFTWARE VERIFICATION ABSTRACT A34121

NAME OF SOFTWARE
  QUANTITY SURVEYING PACKAGE

TYPE OF SOFTWARE
  BILLS OF QUANTITY PRODUCTION

PURPOSE OF SOFTWARE
  TO PRODUCE DRAFT BILLS OF QUANTITY FOR QUANTITY SURVEYORS FROM
  DIMENSION SHEETS, USING THE R3B CODE STRUCTURE

CONFIGURATION AND OPERATING SYSTEM
  HONEYWELL 200 SERIES

  HAS RUN SUCCESSFULLY ON HONEYWELL 120
  AMOUNT OF PRIMARY STORAGE 9K-16K CHARACTERS
  4 MAGNETIC TAPE DRIVES
  1 LINE PRINTER
  1 CARD READER
  1 PAPER TAPE READER
  RUN UNDER OPERATING SYSTEM MOD 1 TR

  HAS RUN SUCCESSFULLY ON HONEYWELL 200
  AMOUNT OF PRIMARY STORAGE 17K-32K CHARACTERS
  5 MAGNETIC TAPE DRIVES
  1 LINE PRINTER
  1 CARD READER
  1 PAPER TAPE READER
  RUN UNDER OPERATING SYSTEM MOD 1 TR

MODE OF USAGE
  BATCH

LANGUAGE
  EASYCODER

AVAILABILITY
  PROGRAM AVAILABLE ON A BUREAU SERVICE

SUPPLIERS COMMENT
  THE SOFTWARE HAS BEEN REGULARLY UPDATED OVER A PERIOD OF SEVERAL
  YEARS IN CO-OPERATION WITH A CONSORTIUM OF QUANTITY SURVEYORS,
  ALL OF WHICH REGULARLY USE THE PACKAGE FACILITIES

     COPYRIGHT NCC 1972   PRINTED ON 19/04/72

NCC STAGE 1 SOFTWARE VERIFICATION ABSTRACT A34122

NAME OF SOFTWARE
  SOLVE BY INFLUENCE COEFFICIENTS

TYPE OF SOFTWARE
  ENGINEERING APPLICATION

PURPOSE OF SOFTWARE
  ANALYSES CONTINUOUS BEAMS DESCRIBED BY PROPERTIES AND APPLIED
  MOMENTS AT REGULARLY SPACED SECTIONS.TABULATES AND PLOTS MOMENTS,
  SHEARS, DEFLECTIONS, AND STRESSES, AND ACCUMULATES LOAD CASES

CONFIGURATION AND OPERATING SYSTEM
  ICL ATLAS

  HAS RUN SUCCESSFULLY ON ATLAS 2
  AMOUNT OF PRIMARY STORAGE 17K-32K WORDS
  1 DISC DRIVE, 10K-100K WORDS STORAGE
  1 LINE PRINTER
  1 TELETYPE
  1 GRAPH PLOTTER
  RUN UNDER CAMBRIDGE MIXED LANGUAGE SYSTEM

MODE OF USAGE
  REAL-TIME

LANGUAGE
  ANSI FORTRAN

AVAILABILITY
  PROGRAM AVAILABLE ON A BUREAU SERVICE

NCC STAGE 1 SOFTWARE VERIFICATION ABSTRACT A34123

NAME OF SOFTWARE
  INTERACTIVE PILE GROUP ANALYSIS

TYPE OF SOFTWARE
  ENGINEERING APPLICATION

PURPOSE OF SOFTWARE
  GENERATES LOAD CASES FROM STANDARD COMPONENTS AND ANALYSES THEIR
  ACTION ON PILE GROUPS. CONFIGURATION OF LOAD COMPONENTS AND
  PILES RAPIDLY CHANGED INTERACTIVELY. ALL DATA AND INTERACTIVE
  COMMANDS IN PROBLEM ORIENTED LANGUAGE

CONFIGURATION AND OPERATING SYSTEM
  ICL ATLAS

  HAS RUN SUCCESSFULLY ON ATLAS 2
  AMOUNT OF PRIMARY STORAGE 9K-16K WORDS
  1 LINE PRINTER
  1 TELETYPE
  RUN UNDER CAMBRIDGE MIXED LANGUAGE SYSTEM

MODE OF USAGE
  INTERACTIVE

LANGUAGE
  ANSI FORTRAN

AVAILABILITY
  PROGRAM AVAILABLE ON A BUREAU SERVICE

    COPYRIGHT NCC 1972   PRINTED ON 19/04/72

NCC STAGE 1 SOFTWARE VERIFICATION ABSTRACT A34124

NAME OF SOFTWARE
  BAR BENDING SCHEDULES

TYPE OF SOFTWARE
  ENGINEERING APPLICATION

PURPOSE OF SOFTWARE
  CHECKS DATA AND CARRIES OUT SOME OF THE ARITHMETIC FOR SCHEDULES
  OF REINFORCING BARS TO BS 4466

CONFIGURATION AND OPERATING SYSTEM
  ICL ATLAS

  HAS RUN SUCCESSFULLY ON ATLAS 2
  AMOUNT OF PRIMARY STORAGE 9K-16K WORDS
  1 DISC DRIVE, 10K-100K WORDS STORAGE
  1 LINE PRINTER
  1 CARD PUNCH
  1 TELETYPE
  RUN UNDER CAMBRIDGE MIXED LANGUAGE SYSTEM

MODE OF USAGE
  REAL-TIME

LANGUAGE
  ANSI FORTRAN

AVAILABILITY
  PROGRAM MAY BE AVAILABLE FOR USE OUTSIDE SUPPLIERS ORGANISATION.
  PROGRAM AVAILABLE ON A BUREAU SERVICE

     COPYRIGHT NCC 1972   PRINTED ON 19/04/72

NCC STAGE 1 SOFTWARE VERIFICATION ABSTRACT A34125

NAME OF SOFTWARE
   INFLUENCE LINES

TYPE OF SOFTWARE
   ENGINEERING APPLICATION

PURPOSE OF SOFTWARE
   CALCULATES AND PLOTS INFLUENCE LINES OF BENDING MOMENT AND SHEAR
   FORCE FOR CONTINUOUS BEAMS OF VARYING SECTION

CONFIGURATION AND OPERATING SYSTEM
   ICL ATLAS

   HAS RUN SUCCESSFULLY ON ATLAS 2
   AMOUNT OF PRIMARY STORAGE 17K-32K WORDS
   1 DISC DRIVE, 10K-100K WORDS STORAGE
   1 GRAPH PLOTTER
   1 TELETYPE
   RUN UNDER CAMBRIDGE MIXED LANGUAGE SYSTEM

MODE OF USAGE
   REAL-TIME

LANGUAGE
   ANSI FORTRAN

AVAILABILITY
   PROGRAM AVAILABLE ON A BUREAU SERVICE

      COPYRIGHT NCC 1972   PRINTED ON 19/04/72

NCC STAGE 1 SOFTWARE VERIFICATION ABSTRACT A34126

NAME OF SOFTWARE
   PRESTRESSED BEAM DESIGN

TYPE OF SOFTWARE
   ENGINNEERING APPLICATION

PURPOSE OF SOFTWARE
   CALCULATES EFFECTS OF PRESTRESSING TENDONS ON CONTINUOUS BEAMS.
   TENDONS CHANGED INTERACTIVELY AND DISPLAYED ON STORAGE TUBE,
   TOGETHER WITH RESULTANT STRESS. DESIGNS MAY BE DUMPED,
   RETRIEVED AND PRINTED OUT

CONFIGURATION AND OPERATING SYSTEM
   ICL ATLAS

   HAS RUN SUCCESSFULLY ON ATLAS 2
   AMOUNT OF PRIMARY STORAGE 17K-32K WORDS
   1 DISC DRIVE, 10K-100K WORDS STORAGE
   1 LINE PRINTER
   1 PAPER TAPE READER
   1 GRAPH PLOTTER
   1 VDU
   RUN UNDER CAMBRIDGE MIXED LANGUAGE SYSTEM

MODE OF USAGE
   INTERACTIVE

LANGUAGE
   ANSI FORTRAN

AVAILABILITY
   PROGRAM AVAILABLE AS A BUREAU SERVICE

SUPPLIERS COMMENT
   FIRMS NAMED AS SUPPLIER AND AGENT ARE IN FACT JOINT OWNERS

NCC STAGE 1 SOFTWARE VERIFICATION ABSTRACT A34127

NAME OF SOFTWARE
   STANDARD PRESTRESSED CONCRETE BEAM DESIGN

TYPE OF SOFTWARE
   ENGINEERING APPLICATION

PURPOSE OF SOFTWARE
   ENABLES SECTION PROPERTIES FOR A SET OF STANDARD PRESTRESSED
   CONCRETE BEAMS TO BE STORED IN DATA BANK. SELECTS APPROPRIATE
   BEAM AND DESIGNS PRESTRESSING SYSTEM FOR GIVEN CONDITIONS.

CONFIGURATION AND OPERATING SYSTEM
   ICL ATLAS

   HAS RUN SUCCESSFULLY ON ATLAS 2
   AMOUNT OF PRIMARY STORAGE 9K-16K WORDS
   1 DISC DRIVE,<10K WORDS STORAGE
   TELETYPES
   RUN UNDER CAMBRIDGE MIXED LANGUAGE SYSTEM

MODE OF USAGE
   REAL-TIME

LANGUAGE
   ANSI FORTRAN

AVAILABILITY
   PROGRAM MAY BE AVAILABLE FOR USE OUTSIDE SUPPLIERS ORGANISATION
   PROGRAM AVAILABLE AS A BUREAU SERVICE

      COPYRIGHT NCC 1972   PRINTED ON 19/04/72

NCC STAGE 1 SOFTWARE VERIFICATION ABSTRACT A34128

NAME OF SOFTWARE
  SECTION DESIGN AND OPTIMISATION

TYPE OF SOFTWARE
  ENGINEERING APPLICATION

PURPOSE OF SOFTWARE
  DESIGNS LARGE STRUCTURAL SECTIONS FOR PLANE BENDING UNDER GIVEN
  LOADS AND STRESSES; INCLUDES MODULAR RATIO CHANGES,DEAD LOAD
  CALCULATION AND PRE-STRESSED DESIGN. CAN ALSO COST DESIGNS AND
  SEARCH FOR MOST ECONOMIC SECTION.

CONFIGURATION AND OPERATING SYSTEM
  ICL ATLAS

  HAS RUN SUCCESSFULLY ON ATLAS 2
  AMOUNT OF PRIMARY STORAGE 9K-16K WORDS
  TELETYPES
  RUN UNDER CAMBRIDGE MIXED LANGUAGE SYSTEM

MODE OF USAGE
  REAL-TIME

LANGUAGE
  ANSI FORTRAN

AVAILABILITY
  PROGRAM MAY BE AVAILABLE FOR USE OUTSIDE SUPPLIERS ORGANISATION
  PROGRAM AVAILABLE AS A BUREAU SERVICE

    COPYRIGHT NCC 1972   PRINTED ON 19/04/72

NCC STAGE 1 SOFTWARE VERIFICATION ABSTACT A34129

NAME OF SOFTWARE
  WESTERGAARD ANALYSIS OF SLABS

TYPE OF SOFTWARE
  ENGINEERING APPLICATION

PURPOSE OF SOFTWARE
  APPLIES GENERAL WESTERGAARD FORMULAE FOR WHEEL LOADS ON
  SLABS. SUMS MULTIPLE WHEELS AND CALCULATES PRINCIPAL
  MOMENTS

CONFIGURATION AND OPERATING SYSTEM
  ICL ATLAS

  HAS RUN SUCCESSFULLY ON ATLAS 2
  AMOUNT OF PRIMARY STORAGE 17K-32K WORDS
  1 TELETYPE
  RUN UNDER CAMBRIDGE MULTI-ACCESS SYSTEM

MODE OF USAGE
  REAL-TIME

LANGUAGE
  ALGOL

AVAILABILITY
  PROGRAM MAY BE AVAILABLE FOR USE OUTSIDE SUPPLIERS ORGANISATION
  PROGRAM AVAILABLE AS A BUREAU SERVICE

SUPPLIERS COMMENT
  PROGRAM WOULD PROBABLY FIT INTO 4K WITH EFFICIENT COMPILER

NCC STAGE 1 SOFTWARE VERIFICATION ABSTRACT A34130

NAME OF SOFTWARE
    GENERAL PURPOSE CORE SORT (ICL1900)

TYPE OF SOFTWARE
    UTILITY

PURPOSE OF SOFTWARE
    SORTS LIMITED SIZED MAGNETIC TAPE FILES SO AS TO MINIMISE BOTH
    OPERATOR INTERVENTION AND PERIPHERAL USAGE. RECORDS MAY BE
    SORTED IN ASCENDING OR DESCENDING SEQUENCE. CAN USE UP TO FOUR
    SORT KEYS, EACH WITH UP TO 32 CHARACTERS.

CONFIGURATION AND OPERATING SYSTEM
    ICL 1900

    HAS RUN SUCCESSFULLY ON ICL 1901
    AMOUNT OF PRIMARY STORAGE 9K-16K WORDS
    1 MAGNETIC TAPE DRIVE
    1 CARD READER
    1 PAPER TAPE READER
    PAPER TAPE READER IS AN ALTERNATIVE TO CARD READER.
    RUN UNDER OPERATING SYSTEM EXECUTIVE

MODE OF USAGE
    BATCH

LANGUAGE
    PLAN 3

AVAILABILITY
    PROGRAM MAY BE AVAILABLE FOR USE OUTSIDE SUPPLIERS ORGANISATION

SUPPLIERS COMMENT
    ALTHOUGH THE STANDARD PROGRAM REQUIRES 13.8K, ALTERNATIVE VERSIONS
    WITH A GREATER OR LESSER CORE REQUIREMENT MAY BE PRODUCED BY TWO
    AMENDMENTS TO THE SOURCE PROGRAM

        COPYRIGHT NCC 1972   PRINTED ON 19/04/72

NCC STAGE 1 SOFTWARE VERIFICATION ABSTRACT A34131

NAME OF SOFTWARE
  PORTFOLIO PERFORMANCE

TYPE OF SOFTWARE
  FINANCIAL APPLICATION

PURPOSE OF SOFTWARE
  EVALUATES THE TRUE INCOME AND CAPITAL RETURN ON AN
  INVESTMENT PORTFOLIO ALLOWING FOR NEW MONEY. COMPARES RETURN WITH
  A NOTIONAL RETURN FROM THE SAME PORTFOLIO IF INVESTED IN
  EQUITY AND FIXED INTEREST INDICES.

CONFIGURATION AND OPERATING SYSTEM
  IBM 360

  HAS RUN SUCCESSFULLY ON IBM 360/65, IBM 360/40, IBM 360/30
  AMOUNT OF PRIMARY STORAGE 17K-32K BYTES
  1 LINE PRINTER
  1 CARD READER
  RUN UNDER OPERATING SYSTEM OS

MODE OF USAGE
  BATCH

LANGUAGE
  FORTRAN IV

AVAILABILITY
  PROGRAM MAY BE AVAILABLE FOR USE OUTSIDE SUPPLIERS ORGANISATION
  PROGRAM AVAILABLE AS A BUREAU SERVICE.

NCC STAGE 1 SOFTWARE VERIFICATION ABSTRACT A34132

NAME OF SOFTWARE
  SALES LEDGER AND CREDIT CONTROL

TYPE OF SOFTWARE
  ACCOUNTING

PURPOSE OF SOFTWARE
  TO PROVIDE STATEMENTS AND AGED BALANCES

CONFIGURATION AND OPERATING SYSTEM
  ICL 1900

  HAS RUN SUCCESSFULLY ON ICL 1901A
  AMOUNT OF PRIMARY STORAGE 4K-8K WORDS,OVERLAYS USED
  4 MAGNETIC TAPE DRIVES
  1 LINE PRINTER
  1 CARD READER
  RUN UNDER OPERATING SYSTEM EXECUTIVE

MODE OF USAGE
  BATCH

LANGUAGE
  COMPACT COBOL

AVAILABILITY
  PROGRAM MAY BE AVAILABLE FOR USE OUTSIDE SUPPLIERS ORGANISATION
  PROGRAM AVAILABLE AS A BUREAU SERVICE.

  COPYRIGHT NCC 1972   PRINTED ON 19/04/72

NCC STAGE 1 SOFTWARE VERIFICATION ABSTRACT A34133

NAME OF SOFTWARE
   BOUGHT AND NOMINAL LEDGER

TYPE OF SOFTWARE
   ACCOUNTING

PURPOSE OF SOFTWARE
   TO PROVIDE DAY BOOKS , ACCOUNTS DUE FOR PAYMENT, NOMINAL
   LEDGER

CONFIGURATION AND OPERATING SYSTEM
   ICL 1900

   HAS RUN SUCCESSFULLY ON ICL 1901A
   AMOUNT OF PRIMARY STORAGE 4K-8K WORDS
   4 MAGNETIC TAPE DECKS
   1 LINE PRINTER
   1 CARD READER

MODE OF USAGE
   BATCH

LANGUAGE
   COMPACT COBOL AND NICOL

AVAILABILITY
   PROGRAM MAY BE AVAILABLE FOR USE OUTSIDE SUPPLIERS
   ORGANISATION. PROGRAM AVAILABLE AS A BUREAU SERVICE

   COPYRIGHT NCC 1972   PRINTED ON 19/04/72

NCC STAGE 1 SOFTWARE VERIFICATION ABSTRACT A34134

NAME OF SOFTWARE
    CASH TRANSFER TAPE CONVERSION SOFTWARE FOR INTERBANK
    CREDIT AND DIRECT DEBIT TRANSACTIONS

TYPE OF SOFTWARE
    ACCOUNTING,FILE HANDLING,UTILITY

PURPOSE OF SOFTWARE
    CONVERTS MAGNETIC TAPE FILES PRODUCED BY COBOL OR PLAN PRO-
    GRAMS AND STANDARD ICL HOUSEKEEPING TO THE SPECIAL FORMAT
    REQUIRED BY INTERBANK COMPUTER BUREAU. SAVES PRINTING
    CREDIT TRANSFERS FOR PAYROLL, SUPPLIERS, ETC., OR DIRECT
    DEBIT SLIPS

CONFIGURATION AND OPERATING SYSTEM
    ICL 1900

    HAS RUN SUCCESSFULLY ON ICL 1902A
    AMOUNT OF PRIMARY STORAGE 4K-8K WORDS
    2 MAGNETIC TAPE DECKS
    1 LINE PRINTER
    RUN UNDER OPERATING SYSTEM EXECUTIVE

MODE OF USAGE
    BATCH

LANGUAGE
    PLAN

AVAILABILITY
    PROGRAM MAY BE AVAILABLE FOR USE OUTSIDE SUPPLIERS
    ORGANISATION. PROGRAM AVAILABLE AS A BUREAU SERVICE

SUPPLIERS COMMENT
    PROGRAM CREATES SPECIAL HEADER AND TRAILER LABELS,
    CHECKS THE FILE FOR DEBIT/CREDIT BALANCE AND CONVERTS
    THE CHARACTER SET. A SMALL DOCKET FOR DESPATCH WITH THE
    TAPE TO THE INTERBANK COMPUTER BUREAU IS PRINTED.
    PROGRAM IS AVAILABLE IN OBJECT FORM ON CARD OR
    MAGNETIC TAPE,WITH FULL OPERATING INSTRUCTIONS AND
    FREE MAINTENANCE FOR 2 YEARS.
    PRICE £200 INCLUSIVE OR BUREAU USE.

                    PRINTED ON 19/04/72

NCC STAGE 1 VERIFICATION ABSTRACT A34135

NAME OF SOFTWARE
  ABCONS SYSTEM

TYPE OF SOFTWARE
  ENGINEERING APPLICATION

PURPOSE OF SOFTWARE
  REINFORCED CONCRETE DESIGN AND DETAILING

CONFIGURATION AND OPERATING SYSTEM
  ICL1900, ATLAS

  HAS RUN SUCCESSFULLY ON ICL1905
  AMOUNT OF PRIMARY STORAGE 33K-64K CHARACTERS
  1 DISC DRIVE, 101K-1M WORDS STORAGE
  3 MAGNETIC TAPE DRIVES
  1 LINE PRINTER
  1 CARD READER
  RUN UNDER OPERATING SYSTEM EXECUTIVE

  HAS RUN SUCCESSFULLY ON ATLAS 2
  AMOUNT OF PRIMARY STORAGE 33K-64K WORDS
  4 DISC DRIVES,101K-1M WORDS STORAGE
  2 MAGNETIC TAPE DRIVES
  1 LINE PRINTER
  1 CARD READER
  1 TELETYPE
  RUN UNDER CAMBRIDGE MULTI-ACCESS SYSTEM

MODE OF USAGE
  BATCH

LANGUAGE
  FORTRAN IV

AVAILABILITY
  PROGRAM AVAILABLE AS A BUREAU SERVICE

    COPYRIGHT NCC 1972   PRINTED ON 19/04/72

NCC STAGE 1 SOFTWARE VERIFICATION ABSTRACT A34136

NAME OF SOFTWARE
  ARLINGTON INVENTORY MANAGEMENT SYSTEM

TYPE OF SOFTWARE
  STOCK CONTROL,INVOICING PROCEDURE,ACCOUNTING

PURPOSE OF SOFTWARE
  INVENTORY MANAGEMENT TO AIRCRAFT
  SUPPLY SPECIFICATIONS (ATA200-AIR
  TRANSPORT ASSOCIATION OF AMERICA
  SPECIFICATION 200)

CONFIGURATION AND OPERATING SYSTEM
  IBM 360

  HAS RUN SUCCESSFULLY ON IBM360/20,IBM360/30.
  AMOUNT OF PRIMARY STORAGE 9K-16K BYTES
  4 MAGNETIC TAPE DRIVES
  1 LINE PRINTER
  1 CARD READER
  1 CARD PUNCH
  DISCS ARE ALTERNATIVE TO MAGNETIC TAPES
  RUN UNDER OPERATING SYSTEM 360/20 TOS/BPS, 360/30 DOS/TOS

MODE OF USAGE
  BATCH

LANGUAGE
  RPG/BAL, NEAT/3

AVAILABILITY
  PROGRAM IS AVAILABLE FOR USE OUTSIDE SUPPLIERS ORGANISATION.
  PROGRAM AVAILABLE AS A BUREAU SERVICE.

SUPPLIERS COMMENT
  AIMS PROVIDES MANAGEMENT WITH MANY TYPES OF STATISTICAL AND
  FINANCIAL REPORTS, ALL OF WHICH ARE DESIGNED TO OPTIMISE THE
  MONETARY INVESTMENT IN SPARE PARTS STOCK AND AT THE SAME TIME
  ENSURE THAT DELIVERY PERFORMANCE TO CUSTOMERS IS MAINTAINED.
  DUE TO BE IMPLEMENTED ON NCR CENTURY SHORTLY

NCC STAGE 1 SOFTWARE VERIFICATION ABSTRACT A34137

NAME OF SOFTWARE
   STANDARD MAGNETIC TAPE SORT TIMINGS PROGRAM

TYPE OF SOFTWARE
   UTILITY

PURPOSE OF SOFTWARE
   CALCULATES THE TIME AN ICL SYSTEM 4-50 OR 4-70 MAGNETIC
   TAPE SORT WILL TAKE FROM PARAMETERS SUPPLIED AT RUN TIME (BLOCK
   SIZE,RECORD SIZE,NUMBER OF RECORDS,ETC)

CONFIGURATION AND OPERATING SYSTEM
   ICL SYSTEM 4, RCA SPECTRA 70

   HAS RUN SUCCESSFULLY ON ICL 4-70, RCA SPECTRA 70/45
   AMOUNT OF PRIMARY STORAGE 17K-32K BYTES
   1 MAGNETIC TAPE DRIVE
   1 LINE PRINTER
   1 CARD READER
   RUN UNDER OPERATING SYSTEM J LEVEL

MODE OF USAGE
   BATCH

LANGUAGE
   FORTRAN IV

AVAILABILITY
   PROGRAM MAY BE AVAILABLE FOR USE OUTSIDE SUPPLIERS ORGANISATION
   PROGRAM AVAILABLE AS A BUREAU SERVICE

SUPPLIERS COMMENT
   THE PROGRAM ACCESSES POLYPHASE TABLES HELD ON TAPE

      COPYRIGHT NCC 1972   PRINTED ON 19/04/72

NCC STAGE 1 SOFTWARE VERIFICATION ABSTRACT A34138

NAME OF SOFTWARE
   PSB PERSONNEL INTERROGATION OF MASTER FILES

TYPE OF SOFTWARE
   STATISTICAL APPLICATION (COMMERCIAL), INFORMATION RETRIEVAL

PURPOSE OF SOFTWARE
   GENERALISED INTERROGATION SYSTEM TO ANSWER AD HOC
   ENQUIRIES FROM PERSONNEL WITHIN AN ORGANISATION

CONFIGURATION AND OPERATING SYSTEM
   CDC3600

   HAS RUN SUCCESSFULLY ON CDC3600
   AMOUNT OF PRIMARY STORAGE 17K-32K WORDS,OVERLAYS USED.
   5 MAGNETIC TAPE DRIVES
   1 LINE PRINTER
   1 CARD READER
   RUN UNDER OPERATING SYSTEM FORMON.

MODE OF USAGE
   BATCH

LANGUAGE
   FORTRAN IV

AVAILABILITY
   PROGRAM MAY BE AVAILABLE FOR USE OUTSIDE SUPPLIERS ORGANISATION

SUPPLIERS COMMENT
   SYSTEM WRITTEN TO CATER FOR ANY FILE FORMAT INCLUDING VARIABLE
   LENGTH AND PACKED BINARY. 14 OUTPUT OPTIONS COVER LISTINGS AND
   TABULATIONS.

NCC STAGE 1 SOFTWARE VERIFICATION ABSTRACT A34139

NAME OF SOFTWARE
  REPORT SERVICE - VERY PROMPT

TYPE OF SOFTWARE
  FILE HANDLING

PURPOSE OF SOFTWARE
  DATA RETRIEVAL AND REPORTING FROM ANY FILE WH'CH CAN BE
  READ SEQUENTIALLY

CONFIGURATION AND OPERATING SYSTEM
  IBM 360

  HAS RUN SUCCESSFULLY ON IBM 360/30
  AMOUNT OF PRIMARY STORAGE 17K-32K BYTES,OVERLAYS USED
  2 DISC DRIVES,1.1M-10M BYTES
  1 LINE PRINTER
  1 CARD READER
  RUN UNDER OPERATING SYSTEM DOS RELEASE 21

MODE OF USAGE
  BATCH

LANGUAGE
  COBOL MAINLY,WITH SOME ASSEMBLER

AVAILABILITY
  PROGRAM MAY BE AVAILABLE FOR USE OUTSIDE SUPPLIERS ORGANISATION
  PROGRAM AVAILABLE AS A BUREAU SERVICE

SUPPLIERS COMMENT
  THE HARDWARE CONFIGURATION IS VARIABLE. WORKFILES USED IN
  INSTALLATION AND EXECUTION CAN BE ACCOMMODATED ON 2400,2314 ETC
  DISC DRIVES.THE SYSTEM,INSTALLED IN OVER 30 LOCATIONS IN
  THE U.S.A. HAS BEEN THOROUGHLY INVESTIGATED AND FOUND TO BE
  COMPLETELY RELIABLE.

  HAS RUN ONLY ON IBM 360/30 SO FAR IN UK

     COPYRIGHT NCC 1972   PRINTED ON 19/04/72

NCC STAGE 1 SOFTWARE VERIFICATION ABSTRACT A34140

NAME OF SOFTWARE
  TRIPLAN PROGRAM SYSTEMS AND NATIONAL DISTANCE BANK.

TYPE OF SOFTWARE
  OPERATIONAL RESEARCH APPLICATION.

PURPOSE OF SOFTWARE
  VEHICLE SCHEDULING. THE ALLOCATION OF VEHICLES TO SUBSETS
  OF CUSTOMERS AND/OR PASSENGER STOPS IN SUCH A WAY AS TO
  MINIMISE THE NUMBER OF VEHICLES REQUIRED, OR OTHER COST
  CRITERIA IN ACCORDANCE WITH SPECIFIED DATA AND CONSTRAINTS
  GIVEN DATA AND CONSTRAINTS.

CONFIGURATION AND OPERATING SYSTEM
  ICL 1900

  HAS RUN SUCCESSFULLY ON ICL1902A,ICL1903
  AMOUNT OF PRIMARY STORAGE 17K-32K WORDS
  1 DISC DRIVE,10K-100K WORDS STORAGE
  2 MAGNETIC TAPE DRIVES
  1 LINE PRINTER
  1 CARD READER
  RUN UNDER OPERATING SYSTEM GEORGE 2

MODE OF USAGE
  BATCH

LANGUAGE
  FORTRAN IV

AVAILABILITY
  PROGRAM MAY BE AVAILABLE FOR USE OUTSIDE SUPPLIERS
  ORGANISATION. PROGRAM AVAILABLE AS BUREAU SERVICE.

SUPPLIERS COMMENT
  THE NATIONAL DISTANCE BANK IS A MODEL OF THE BRITISH ROAD
  NETWORK AND CONSISTS OF ALL ROAD DISTANCES BETWEEN 97 MAJOR
  CENTRES. EACH CENTRE HAS A REGION OF UP TO 112 LOCATIONS
  INCLUDING THE CENTRE AND BORDER POINTS SHARED WITH ADJOINING
  REGIONS,TWO OR MORE REGIONS CAN BE MERGED THROUGH BORDER
  PTS.DISTANCES BETWEEN LOCATIONS IN THE SAME REGION,ADJOINING
  OR WIDELY SEPARATED REGIONS ARE AVAILABLE,WHEN DISTANCES ARE
  UP-DATED IN ACCORDANCE WITH CHANGES TO ROADS,BRIDGES,TUNNELS
  OR FERRIES, ONLY DISTANCES TO IMMEDIATELY ADJACENT LOCATIONS
  NEED BE MODIFIED. RE-RUNNING THE NETWORK GENERATOR SEGMENT, DIST
  CORRECTS ALL DISTANCES OF WHICH THE MODIFIED LINKS ARE A
  PART, GIVING GREAT FLEXIBILITY. THE INPUT SEGMENT PRODUCES
  A MAP ON THE LINE PRINTER OF ALL LOCATIONS BY SERIAL
  NUMBERS AND INITIAL INTER-LOCATION DISTANCES,I.E.
  DISTANCES TO ALL ADJACENT LOCATIONS. THE TRIPLAN SYSTEM
  PRODUCES ON THE LINE PRINTER A SCALE ROAD MAP OF THE
  DEPOT AREA AND A PLOT OF EACH TRIP AS IT IS PRODUCED.
  COULD BE ADAPTED TO RUN ON IBM 360/25

NCC STAGE 1 SOFTWARE VERIFICATION ABSTRACT A34141

NAME OF SOFTWARE
   VISCOSITY OF A GAS AT HIGH PRESSURE

TYPE OF SOFTWARE
   ENGINEERING APPLICATION.   SCIENTIFIC APPLICATION.

PURPOSE OF SOFTWARE
   GIVEN THE VISCOSITY OF A GAS AT WORKING TEMPERATURE BUT
   NORMAL PRESSURE- THE PROGRAM CALCULATES THE VISCOSITY AT A
   HIGH PRESSURE.IF GAS IS A MIXTURE VISCOSITY OF THE VARIOUS
   COMPONENTS ARE COMBINED GIVING VISCOSITY AT SAME OR HIGHER
   PRESSURE.

CONFIGURATION AND OPERATING SYSTEM
   ICL 1900

   HAS RUN SUCCESSFULLY ON ICL1904/ICL1905(BARIC INSTALLATION)
   AMOUNT OF PRIMARY STORAGE 9K-16K WORDS
   1 PAPER TAPE READER
   1 LINE PRINTER
   1 CARD READER
   CARD/PAPER TAPE ARE ALTERNATIVES
   NO OPERATING SYSTEM USED.

MODE OF USAGE
   BATCH

LANGUAGE
   ANSI FORTRAN

AVAILABILITY
   PROGRAM MAY BE AVAILABLE FOR USE OUTSIDE SUPPLIERS ORGANISATION.

SUPPLIERS COMMENT
   SUPPORTED BY THE MINISTRY OF AVIATION SUPPLY ADVANCED
   COMPUTER TECHNOLOGY PROJECT.A WIDE VARIETY OF UNITS CAN BE
   USED.

NCC STAGE 1 SOFTWARE VERIFICATION ABSTRACT A34142

NAME OF SOFTWARE
  DENSITY AND VISCOSITY OF WATER AND STEAM.

TYPE OF SOFTWARE
  ENGINEERING APPLICATION.   SCIENTIFIC APPLICATION

PURPOSE OF SOFTWARE
  GIVEN PRESSURE AND TEMPERATURE CALCULATES DENSITY
  AND VISCOSITY OF WATER,SATURATED AND SUPER HEATED STEAM.FOR
  WATER,THEY ARE CALCULATED UP TO 1500 ATMOSPHERES.FOR STEAM,
  VISCOSITY UP TO 1500DEG C,DENSITY UP TO 200 ATMOSPHERES.
  UPPER TEMPERATURE FROM 360DEG C TO 540DEG C.

CONFIGURATION AND OPERATING SYSTEM
  ICL 1900

  HAS RUN SUCCESSFULLY ON ICL1904/ICL1905(BARIC INSTALLATION)
  AMOUNT OF PRIMARY STORAGE 17K-32K WORDS
  1 PAPER TAPE READER
  1 LINE PRINTER
  1 CARD READER
  CARD/PAPER TAPE ARE ALTERNATIVES
  NO OPERATING SYSTEM USED.

MODE OF USAGE
  BATCH

LANGUAGE
  ANSI FORTRAN IV

AVAILABILITY
  PROGRAM MAY BE AVAILABLE FOR USE OUTSIDE SUPPLIERS ORGANISATION

SUPPLIERS COMMENT
  SUPPORTED BY THE MINISTRY OF AVIATION SUPPLY ADVANCED
  COMPUTER TECHNOLOGY PROJECT.PROGRAM COULD BE OVERLAID IF
  REQUIRED.A WIDE VARIETY OF UNITS CAN BE USED FOR EACH
  CALCULATION.

NCC STAGE 1 SOFTWARE VERIFICATION ABSTRACT A34143

NAME OF SOFTWARE
  GAS LAW DEVIATION COEFFICIENT FOR AIR

TYPE OF SOFTWARE
  ENGINEERING APPLICATION. SCIENTIFIC APPLICATION.

PURPOSE OF SOFTWARE
  GIVEN THE ABSOLUTE PRESSURE AND THE TEMPERATURE THIS
  PROGRAM CALCULATES THE GAS LAW DEVIATION COEFFICIENT FOR
  AIR. IT COVERS TEMPERATURE FROM -100DEG C TO 200DEG C,
  PRESSURE FROM 0 TO 1000 ATMOSPHERES. A WIDE VARIETY OF
  UNITS CAN BE USED.

CONFIGURATION AND OPERATING SYSTEM
  ICL1900

  HAS RUN SUCCESSFULLY ON ICL1904/ICL1905(BARIC INTALLATION)
  AMOUNT OF PRIMARY STORAGE 9K-16K WORDS
  1 LINE PRINTER
  1 PAPER TAPE READER
  1 CARD READER
  CARD/PAPER TAPE ARE ALTERNATIVES
  NO OPERATING SYSTEM USED

MODE OF USAGE
  BATCH

LANGUAGE
  ANSI FORTRAN

AVAILABILITY
  PROGRAM MAY BE AVAILABLE FOR USE OUTSIDE SUPPLIERS
  ORGANISATION

SUPPLIERS COMMENT
  SUPPORTED BY THE MINISTRY OF AVIATION SUPPLY ADVANCED COMPUTER
  TECHNOLOGY PROJECT.

NCC STAGE 1 SOFTWARE VERIFICATION ABSTRACT A34144

NAME OF SOFTWARE
  SPECIFIC HEAT RATIO OF A MIXTURE OF GASES.

TYPE OF SOFTWARE
  ENGINEERING APPLICATION.   SCIENTIFIC APPLICATION

PURPOSE OF SOFTWARE
  CALCULATES THE SPECIFIC HEAT RATIO OF A MIXTURE OF GASES FROM
  THE INDIVIDUAL SPECIFIC HEAT RATIOS, THE SPECIFIC HEATS AT
  CONSTANT PRESSURE,THE MOLECULAR WEIGHTS AND THE PERCENTAGE
  OF EACH. FOR AIR THE CONSTANTS ARE PROVIDED.

CONFIGURATION AND OPERATING SYSTEM
  ICL1900

  HAS RUN SUCCESSFULLY ON ICL1904/ICL1905 (BARIC INSTALLATION)
  AMOUNT OF PRIMARY STORAGE 4K-8K WORDS
  1 LINE PRINTER
  1 CARD READER
  1 PAPER TAPE READER
  CARD/PAPER TAPE ARE ALTERNATIVES
  NO OPERATING SYSTEM USED.

MODE OF USAGE
  BATCH

LANGUAGE
  ANSI FORTRAN

AVAILABILITY
  PROGRAM MAY BE AVAILABLE FOR USE OUTSIDE SUPPLIERS
  ORGANISATION.

SUPPLIERS COMMENT
  SUPPORTED BY THE MINISTRY OF AVIATION SUPPLY ADVANCED
  COMPUTER TECHNOLOGY PROJECT. A WIDE VARIETY OF UNITS
  MAY BE USED FOR EACH CALCULATION.

  COPYRIGHT NCC 1972   PRINTED ON 19/04/72

NCC STAGE 1 SOFTWARE VERIFICATION ABSTRACT A34145

NAME OF SOFTWARE
   THE DENSITY OF MOIST GASES

TYPE OF SOFTWARE
   ENGINEERING APPLICATION. SCIENTIFIC APPLICATION.

PURPOSE OF SOFTWARE
   THE DENSITY OF A MOIST GAS IS CALCULATED AT A GIVEN TEMPERATURE
   AND PRESSURE. THE SPECIFIC GRAVITY OF THE DRY GAS,THE GAS LAW
   DEVIATION COEFFICIENT,AND THE HUMIDITY OR MOISTURE CONTENT ARE
   REQUIRED AS INPUT.FOR AIR THE PARAMETERS ARE CALCULATED BY THE
    PROGRAM.

CONFIGURATION AND OPERATING SYSTEM
   ICL 1900

   HAS RUN SUCCESSFULLY ON ICL 1904/ICL 1905 (BARIC INSTALLATION)
   AMOUNT OF PRIMARY STORAGE 9K-16K WORDS
   1 LINE PRINTER
   1 CARD READER
   1 PAPER TAPE READER
   CARD/PAPER TAPE ARE ALTERNATIVES
   NO OPERATING SYSTEM USED

MODE OF USAGE
   BATCH

LANGUAGE
   ANSI FORTRAN

AVAILABILITY
   PROGRAM MAY BE AVAILABLE FOR USE OUTSIDE SUPPLIERS
   ORGANISATION

SUPPLIERS COMMENT
   SUPPORTED BY THE MINISTRY OF AVIATION SUPPLY ADVANCED COMPUTER
   TECHNOLOGY PROJECT. A WIDE VARIETY OF UNITS MAY BE USED FOR
   EACH CALCULATION.

NCC STAGE 1 SOFTWARE VERIFICATION ABSTRACT A34146

NAME OF SOFTWARE
   FLUID FLOW B.S.1042

TYPE OF SOFTWARE
   ENGINEERING APPLICATION.   SCIENTIFIC APPLICATION.

PURPOSE OF SOFTWARE
   CALCULATIONS IN B.S.1042 PART 1 - METHODS FOR THE
   MEASUREMENT OF FLUID FLOW IN PIPES - FOR ORIFICE PLATES,
   NOZZLES AND VENTURI TUBES. PITOT TUBES ARE EXCLUDED.FOR AIR
   STEAM AND WATER,THE FLUID PARAMETERS ARE.CALCULATED.

CONFIGURATION AND OPERATING SYSTEM
   ICL1900,UNIVAC 1100

   HAS RUN SUCCESSFULLY ON UNIVAC 1108 (NEL INSTALLATION)
   AMOUNT OF PRIMARY STORAGE 17K-32K WORDS
   1 LINE PRINTER
   1 CARD READER
   CARD/PAPER TAPE ARE ALTERNATIVES
   RUN UNDER OPERATING SYSTEM EXEC 2

   HAS RUN SUCCESSFULLY ON ICL1904/ICL1905 (BARIC INSTALLATION)
   AMOUNT OF PRIMARY STORAGE 9K-16K WORDS
   1 DISC DRIVE,10K-100K WORDS STORAGE
   1 MAGNETIC TAPE DRIVE
   1 LINE PRINTER
   1 CARD READER
   1 PAPER TAPE READER
   DISC/MAG.TAPE,CARD/PAPER TAPE,ARE ALTERNATIVES
   NO OPERATING SYSTEM USED.

MODE OF USAGE
   BATCH

LANGUAGE
   ANSI FORTRAN

AVAILABILITY
   PROGRAM MAY BE AVAILABLE FOR USE OUTSIDE SUPPLIERS
   ORGANISATION.

SUPPLIERS COMMENT
   SUPPORTED BY THE MINISTRY OF AVIATION SUPPLY ADVANCED
   COMPUTER TECHNOLOGY PROJECT.
   A WIDE VARIETY OF UNITS CAN BE USED FOR EACH CALCULATION
   HAS ALSO RUN ON UNIVAC 1108(UCC,EUSTON ROAD INSTALLATION)

NCC STAGE 1 SOFTWARE VERIFICATION ABSTRACT A34147

NAME OF SOFTWARE
   SHELL AND 3-D FRAME PROGRAM CNME 14

TYPE OF SOFTWARE
   ENGINEERING APPLICATION

PURPOSE OF SOFTWARE
   FESS 2 IS A SECTION PROGRAM OF THE FINITE ELEMENT SOLUTION
   SYSTEM FESS IT PERMITS THE SOLUTION OF THIN SHELLS
   INCLUDING EDGE STIFFENING BEAMS IF PRESENT,BEAM AND
   SHELL GRILLAGE STRUCTURES

CONFIGURATION AND OPERATING SYSTEM
   ICL 1900, IBM 360, UNIVAC 1100, CDC 6600

   HAS RUN SUCCESSFULLY ON ICL 1905
   AMOUNT OF PRIMARY STORAGE 17K-32K WORDS,OVERLAYS USED.
   4 MAGNETIC TAPE DRIVES
   1 LINE PRINTER
   1 CARD READER
   RUN UNDER OPERATING SYSTEM GEORGE 3

   HAS RUN SUCCESSFULLY ON IBM360/65
   AMOUNT OF PRIMARY STORAGE 65K-128K BYTES,OVERLAYS USED.
   3 DISC DRIVES,10K-100K BYTES STORAGE
   1 LINE PRINTER
   1 CARD READER
   1 GRAPH PLOTTER
   RUN UNDER OPERATING SYSTEM OS MFT2

   HAS RUN SUCCESSFULLY ON CDC 6600
   AMOUNT OF PRIMARY STORAGE 65K-128K WORDS
   7 DISC DRIVES,>100M CHARACTERS STORAGE
   6 MAGNETIC TAPE DRIVES
   3 LINE PRINTERS
   2 CARD READERS
   1 CARD PUNCH
   1 PAPER TAPE READER
   1 PAPER TAPE PUNCH
   1 GRAPH PLOTTER
   22 VDU'S
   16 REMOTE TERMINALS(VDU)
   6 LOCAL TERMINALS(VDU)
   RUN UNDER OPERATING SYSTEM SCOPE

MODE OF USAGE
   BATCH

LANGUAGE
   FORTRAN IV

AVAILABILITY
   PROGRAM MAY BE AVAILABLE FOR USE OUTSIDE SUPPLIERS

ORGANISATION
PROGRAM AVAILABLE AS A BUREAU SERVICE

SUPPLIERS COMMENT
THIS PROGRAM WAS DEVELOPED ON A CIRIA RESEARCH GRANT AND IS
AVAILABLE TO CIRIA MEMBERS ON SPECIAL TERMS IT IS PART OF A
LARGER GENERAL ANALYSIS SYSTEM

COPYRIGHT NCC 1972   PRINTED ON 19/04/72

NCC STAGE 1 SOFTWARE VERIFICATION ABSTRACT A34148

NAME OF SOFTWARE
    APSE (AUTOMATIC PROGRAMMING & SCALING OF EQUATIONS)

TYPE OF SOFTWARE
    SCIENTIFIC APPLICATION,COMPILER

PURPOSE OF SOFTWARE
    GIVEN A PROBLEM IN THE FORM OF A SET OF DIFFERENTIAL AND OTHER
    EQUATIONS WITH SCALING INFORMATION,PRODUCES SCALED MACHINE
    EQUATIONS FOR AN ANALOG COMPUTER,STATIC CHECK VALUES,AND AN
    ASSIGNMENT OF ANALOG COMPONENTS.

CONFIGURATION AND OPERATING SYSTEM
    ICL KDF9, IBM360, ICL1900, UNIVAC1108, GE615

    HAS RUN SUCCESSFULLY ON ICL 1905F
    AMOUNT OF PRIMARY STORAGE 17K-32K WORDS,OVERLAYS USED.
    1 DISC DRIVE,10K-100K WORDS STORAGE
    1 LINE PRINTER
    1 CARD READER
    RUN UNDER OPERATING SYSTEM GEORGE 3 MARK 5.3

    HAS RUN SUCCESSFULLY ON IBM360/40
    AMOUNT OF PRIMARY STORAGE 129K-256K BYTES,OVERLAYS USED.
    1 DISC DRIVE,101K-1M BYTES STORAGE
    1 LINE PRINTER
    1 CARD READER
    RUN UNDER OPERATING SYSTEM DOS (RELEASE 24)

MODE OF USAGE
    BATCH

LANGUAGE
    ANSI FORTRAN IV

AVAILABILITY
    PROGRAM MAY BE AVAILABLE FOR USE OUTSIDE SUPPLIERS ORGANISATION
    PROGRAM AVAILABLE AS A BUREAU SERVICE

SUPPLIERS COMMENT
    THE PROGRAM CAN BE MODIFIED TO SUIT DIFFERENT GENERAL
    PURPOSE ELECTRONIC ANALOG COMPUTERS,E.G.PACE 231R,EAI680.
    INTRODUCTORY MANUAL AND USERS MANUAL AVAILABLE.

NCC STAGE 1 SOFTWARE VERIFICATION ABSTRACT A34149

NAME OF SOFTWARE
  CROSS-REF

TYPE OF SOFTWARE
  UTILITY

PURPOSE OF SOFTWARE
  CROSS-REFERENCES AND IDENTIFIES INEFFICENCIES IN COBOL SOURCE
  DECKS.THE SYSTEM WILL HANDLE SINGLE DECKS OR WHOLE SUITES

CONFIGURATION AND OPERATING SYSTEM
  IBM360

  HAS RUN SUCCESSFULLY ON IBM 360/40
  AMOUNT OF PRIMARY STORAGE 17K-32K BYTES
  1 DISC DRIVE 1.1M - 10M BYTES STORAGE
  1 LINE PRINTER
  1 CARD READER
  RUN UNDER OPERATING SYSTEM DOS REL 24

MODE OF USAGE
  BATCH

LANGUAGE
  COBOL/ASSEMBLER

AVAILABILITY
  PROGRAM MAY BE AVAILABLE FOR USE OUTSIDE SUPPLIERS
  ORGANISATION.
  PROGRAM AVAILABLE AS A BUREAU SERVICE

SUPPLIERS COMMENT
  THE PRODUCT CURRENTLY OPERATES AT INSTALLATIONS IN FRANCE
  HOLLAND AND THROUGHOUT THE U.S.A. THE PRODUCT IS DOS ONLY,
  REL 19 OR LATER.

  HAS RUN ONLY ON IBM 360/40 SO FAR IN UK

    COPYRIGHT NCC 1972   PRINTED ON 19/04/72

NCC STAGE 1 SOFTWARE VERIFICATION ABSTRACT A34150

NAME OF SOFTWARE
  COBOLDIAGRAMMER

TYPE OF SOFTWARE
  UTILITY

PURPOSE OF SOFTWARE
  FLOWCHARTS AND GIVES OTHER DOCUMENTARY INFORMATION FOR COBOL
  SOURCE DECKS

CONFIGURATION AND OPERATING SYSTEM
  IBM360

  HAS RUN SUCCESSFULLY ON IBM 360/40 IN THIS COUNTRY
  AMOUNT OF PRIMARY STORAGE 17K - 32K BYTES
  1 DISC DRIVE,1.1M - 10M BYTES STORAGE
  1 LINE PRINTER
  RUN UNDER OPERATING SYSTEM DOS REL 24

MODE OF USAGE
  BATCH

LANGUAGE
  ASSEMBLER

AVAILABILITY
  PROGRAM MAY BE AVAILABLE FOR USE OUTSIDE SUPPLIERS
  ORGANISATION
  PROGRAM AVAILABLE AS A BUREAU SERVICE

SUPPLIERS COMMENT
  THE SYSTEM CAN OPERATE UNDER OS AS WELL AS DOS USING
  WORKSPACE ON 2311 OR 2314 DISC DRIVES.IBM 360 MODELS 20
  AND 44 ARE NOT SUPPORTED
  THE SYSTEM CURRENTLY IS IN USE IN FRANCE AND HOLLAND.

  HAS RUN ONLY ON IBM 360/40 SO FAR IN UK

NCC STAGE 1 SOFTWARE VERIFICATION ABSTRACT A34152

NAME OF SOFTWARE
    RESOURCE ALLOCATION PIPING ISOMETRIC DRAWINGS

TYPE OF SOFTWARE
    ENGINEERING APPLICATION

PURPOSE OF SOFTWARE
    RAPID IS A SYSTEM WHICH AUTOMATES THE PRODUCTION OF ISOMETRIC
    DRAWINGS AND THE ORDERING OF MATERIALS REQUIRED FOR A PLANT.

CONFIGURATION AND OPERATING SYSTEM
    ICL1900, UNIVAC1100,CDC3300

    HAS RUN SUCCESSFULLY ON ICL1905F
    AMOUNT OF PRIMARY STORAGE 17K-32K WORDS,OVERLAYS USED
    1 DISC DRIVE, 101K-1M WORDS STORAGE
    2 MAGNETIC TAPES
    1 LINE PRINTER
    1 CARD READER
    1 GRAPH PLOTTER
    RUN UNDER OPERATING SYSTEM GEORGE 2 AND 3

MODE OF USAGE
    BATCH

LANGUAGE
    ANSI FORTRAN X3.9-1966 THROUGHOUT

AVAILABILITY
    PROGRAM MAY BE AVAILABLE FOR USE OUTSIDE SUPPLIERS ORGANISATION
    PROGRAM AVAILABLE AS A BUREAU SERVICE

SUPPLIERS COMMENT
    RAPID PROVIDES FACILITIES FOR PRELIMINARY MATERIAL TAKE OFF THE
    PRODUCTION OF ISOMETRIC DRAWINGS AND ASSOCIATED MATERIAL LISTINGS.
    FINAL MATERIAL TAKE OFF AND AUTOMATIC PRODUCTION OF REQUISITIONS.
    THE DATA BANK CAN CONTAIN PIPING SPECIFICATIONS TO ASA OR DIN
    STANDARDS AND IMPERIAL OR METRIC UNITS CAN BE HANDLED AS
    REQUIRED.

NCC STAGE 1 SOFTWARE VERIFICATION ABSTRACT A34153

NAME OF SOFTWARE
   RANDAX MODULAR ACCOUNTING PLAN PAYROLL

TYPE OF SOFTWARE
   PAYROLL

PURPOSE OF SOFTWARE
   THIS SUITE WILL HANDLE WEEKLY (HOURLY OR FIXED PAY,PREMIUM
   OVERTIME OR ACTUAL OVERTIME),FORTNIGHTLY,FOUR WEEKLY AND MONTHLY
   PAYROLLS. DEALS WITH 11 ITEMS TO GROSS PAY, 14 DEDUCTIONS,
   ROUNDING AND CAN PRODUCE PAYSLIPS,ENVELOPES,TAX FORMS ETC
   ETC.

CONFIGURATION AND OPERATING SYSTEM
   BURROUGHS 500

   HAS RUN SUCCESSFULLY ON B2500,B3500
   AMOUNT OF PRIMARY STORAGE 33K-64K BYTES
   1 DISC DRIVE,10K-100K BYTES STORAGE
   3 MAGNETIC TAPE DRIVES
   1 LINE PRINTER
   1 CARD READER
   1 TELETYPE
   FIXED DISC USED
   RUN UNDER OPERATING SYSTEM BURROUGHS MCP

MODE OF USAGE
   BATCH

LANGUAGE
   COBOL

AVAILABILITY
   PROGRAM MAY BE AVAILABLE FOR USE OUTSIDE SUPPLIERS ORGANISATION.
   PROGRAM AVAILABLE AS A BUREAU SERVICE.

SUPPLIERS COMMENT
   THIS PAYROLL COMES WITH A USER REFERENCE MANUAL, A TRAINING AND
   INSTRUCTION MANUAL AND CASSETTE TAPE FOR PHILIPS TYPE RECORDERS.
   THESE PROVIDE USER WITH ALL HIS NEEDS FOR TRAINING HIS STAFF.
   FOR MORE INFORMATION PLEASE CONTACT SUPPLIER WHO WILL
   FORWARD A DETAILED WRITE UP.

NCC STAGE 1 SOFTWARE VERIFICATION ABSTRACT A34154

NAME OF SOFTWARE
  AUTOMATIC INPUT VALIDATION
  UTILITY
  PROGRAM GENERATOR

PURPOSE OF SOFTWARE
  GENERATES AN INPUT VALIDATION PROGRAM IN COBOL.THE PROCEDURE
  DIVISION IS IN ASSEMBLER OR PLAN

CONFIGURATION AND OPERATING SYSTEM
  IBM 360, ICL SYSTEM 4, ICL 1900

  HAS RUN SUCCESSFULLY ON IBM 360/50, IBM 360/65
  AMOUNT OF PRIMARY STORAGE 33K-64K BYTES
  1 DISC DRIVE,<10K BYTES STORAGE
  1 LINE PRINTER
  1 CARD READER
  RUN UNDER OPERATING SYSTEM OS MFT2

  HAS RUN SUCCESSFULLY ON ICL 1902A
  AMOUNT OF PRIMARY STORAGE 9K-16K WORDS
  1 DISC DRIVE,10K-100K CHARACTERS STORAGE
  4 MAGNETIC TAPE DRIVES
  1 LINE PRINTER
  1 CARD READER
  1 PAPER TAPE READER
  RUN UNDER OPERATING SYSTEM GEORGE 2 OR EXEC

  HAS RUN SUCCESSFULLY ON IBM 360/40
  AMOUNT OF PRIMARY STORAGE 33K-64K BYTES
  1 DISC DRIVE,10K-100K BYTES STORAGE
  1 LINE PRINTER
  1 CARD READER
  1 PAPER TAPE READER
  RUN UNDER OPERATING SYSTEM DOS

  HAS RUN SUCCESSFULLY ON ICL SYSTEM 4/50, ICL SYSTEM 4/70
  AMOUNT OF PRIMARY STORAGE 33K-64K BYTES
  1 DISC DRIVE,10K-100K BYTES STORAGE
  4 MAGNETIC TAPE DRIVES
  1 LINE PRINTER
  1 CARD READER
  1 PAPER TAPE READER
  RUN UNDER J OPERATING SYSTEM

MODE OF USAGE
  BATCH

LANGUAGE
  COBOL AND ASSEMBLER OR PLAN

AVAILABILITY
  PROGRAM MAY BE AVAILABLE FOR USE OUTSIDE SUPPLIERS

ORGANISATION.PROGRAM AVAILABLE AS A BUREAU SERVICE

SUPPLIERS COMMENT
GIVES LARGE COST SAVINGS TO ANY D.P. DEPARTMENT.EASY
TO LEARN. A NON PROGRAMMER CAN WRITE A VALIDATION PROGRAM
IN ONE DAY WITH NOR-VET

COPYRIGHT NCC 1972   PRINTED ON 19/04/72

NCC STAGE 1 SOFTWARE VERIFICATION ABSTRACT A34155

NAME OF SOFTWARE
  SALES ACCOUNTING

TYPE OF SOFTWARE
  ACCOUNTING

PURPOSE OF SOFTWARE
  OPEN-ITEM SALES LEDGER WITH PARAMETER DRIVEN ANALYSIS
  PART OF A TOTALLY INTEGRATED SUITE OF PACKAGES

CONFIGURATION AND OPERATING SYSTEM
  IBM 360, ICL SYSTEM 4, ICL 1900

  HAS RUN SUCCESSFULLY ON IBM360/50, IBM 360/65
  AMOUNT OF PRIMARY STORAGE 65K-128K BYTES
  1 DISC DRIVE,10K-100K BYTES STORAGE
  1 LINE PRINTER
  1 CARD READER
  RUN UNDER OPERATING SYSTEM IBM OS MFT2

  HAS RUN SUCCESSFULLY ON IBM 360/40
  AMOUNT OF PRIMARY STORAGE 33K-64K BYTES OVERLAYS USED
  1 DISC DRIVE,10K-100K BYTES STORAGE
  1 LINE PRINTER
  1 CARD READER
  RUN UNDER OPERATING SYSTEM DOS

  HAS RUN SUCCESSFULLY ON ICL 1902A
  AMOUNT OF PRIMARY STORAGE 9K-16K WORDS OVERLAYS USED
  1 DISC DRIVE,10K-100K CHARACTERS STORAGE
  5 MAGNETIC TAPE DRIVES
  1 LINE PRINTER
  1 CARD READER
  RUN UNDER OPERATING SYSTEM EXECUTIVE

  HAS RUN SUCCESSFULLY ON ICL SYSTEM 4/50,ICL SYSTEM 4/70
  AMOUNT OF PRIMARY STORAGE 65K-128K BYTES
  1 DISC DRIVE,10K-100K BYTES STORAGE
  5 MAGNETIC TAPE DRIVES
  1 LINE PRINTER
  1 CARD READER
  RUN UNDER J OPERATING SYSTEM

MODE OF USAGE
  BATCH

LANGUAGE
  COBOL,LITTLE ASSEMBLER OR PLAN

AVAILABILITY
  PROGRAM MAY BE AVAILABLE FOR USE OUTSIDE SUPPLIERS
  ORGANISATION.PROGRAM AVAILABLE AS A BUREAU SERVICE

SUPPLIERS COMMENT
   PART OF A TOTALLY INTEGRATED SYSTEM OF ACCOUNTING
   PACKAGES IN COBOL MODULES

      COPYRIGHT NCC 1972   PRINTED ON 19/04/72

NCC STAGE 1 SOFTWARE VERIFICATION ABSTRACT A34156

NAME OF SOFTWARE
  PURCHASE ACCOUNTING

TYPE OF SOFTWARE
  ACCOUNTING

PURPOSE OF SOFTWARE
  OPEN ITEM PURCHASE LEDGER,AUTOMATIC PAYMENT OPTIONS,CREDIT
  TRANSFERS,NOMINAL LEDGER,TEN DIFFERENT ANALYSES

CONFIGURATION AND OPERATING SYSTEM
  IBM 360, ICL SYSTEM 4, ICL 1900

  HAS RUN SUCCESSFULLY ON IBM 360/50, IBM 360/65
  AMOUNT OF PRIMARY STORAGE >256K BYTES
  1 DISC DRIVE,10K-100K BYTES STORAGE
  5 MAGNETIC TAPE DRIVES
  1 LINE PRINTER
  1 CARD READER
  1 PAPER TAPE READER
  RUN UNDER OPERATING SYSTEM IBM OS MFT2

  HAS RUN SUCCESSFULLY ON IBM360/40
  AMOUNT OF PRIMARY STORAGE 33K-64K BYTES, OVERLAYS USED
  1 DISC DRIVE,10K-100K BYTES STORAGE
  5 MAGNETIC TAPE DRIVES
  1 LINE PRINTER
  1 CARD READER
  RUN UNDER OPERATING SYSTEM DOS

  HAS RUN SUCCESSFULLY ON ICL 1902A
  AMOUNT OF PRIMARY STORAGE 9K-16K WORDS,OVERLAYS USED
  1 DISC DRIVE,10K-100K CHARACTERS STORAGE
  5 MAGNETIC TAPE DRIVES
  1 LINE PRINTER
  1 CARD READER
  1 PAPER TAPE READER
  RUN UNDER OPERATING SYSTEM EXECUTIVE

  HAS RUN SUCCESSFULLY ON ICL SYSTEM 4/50, ICL SYSTEM 4/70
  AMOUNT OF PRIMARY STORAGE 65K-128K BYTES
  1 DISC DRIVE,10K-100K BYTES STORAGE
  5 MAGNETIC TAPE DRIVES
  1 LINE PRINTER
  1 CARD READER
  1 PAPER TAPE READER
  RUN UNDER J OPERATING SYSTEM

MODE OF USAGE
  BATCH

LANGUAGE
  SUBSET COBOL,LITTLE ASSEMBLER OR PLAN

AVAILABILITY
  PROGRAM MAY BE AVAILABLE FOR USE OUTSIDE
  SUPPLIERS ORGANISATION

SUPPLIERS COMMENT
  PART OF A TOTALLY INTEGRATED SYSTEM OF ACCOUNTING PACKAGES IN COBOL
  MODULES

      COPYRIGHT NCC 1972   PRINTED ON 19/04/72

NCC STAGE 1 SOFTWARE VERIFICATION ABSTRACT A34158

NAME OF SOFTWARE
   SELCOPY SELECT AND COPY UTILITY

TYPE OF SOFTWARE
   UTILITY

PURPOSE OF SOFTWARE
   INFORMATION RETRIEVAL,USING A USER-SUPPLIED PARAMETER LIST
   TO CONTROL SELECTION AND COPYING OF RECORDS AND/OR DATA ITEMS
   BETWEEN DEVICES. USES ARE SYSTEMS TESTING,FILE MAINTENANCE,
   SYSTEM MAINTENANCE,FILE ENQUIRIES ETC.

CONFIGURATION AND OPERATING SYSTEM
   IBM 360

   HAS RUN SUCCESSFULLY ON IBM 360/30, IBM 360/50, IBM 360/40
   AMOUNT OF PRIMARY STORAGE 33K-64K BYTES,OVERLAYS USED
   1 DISC DRIVE,101K-1M BYTES STORAGE
   1 LINE PRINTER
   1 CARD READER
   RUN UNDER OPERATING SYSTEM IBM DOS 360

MODE OF USAGE
   BATCH

LANGUAGE
   IBM 360 DOS BAL

AVAILABILITY
   PROGRAM MAY BE AVAILABLE FOR USE OUTSIDE SUPPLIERS ORGANISATION
   PROGRAM AVAILABLE AS A BUREAU SERVICE

SUPPLIERS COMMENT
   CAN BE REDUCED TO A 32K MACHINE SIZE WITH OVERLAY. WILL BE
   AVAILABLE FOR O.S. HAS MANY SPECIAL FEATURES.IT IS SUBJECT TO
   CONSTANT MAINTENANCE FOR ADDITIONAL FEATURES AND IMPROVEMENTS.

       COPYRIGHT NCC 1972   PRINTED ON 19/04/72

NCC STAGE 1 SOFTWARE VERIFICATION ABSTRACT A34159

NAME OF SOFTWARE
  EASYPAY

TYPE OF SOFTWARE
  PAYROLL

PURPOSE OF SOFTWARE
  TO CALCULATE WEEKLY AND/OR MONTHLY PAYROLLS AND PRINT
  PAYSLIPS,DEPARTMENTAL AND COIN ANALYSES,COSTING AND
  PRODUCTIVITY REPORTS,QUARTERLY NHI SUMMARIES AND YEAR-END TAX
  RETURNS. SYSTEM CAN PROCESS UP TO 98 COMPANIES IN ONE RUN

CONFIGURATION AND OPERATING SYSTEM
  ICL 1900, IBM 360

  HAS RUN SUCCESSFULLY ON ICL 1903
  AMOUNT OF PRIMARY STORAGE 9K-16K WORDS
  3 MAGNETIC TAPE DRIVES
  1 LINE PRINTER
  1 CARD READER
  RUN UNDER OPERATING SYSTEM EXECUTIVE

  HAS RUN SUCCESSFULLY ON IBM 360/30
  AMOUNT OF PRIMARY STORAGE 33K-64K BYTES
  1 DISC DRIVE,<10K BYTES STORAGE
  2 MAGNETIC TAPE DRIVES
  1 LINE PRINTER
  1 CARD READER
  RUN UNDER OPERATING SYSTEM DOS

MODE OF USAGE
  BATCH

LANGUAGE
  COBOL

AVAILABILITY
  PROGRAM MAY BE AVAILABLE FOR USE OUTSIDE SUPPLIERS
  ORGANISATION.PROGRAM AVAILABLE AS A BUREAU SERVICE

NCC STAGE 1 SOFTWARE VERIFICATION ABSTRACT A34160

NAME OF SOFTWARE
  ACS NOMINAL LEDGER WITH BUDGETARY CONTROL

TYPE OF SOFTWARE
  ACCOUNTING

PURPOSE OF SOFTWARE
  USED AS THE CENTRE OF AN ACCOUNTING SYSTEM OR BY ITSELF,IT MAINTAIN
  A NOMINAL LEDGER AND PRODUCES TRIAL BALANCES,A PROFIT AND LOSS
  ACCOUNT AND A BALANCE SHEET,MONITORING PROGRESS AGAINST BUDGET
  ON A PERIOD ONLY AND A YEAR TO DATE BASIS

CONFIGURATION AND OPERATING SYSTEM
  IBM 360

  HAS RUN SUCCESSFULLY ON IBM 360/30
  AMOUNT OF PRIMARY STORAGE 17K-32K BYTES
  2 DISC DRIVES, 11M-100M BYTES STORAGE
  1 LINE PRINTER
  1 CARD READER
  RUN UNDER OPERATING SYSTEM IBM 360 DOS

MODE OF USAGE
  BATCH

LANGUAGE
  IBM 360 DOS ASSEMBLER

AVAILABILITY
  PROGRAM MAY BE AVAILABLE FOR USE OUTSIDE SUPPLIERS
  ORGANISATION.PROGRAM AVAILABLE AS A BUREAU SERVICE

SUPPLIERS COMMENT
  AN OS VERSION IS PLANNED FOR THE NEAR FUTURE

      COPYRIGHT NCC 1972   PRINTED ON 19/04/72

NCC STAGE 1 SOFTWARE VERIFICATION ABSTRACT A34161

NAME OF SOFTWARE
  PROJECT-MASTER

TYPE OF SOFTWARE
  PROJECT CONTROL

PURPOSE OF SOFTWARE
  MONITORS COSTS AND PROGRESS AGAINST BUDGET OF PROJECTS
  EMPLOYING PERSONNEL AND/OR CAPITAL EQUIPMENT. ORIGINALLY
  DESIGNED FOR COMPUTER BUREAU WORK,IT HAS THE FACILITY FOR
  DIRECT USER BILLING/INVOICING BUT MAY BE USED IN WIDER
  APPLICATIONS

CONFIGURATION AND OPERATING SYSTEM
  IBM 360

  HAS RUN SUCCESSFULLY ON IBM 360/30,IBM 360/40
  AMOUNT OF PRIMARY STORAGE 33K-64K BYTES
  3 DISC DRIVES, 11M-100M BYTES STORAGE
  1 LINE PRINTER
  1 CARD READER
  RUN UNDER OPERATING SYSTEM IBM 360 DOS

MODE OF USAGE
  BATCH

LANGUAGE
  IBM 360 DOS ASSEMBLER,RPG

AVAILABILITY
  PROGRAM MAY BE AVAILABLE FOR USE OUTSIDE SUPPLIERS
  ORGANISATION.PROGRAM AVAILABLE AS A BUREAU SERVICE

NCC STAGE 1 SOFTWARE VERIFICATION VERIFICATION ABSTRACT A34162

NAME OF SOFTWARE
   ACS DOS 360 MODULE TEST BED

TYPE OF SOFTWARE
   MODULE TEST BED

PURPOSE OF SOFTWARE
   TO TEST PROGRAM MODULES INDEPENDENTLY BY BUILDING AND PRINTING
   PARAMETER LISTS,HANDLING PROGRAM CHECKS AND PRINTING DETAILS
   OF THEM

CONFIGURATION AND OPERATING SYSTEM
   IBM 360

   HAS RUN SUCCESSFULLY ON IBM360/30
   AMOUNT OF PRIMARY STORAGE 17K-32K BYTES
   1 DISC DRIVE, 10K-100K BYTES STORAGE
   1 LINE PRINTER
   1 CARD READER
   RUN UNDER OPERATING SYSTEM IBM 360 DOS

MODE OF USAGE
   BATCH

LANGUAGE
   IBM 360 BAL

AVAILABILITY
   PROGRAM MAY BE AVAILABLE FOR USE OUTSIDE SUPPLIERS
   ORGANISATION.PROGRAM AVAILABLE AS A BUREAU SERVICE

SUPPLIERS COMMENT
   HAS PRINT ROUTINES TO REPLACE UNAVAILABLE MODULES.HANDLES UP TO
   40 PARAMETERS

       COPYRIGHT NCC 1972   PRINTED ON 19/04/72

NCC STAGE 1 SOFTWARE VERIFICATION ABSTRACT A34163

NAME OF SOFTWARE
   ACS OS 360 MODULE TEST BED

TYPE OF SOFTWARE
   MODULE TEST BED

PURPOSE OF SOFTWARE
   TO TEST PROGRAM MODULES INDEPENDENTLY BY BUILDING AND PRINTING
   PARAMETER LISTS,HANDLING PROGRAM CHECKS AND PRINTING DETAILS
   OF THEM, AND LIMITING MODULE EXECUTION TIME

CONFIGURATION AND OPERATING SYSTEM
   IBM 360

   HAS RUN SUCCESSFULLY ON IBM 360/50,IBM 360/40
   AMOUNT OF PRIMARY STORAGE 65K-128K BYTES
   1 DISC DRIVE, 101K-1M BYTES STORAGE
   1 LINE PRINTER
   1 CARD READER
   RUN UNDER OPERATING SYSTEM IBM 360 OS

MODE OF USAGE
   BATCH

LANGUAGE
   IBM 360 OS ASSEMBLER

AVAILABILITY
   PROGRAM MAY BE AVAILABLE FOR USE OUTSIDE SUPPLIERS
   ORGANISATION.PROGRAM AVAILABLE AS A BUREAU SERVICE

SUPPLIERS COMMENT
   PRODUCES EDIT LIST OF INPUT CARDS. ALLOWS FIELDS TO BE SPECIFIED
   AS-CHARACTER,PACKED DECIMAL,HEXADECIMAL,FULLWORD,HALFWORD,BINARY
   BYTE. CAN RETAIN OUTPUT PARAMETERS USED FOR PREVIOUS EXECUTION

NCC STAGE 1 SOFTWARE VERIFICATION ABSTRACT A34164

NAME OF SOFTWARE
  STANDARD CARD INPUT

TYPE OF SOFTWARE
  UTILITY

PURPOSE OF SOFTWARE
  READS 80 COLUMN CARDS (OR CARD IMAGES FROM MAGNETIC TAPE),
  PERFORMS CERTAIN CHECKS/RECONCILIATIONS,AND OUTPUTS 80 BYTE
  IMAGES TO TAPE. REPORTS ARE OUTPUT TO TYPEWRITER LOG AND/OR
  SYSTEM JOURNAL

CONFIGURATION AND OPERATING SYSTEM
  ICL SYSTEM 4

  HAS RUN SUCCESSFULLY ON ICL SYSTEM 4/50, ICL SYSTEM 4/70
  AMOUNT OF PRIMARY STORAGE 17K-32K BYTES,OVERLAYS USED
  1 MAGNETIC TAPE DRIVE
  1 CARD READER
  1 ADDITIONAL TAPE DRIVE IF INPUT FROM TAPE
  RUN UNDER OPERATING SYSTEM J LEVEL

MODE OF USAGE
  BATCH

LANGUAGE
  USERCODE

AVAILABILITY
  PROGRAM MAY BE AVAILABLE FOR USE OUTSIDE SUPPLIERS
  ORGANISATION.PROGRAM AVAILABLE AS A BUREAU SERVICE

NCC STAGE 1 SOFTWARE VERIFICATION ABSTRACT A34165

NAME OF SOFTWARE
   TAPE EDIT PATTERN SEARCH

TYPE OF SOFTWARE
   UTILITY

PURPOSE OF SOFTWARE
   DESIGNED FOR USE IN PRINTING OUT PARTICULAR SECTIONS OF A
   FILE ACCORDING TO CONTROL INFORMATION, WHERE THE AMOUNT OF DATA
   IS VERY LARGE AND OTHER FILE EDIT FACILITIES DO NOT PROVIDE AN
   EASY WAY OF OBTAINING THE NECESSARY PRINTOUT

CONFIGURATION AND OPERATING SYSTEM
   ICL SYSTEM 4

   HAS RUN SUCCESSFULLY ON ICL SYSTEM 4/50, ICL SYSTEM 4/70
   AMOUNT OF PRIMARY STORAGE 9K-16K BYTES
   1 MAGNETIC TAPE DRIVE
   1 LINE PRINTER
   RUN UNDER OPERATING SYSTEM J LEVEL

MODE OF USAGE
   BATCH

LANGUAGE
   USERCODE

AVAILABILITY
   PROGRAM MAY BE AVAILABLE FOR USE OUTSIDE SUPPLIERS
   ORGANISATION.PROGRAM AVAILABLE AS A BUREAU SERVICE

      COPYRIGHT NCC 1972   PRINTED ON 19/04/72

NCC STAGE 1 SOFTWARE VERIFICATION ABSTRACT A34166

NAME OF SOFTWARE
   STANDARD PRINT PROGRAM

TYPE OF SOFTWARE
   UTILITY

PURPOSE OF SOFTWARE
   TO ENABLE A 7 OR 9 TRACK MAGNETIC TAPE, PREPARED IN A SUITABLE
   FORMAT, TO BE PRINTED USING A 132 OR 160 COLUMN LINE PRINTER

CONFIGURATION AND OPERATING SYSTEM
   ICL SYSTEM 4

   HAS RUN SUCCESSFULLY ON ICL SYSTEM 4/50.ICL SYSTEM 4/70
   AMOUNT OF PRIMARY STORAGE 17K-32K BYTES
   1 MAGNETIC TAPE DRIVE
   1 LINE PRINTER
   RUN UNDER OPERATING SYSTEM J LEVEL

MODE OF USAGE
   BATCH

LANGUAGE
   USERCODE

AVAILABILITY
   PROGRAM MAY BE AVAILABLE FOR USE OUTSIDE SUPPLIERS
   ORGANISATION.PROGRAM AVAILABLE AS A BUREAU SERVICE

SUPPLIERS COMMENT
   RESTART AND COMPREHENSIVE SELECTIVE PRINTING FACILITIES ARE
   PROVIDED TOGETHER WITH A NUMBER OF OPTIONAL PROGRAMMER AND
   OPERATOR AIDS

      COPYRIGHT NCC 1972   PRINTED ON 19/04/72

NCC STAGE 1 SOFTWARE VERIFICATION ABSTRACT A34167

NAME OF SOFTWARE
  QUB GRAPH PLOTTING SYSTEM

TYPE OF SOFTWARE
  GRAPH PLOTTING

PURPOSE OF SOFTWARE
  IT PROVIDES A SIMPLE USER INTERFACE WITH ICL GRAPH PLOTTING
  SOFTWARE BY STANDARDISING MANY OF THE MECHANICAL OPERATIONS
  (SUCH AS SCALING ETC) WHICH HAVE TO BE UNDERGONE WHEN
  PLOTTING GRAPHS

CONFIGURATION AND OPERATING SYSTEM
  ICL 1900

  HAS RUN SUCCESSFULLY ON ICL 1905, ICL 1907
  AMOUNT OF PRIMARY STORAGE 9K-16K WORDS
  1 DISC DRIVE, 10K-100K WORDS STORAGE
  1 MAGNETIC TAPE DRIVE
  1 GRAPH PLOTTER
  RUN UNDER QUEEN'S UNIVERSITY BATCH OPERATING SYSTEM-QUBE

MODE OF USAGE
  BATCH

LANGUAGE
  FORTRAN IV

AVAILABILITY
  PROGRAM MAY BE AVAILABLE FOR USE OUTSIDE SUPPLIERS
  ORGANISATION.PROGRAM AVAILABLE AS A BUREAU SERVICE

SUPPLIERS COMMENT
  FUNCTIONAL MODULES FOR PRODUCTION OF SPECIFIC TYPES OF
  GRAPHICAL REPRESENTATION MAY BE EASILY ADDED TO THE SYSTEM.A
  FULL USER MANUAL IS AVAILABLE. THE PACKAGE PREPARES MAGNETIC
  TAPE OUTPUT FOR PSEUDO OFF-LINE OPERATION TO CALCOMP 545
  PLOTTER. OTHER PLOTTER MODEL AND TAPE SYSTEM MODELS MAY BE USED
  WITH ONLY MINOR PROGRAM MODIFICATIONS.

NCC STAGE 1 SOFTWARE VERIFICATION ABSTRACT A34168

NAME OF SOFTWARE
   BATCH DISTILLATION AT CONSTANT REFLUX RATIO - QUANTITY
   DISTILLED AND BULK DISTILLATE COMPOSITION

TYPE OF SOFTWARE
   SCIENTIFIC APPLICATION

PURPOSE OF SOFTWARE
   TO CALCULATE THE COURSE OF A BINARY, BATCHWISE DISTILLATION
   WHERE THE REFLUX RATIO IS HELD CONSTANT AND OVERHEAD
   COMPOSITION CHANGES PROGRESSIVELY AS THE PROPORTION OF
   MORE VOLATILE COMPONENT IN THE SYSTEM FALLS

CONFIGURATION AND OPERATING SYSTEM
   ICL 803B, ICL 503

   HAS RUN SUCCESSFULLY ON ICL 803B
   AMOUNT OF PRIMARY STORAGE 4K-8K WORDS
   1 PAPER TAPE READER
   1 PAPER TAPE PUNCH
   NO OPERATING SYSTEM USED

   HAS RUN SUCCESSFULLY ON ICL 503
   AMOUNT OF PRIMARY STORAGE 4K-8K WORDS
   1 PAPER TAPE READER
   1 PAPER TAPE PUNCH
   NO OPERATING SYSTEM USED

MODE OF USAGE
   BATCH

LANGUAGE
   ELLIOTT AUTOCODE MARK 3

AVAILABILITY
   PROGRAM MAY BE AVAILABLE FOR USE OUTSIDE SUPPLIERS
   ORGANISATION.PROGRAM AVAILABLE AS A BUREAU SERVICE

NCC STAGE 1 SOFTWARE VERIFICATION ABSTRACT A34169

NAME OF SOFTWARE
  ASCOP - A STATISTICAL COMPUTING PROCEDURE

TYPE OF SOFTWARE
  STATISTICAL APPLICATION (SCIENTIFIC)

PURPOSE OF SOFTWARE
  A COMPUTING SYSTEM FOR DATA MANAGEMENT AND STATISTICAL
  ANALYSIS.

CONFIGURATION AND OPERATING SYSTEM
  ATLAS, IBM 360, ICL 1900

  HAS RUN SUCCESSFULLY ON ATLAS 1
  AMOUNT OF PRIMARY STORAGE 33K-64K WORDS, OVERLAYS USED
  1 DISC DRIVE,11M-100M WORDS STORAGE
  16 MAGNETIC TAPE DRIVES
  2 PAPER TAPE READERS
  4 DRUMS
  2 LINE PRINTERS
  2 PAPER TAPE PUNCHES
  10 TELETYPES
  2 CARD READERS
  2 VDU'S
  2 CARD PUNCHES
  1 GRAPH PLOTTER
  RUN UNDER OPERATING SYSTEM HARTRAN

  HAS RUN SUCCESSFULLY ON IBM 360/75
  AMOUNT OF PRIMARY STORAGE >256K BYTES,OVERLAYS USED
  2 DISC DRIVES,>100M BYTES STORAGE
  8 MAGNETIC TAPE DRIVES
  1 DRUM
  2 LINE PRINTERS
  3 TELETYPES
  2 CARD READERS
  1 CARD PUNCH
  1 GRAPH PLOTTER
  RUN UNDER OPERATING SYSTEM OS MFT2 RELEASE 17/18.

MODE OF USAGE
  BATCH

LANGUAGE
  FORTRAN IV, ASSEMBLER CODE

AVAILABILITY
  PROGRAM MAY BE AVAILABLE FOR USE OUTSIDE SUPPLIERS ORGANISATION
  PROGRAM AVAILABLE AS A BUREAU SERVICE

NCC STAGE 1 SOFTWARE VERIFICATION ABSTRACT A34170

NAME OF SOFTWARE
  THESAURUS MANAGEMENT SYSTEM

TYPE OF SOFTWARE
  INFORMATION RETRIEVAL, FILE HANDLING

PURPOSE OF SOFTWARE
  PRODUCES THESAURUS IN ENGINEERS JOINT COUNCIL FORMAT.
  GIVEN ANY ONE RELATIONSHIP OF THE THREE RECIPROCAL
  RELATIONSHIPS (USE/USE FOR;BROADER TERM/NARROWER TERM;
  RELATED TERM/RELATED TERM). ELIMINATES MANUAL CROSS POSTING
  AND OUTPUTS ALPHABETIC & HIERARCHICAL LISTINGS.

CONFIGURATION AND OPERATING SYSTEM
  ICL 1900

  HAS RUN SUCCESSFULLY ON ICL 1905F.
  AMOUNT OF PRIMARY STORAGE 33K-64K WORDS
  3 DISC DRIVES, 11M-100M WORDS STORAGE
  6 MAGNETIC TAPE DRIVES
  1 LINE PRINTER
  1 CARD READER
  1 CARD PUNCH
  1 PAPER TAPE READER
  1 PAPER TAPE PUNCH
  8 TELETYPES
  RUN UNDER OPERATING SYSTEM GEORGE 3 MARK 6.2

MODE OF USAGE
  BATCH

LANGUAGE
  FORTRAN

AVAILABILITY
  PROGRAM MAY BE AVAILABLE FOR USE OUTSIDE SUPPLIERS
  ORGANISATION.PROGRAM AVAILABLE AS A BUREAU SERVICE

    COPYRIGHT NCC 1972   PRINTED ON 19/04/72

NCC STAGE 1 SOFTWARE VERIFICATION ABSTRACT A34171

NAME OF SOFTWARE
  NETWORK ANALYSIS OF PROJECTS

TYPE OF SOFTWARE
  PERT,CRITICAL PATH

PURPOSE OF SOFTWARE
  CAPSTAN IS A SIMPLE TO USE NETWORK ANALYSIS PROGRAM WITH
  FACILITIES FOR RESOURCE SCHEDULING.
  THE PROGRAM PRODUCES VARIOUS TYPES OF OUTPUT FOR USE
  BY MANAGEMENT IN PROJECT CONTROL

CONFIGURATION AND OPERATING SYSTEM
  IBM 360, ICL 1900

  HAS RUN SUCCESSFULLY ON IBM 360/50,IBM 360/65,IBM 360/75
  AMOUNT OF PRIMARY STORAGE 129K - 256K BYTES,OVERLAYS USED
  1 DISC DRIVE,101K-1M BYTES STORAGE
  1 LINE PRINTER
  1 CARD READER
  1 TELETYPE
  RUN UNDER OPERATING SYSTEM MVT RELEASE 19

  HAS RUN SUCCESSFULLY ON ICL 1905F
  AMOUNT OF PRIMARY STORAGE 33K-64K WORDS,OVERLAYS USED
  1 DISC DRIVE, 10K-100K WORDS STORAGE
  1 LINE PRINTER
  1 CARD READER
  1 TELETYPE
  RUN UNDER OPERATING SYSTEM GEORGE 3

MODE OF USAGE
  BATCH

LANGUAGE
  FORTRAN IV

AVAILABILITY
  PROGRAM MAY BE AVAILABLE FOR USE OUTSIDE SUPPLIERS
  ORGANISATION.
  PROGRAM AVAILABLE AS A BUREAU SERVICE

SUPPLIERS COMMENT
  WILL RUN UNDER MOST SYSTEMS WITH FORTRAN COMPILER

      COPYRIGHT NCC 1972   PRINTED ON 19/04/72

NCC STAGE 1 SOFTWARE VERIFICATION ABSTRACT A34172

NAME OF SOFTWARE
  PROJECT ENGINEER SCHEDULING TECHNIQUE

TYPE OF SOFTWARE
  PERT,CPA

CONFIGURATION AND OPERATING SYSTEM
  IBM 360

  HAS RUN SUCCESSFULLY ON IBM 360/65,IBM 360/75
  AMOUNT OF PRIMARY STORAGE 65K-128K BYTES
  4 DISC DRIVES,101K-1M BYTES STORAGE
  1 LINE PRINTER
  1 CARD READER
  1 CARD PUNCH
  4 DISC FILES USED
  RUN UNDER OPERATING SYSTEM MFT 11 R17.

MODE OF USAGE
  BATCH

LANGUAGE
  FORTRAN IV

AVAILABILITY
  PROGRAM MAY BE AVAILABLE FOR USE OUTSIDE SUPPLIERS
  ORGANISATION.
  PROGRAM AVAILABLE AS A BUREAU SERVICE.

NCC STAGE 1 SOFTWARE VERIFICATION ABSTRACT A34173

NAME OF SOFTWARE
   CASHFLO,   A DIGITAL COMPUTER PROGRAM FOR ASSESSING
   THE PROFITABILITY OF FINANCIAL INVESTMENT.

TYPE OF SOFTWARE.
   ACCOUNTING

PURPOSE OF SOFTWARE
   FOR A GIVEN SEQUENCE OF CAPITAL OUTLAYS AND GROSS PROFITS
   AND FOR GIVEN TAX CONDITIONS AND PROPORTIONS OF DEBT AND EQUITY,
   CAPITAL RESULTS ARE OBTAINED FOR (1) NET PRESENT VALUE FOR
   A GIVEN DISCOUNT RATE (2) INTERNAL RATE OF RETURN FOR A GIVEN
   COST OF EQUITY CAPITAL AND (3) LEVEL OF GROSS PROFIT TO
   ACHIEVE RATE OF RETURN.

CONFIGURATION AND OPERATING SYSTEM
   ICL SYSTEM 4, IBM 360

   HAS RUN SUCCESSFULLY ON ICL SYSTEM 4/70
   AMOUNT OF PRIMARY STORAGE 33K-64K BYTES
   1 LINE PRINTER
   1 CARD READER
   RUN UNDER OPERATING SYSTEM J 1400

   HAS RUN SUCCESSFULLY ON IBM 360/50
   AMOUNT OF PRIMARY STORAGE 33K-64K BYTES
   1 LINE PRINTER
   1 CARD READER
   RUN UNDER OPERATING SYSTEM DOS

MODE OF USAGE
   BATCH

LANGUAGE
   FORTRAN IV

AVAILABILITY
   PROGRAM MAY BE AVAILABLE FOR USE OUTSIDE SUPPLIERS
   ORGANISATION.
   PROGRAM AVAILABLE AS A BUREAU SERVICE

      COPYRIGHT NCC 1972   PRINTED ON 19/04/72

NCC STAGE 1 SOFTWARE VERIFICATION ABSTRACT A34174

NAME OF SOFTWARE
   BUSINESS SIMULATION EXERCISE - DYNAMIC RESTAURANT MODEL SERIES 3

TYPE OF SOFTWARE
   BUSINESS GAMES

PURPOSE OF SOFTWARE
   A MORE ADVANCED MODEL THAN SERIES 2 (NCC ABSTRACT A34071).AS
   FOR SERIES 2 WITH ADDED REFINEMENTS WHICH COVER MARKET
   CAPACITY AND CONTROL,CALCULATION OF MARKET SHARE, DIVIDENDS,
   BUSINESS RE-SALE, INDIRECT PRODUCTION COSTS, STORAGE,
   WASTE ETC.

CONFIGURATION AND OPERATING SYSTEM
   ICL 1900

   HAS RUN SUCCESSFULLY ON ICL 1903A
   AMOUNT OF PRIMARY STORAGE 9K-16K WORDS
   2 MAGNETIC TAPE DRIVES
   1 LINE PRINTER
   1 CARD READER
   RUN UNDER OPERATING SYSTEM GEORGE 2 MK.8C AND GEORGE 3

MODE OF USAGE
   BATCH

LANGUAGE
   FORTRAN IV

AVAILABILITY
   PROGRAM AVAILABLE AS A BUREAU SERVICE

SUPPLIERS COMMENT
   THIS MODEL IS ONE OF A NUMBER GIVING A NATURAL PROGRESSION FROM
   SIMPLE TO MORE COMPLEX SITUATIONS.
   SUITABLE FOR THE MORE ADVANCED STUDENT.
   MODIFIED VERSION USED FOR THE FINAL SECTION OF THE NATIONAL
   CATERING BUSINESS GAME 1972.

      COPYRIGHT NCC 1972   PRINTED ON 19/04/72

NCC STAGE 1 SOFTWARE VERIFICATION ABSTRACT A34175

NAME OF SOFTWARE
   SMITHS INDUSTRIES PAPER TAPE LISTING PROGRAM

TYPE OF SOFTWARE
   UTILITY

PURPOSE OF SOFTWARE
   READS ICL 8 TRACK PAPER TAPE AND LISTS IT ON A LINE PRINTER.
   THE PROGRAM HIGHLIGHTS ANY PARITY ERRORS AND RECOVERS FROM
   THEM AUTOMATICALLY. RECORDS OF ANY LENGTH MAY BE PRINTED,
   EACH PRINT LINE CONSISTING OF 100 CHARACTERS.

CONFIGURATION AND OPERATING SYSTEM
   ICL 1900

   HAS RUN SUCCESSFULLY ON ICL 1904E
   AMOUNT OF PRIMARY STORAGE <4K WORDS
   1 MAGNETIC TAPE DRIVE
   1 LINE PRINTER
   1 PAPER TAPE READER
   RUN UNDER OPERATING SYSTEMS MANUAL EXECUTIVE AND GEORGE 2 MK 9B

MODE OF USAGE
   BATCH

LANGUAGE
   PLAN 3

AVAILABILITY
   PROGRAM MAY BE AVAILABLE FOR USE OUTSIDE SUPPLIERS
   ORGANISATION.PROGRAM AVAILABLE AS A BUREAU SERVICE

SUPPLIERS COMMENT
   THE FIRST PAGE OF ALL LISTING CONTAINS AN EXPLANATION
   OF HOW THE VARIOUS SHIFT CHARACTERS ARE PRINTED
   PAGES CONTAINING DATA HAVE A "CURSOR" LINE OF THE NUMBERS
   0 TO 99 PRINTED AT THE TOP AND BOTTOM

      COPYRIGHT NCC 1972   PRINTED ON 19/04/72

NCC STAGE 1 SOFTWARE VERIFICATION ABSTRACT A34177

NAME OF SOFTWARE
  STANDARD COST BUILD UP AND INDENTED COST PRESENTATION

TYPE OF SOFTWARE
  ACCOUNTING

PURPOSE OF SOFTWARE
  BUILDS UP THE CONSTITUENT COSTS INCURRED AND VALUE OF
  RESOURCES UTILISED AT ALL LEVELS OF MANUFACTURE.PRINTS
  A COMPREHENSIVE COST CARD AND PRODUCES A PICTORIAL
  REPRESENTATION OF A PRODUCTS STRUCTURE SHOWING THE MAJOR
  COST ELEMENTS BY LEVEL

CONFIGURATION AND OPERATING SYSTEM
  ICL 1900

  HAS RUN SUCCESSFULLY ON ICL 1904E
  AMOUNT OF PRIMARY STORAGE 17K-32K WORDS
  2 DISC DRIVES,<10K WORDS STORAGE
  6 MAGNETIC TAPE DRIVES
  1 LINE PRINTER
  1 CARD READER
  RUN UNDER OPERATING SYSTEM GEORGE 2 MK 9B

MODE OF USAGE
  BATCH

LANGUAGE
  COBOL,PLAN(SUBROUTINES)

AVAILABILITY
  PROGRAM MAY BE AVAILABLE FOR USE OUTSIDE SUPPLIERS
  ORGANISATION.PROGRAM AVAILABLE AS A BUREAU SERVICE

SUPPLIERS COMMENT
  THE PRODUCTION OF COST CARDS IS SELECTIVE ON CODE OR CLASS.
  NEW RATES CAN BE APPLIED TO SIMULATE CHANGES-VARIANCE REPORT
  PRODUCED
  PICTORIAL REPRESENTATION OF COSTS IS SELECTIVE ON CODE AND
  CLASS

        COPYRIGHT NCC 1972   PRINTED ON 19/04/72

NCC STAGE 1 SOFTWARE VERIFICATION ABSTRACT A34178

NAME OF SOFTWARE
  DATA MANAGEMENT FOR FILE INDEPENDENT PROGRAMS

TYPE OF SOFTWARE
  LOGICAL RECORD HANDLING,FILE HANDLING

PURPOSE OF SOFTWARE
  SUPPORT AND HANDLING OF HIERARCHICAL SEGMENTED
  LOGICAL RECORDS OF ANY LENGTH. PROVIDES AN INTERFACE
  TO ANY PHYSICAL FILE MANAGEMENT. ALLOWS DYNAMIC RECORD
  AND FILE CHANGES WITH MINIMUM PROGRAM MODIFICATION

CONFIGURATION AND OPERATING SYSTEM
  IBM 360

  HAS RUN SUCCESSFULLY ON IBM 360/40, IBM 360/50
  AMOUNT OF PRIMARY STORAGE 129K-256K BYTES ,OVERLAYS USED
  8 DISC DRIVES ,11M-100M BYTES STORAGE
  MAGNETIC TAPE OR DISC FILES
  RUN UNDER OPERATING SYSTEM DOS2 AND MFT2

MODE OF USAGE
  BATCH

LANGUAGE
  BASIC ASSEMBLER LANGUAGE BAL

AVAILABILITY
  PROGRAM MAY BE AVAILABLE FOR USE OUTSIDE SUPPLIERS
  ORGANISATION

SUPPLIERS COMMENT
  DATAFLIP IS OF HELP AT COMPUTER SYSTEMS DESIGN STAGE
  IN THAT IT SEPARATES AND RESOLVES THE TWO OPPOSING
  PROBLEMS OF FILE DESIGN; LOGICAL RECORD FORMAT AND
  PHYSICAL FILE CHARACTERISTICS AND MAINTAINS THESE TWO AS
  SEPARATE INDIVIDUALLY CHANGEABLE SYSTEMS
  DEVICE INDEPENDENT PROGRAM SUPPLIED IN SOURCE
  FORM
  SOFTWARE TAILORED TO SUIT NEEDS FROM 5K TO 15K CORE

NCC STAGE 1 SOFTWARE VERIFICATION ABSTRACT A34182

NAME OF SOFTWARE
   ATKINS STRUCTURAL ANALYSIS SYSTEM

TYPE OF SOFTWARE
   ENGINEERING APPLICATION

PURPOSE OF SOFTWARE
   ASAS IS A GENERAL SYSTEM FOR THE STRESS ANALYSIS OF
   ENGINEERING STRUCTURES/COMPONENTS USING THE MATRIX DISPLACEMENT
   FINITE ELEMENT METHOD.PRESSURE,TEMPERATURE AND NODAL
   LOADS ARE PERMITTED

CONFIGURATION AND OPERATING SYSTEM
   UNIVAC 1108, IBM 360, XDS SIGMA

   HAS RUN SUCCESSFULLY ON UNIVAC 1108
   AMOUNT OF PRIMARY STORAGE 33K-64K WORDS, OVERLAYS USED
   1 LINE PRINTER
   1 CARD READER
   1 DRUM
   RUN UNDER OPERATING SYSTEM EXEC.8 VER.25.87.37NLB2

   HAS RUN SUCCESSFULLY ON SIGMA 5 AND 7
   AMOUNT OF PRIMARY STORAGE 33K-64K WORDS, OVERLAYS USED
   1 DISC DRIVE,1.1M-10M WORDS STORAGE
   1 LINE PRINTER
   1 CARD READER
   RUN UNDER OPERATING SYSTEM BPM/BTM

MODE OF USAGE
   BATCH

LANGUAGE
   FORTRAN IV

AVAILABILITY
   PROGRAM AVAILABLE AS A BUREAU SERVICE
   PROGRAM MAY BE AVAILABLE FOR USE OUTSIDE SUPPLIERS
   ORGANISATION

SUPPLIERS COMMENT
   ASAS IS A LARGE SCALE SYSTEM INVOLVING ABOUT 15 MAN-YEARS
   OF EFFORT TO DATE. WITH MAJOR SUPPORT FROM THE ENGINEERING
   INDUSTRY,EXTENSIVE DEVELOPMENT AND APPLICATION WORK
   IS CONTINUING. THE ASAS TEAM OF ABOUT 12 FULL-TIME STAFF
   PROVIDES A FULL CONSULTANCY AND INFORMATION SERVICE

NCC STAGE 1 SOFTWARE VERIFICATION ABSTRACT A34183

NAME OF SOFTWARE
  SYMAP (SYNAGRAPHIC MAPPING SYSTEM) CONFORMANT MAPPING

TYPE OF SOFTWARE
  LINEPRINTER MAPPING SYSTEM

PURPOSE OF SOFTWARE
  TO GENERATE MAP DISPLAYS USING A STANDARD LINE PRINTER
  SHOWING THE VALUES OF SPATIALLY DISTRIBUTED DATA
  ACCORDING TO THEIR ACTUAL GEOGRAPHIC LOCATION ON A
  BASE MAP

CONFIGURATION AND OPERATING SYSTEM
  IBM 360,ICL 1900,ICL SYSTEM 4

  HAS RUN SUCCESSFULLY ON IBM 360/40
  AMOUNT OF PRIMARY STORAGE 33K-64K BYTES, OVERLAYS USED
  3 MAGNETIC TAPE DRIVES
  1 LINE PRINTER
  1 CARD READER
  RUN UNDER OPERATING SYSTEM DOS

  HAS RUN SUCCESSFULLY ON ICL 1905F
  AMOUNT OF PRIMARY STORAGE 17K-32K WORDS, OVERLAYS USED
  3 MAGNETIC TAPE DRIVES
  1 LINE PRINTER
  1 CARD READER
  RUN UNDER OPERATING SYSTEM GEORGE III

  HAS RUN SUCCESSFULLY ON ICL SYSTEM 4/50
  AMOUNT OF PRIMARY STORAGE 65K-128K BYTES, OVERLAYS USED
  3 MAGNETIC TAPE DRIVES
  1 LINE PRINTER
  1 CARD READER
  RUN UNDER OPERATING SYSTEM J 1300

MODE OF USAGE
  BATCH

LANGUAGE
  FORTRAN

AVAILABILITY
  PROGRAM MAY BE AVAILABLE FOR USE OUTSIDE SUPPLIERS
  ORGANISATION.PROGRAM AVAILABLE AS A BUREAU SERVICE

SUPPLIERS COMMENT
  USES STANDARD LINE PRINTER CHARACTERS AND OVERPRINTING
  TO OBTAIN A WHITE TO BLACK TONE RANGE WHICH
  CAN CORRESPOND TO A SMALL TO LARGE DATA VALUE RANGE.
  CONFORMANT MAPPING IMPLIES THAT EACH DATA VALUE
  REFERS TO SOME PREDEFINED SPATIAL UNIT(AREA,LINE,OR POINT).
  A MAP IS PRODUCED BY FILLING EACH UNIT WITH A SYMBOL

DEPENDENT UPON THE VALUE RELATING TO THAT UNIT

NCC STAGE 1 SOFTWARE VERIFICATION ABSTRACT A34185

NAME OF SOFTWARE
  EMPLOYMENT SURVEY

TYPE OF SOFTWARE
  STATISTICAL APPLICATION (COMMERCIAL)

PURPOSE OF SOFTWARE
  TO PRODUCE ANALYSES OF EMPLOYMENT DATA; INFORMATION HELD
  WITHIN ENUMERATION DISTRICT, GRID REFERENCE, MINIMUM
  LIST HEADING,STANDARD INDUSTRIAL CLASSIFICATION.

CONFIGURATION AND OPERATING SYSTEM
  ICL 1900

  HAS RUN SUCCESSFULLY ON ICL 1902A
  AMOUNT OF PRIMARY STORAGE 17K-32K WORDS
  2 DISC DRIVES,11M-100M CHARACTERS STORAGE
  4 MAGNETIC TAPE DRIVES
  1 LINE PRINTER
  1 PAPER TAPE READER
  RUN UNDER OPERATING SYSTEM GEORGE 2

MODE OF USAGE
  BATCH

LANGUAGE
  COBOL/FIND-2

AVAILABILITY
  PROGRAM MAY BE AVAILABLE FOR USE OUTSIDE SUPPLIERS
  ORGANISATION

     COPYRIGHT NCC 1972   PRINTED ON 19/04/72

NCC STAGE 1 SOFTWARE VERIFICATION ABSTRACT A34186

NAME OF SOFTWARE
    POPULATION PROJECTION

TYPE OF SOFTWARE
    STATISTICAL APPLICATION (SCIENTIFIC)

PURPOSE OF SOFTWARE
    TO PROJECT THE POPULATION OF ANY AREA BY 5 YEAR STAGES
    TO A MAXIMUM OF 30 YEARS

CONFIGURATION AND OPERATING SYSTEM
    ICL 1900

    HAS RUN SUCCESSFULLY ON ICL 1902A
    AMOUNT OF PRIMARY STORAGE 17K-32K WORDS
    2 DISC DRIVES,11M-100M CHARACTERS STORAGE
    4 MAGNETIC TAPE DRIVES
    1   LINE PRINTER
    1 PAPER TAPE READER
    RUN UNDER OPERATING SYSTEM GEORGE 2

MODE OF USAGE
    BATCH

LANGUAGE
    FORTRAN IV

AVAILABILITY
    PROGRAM MAY BE AVAILABLE FOR USE OUTSIDE SUPPLIERS
    ORGANISATION

SUPPLIERS COMMENT
    PRESENT TECHNIQUE BASED ON COHORT SURVIVAL METHOD- WITH
    OR WITHOUT MIGRATION. DOES NOT UTILIZE MARRIAGE RATES.
    SYSTEM BEING CURRENTLY RE-APPRAISED.

        COPYRIGHT NCC 1972   PRINTED ON 19/04/72

NCC STAGE 1 SOFTWARE VERIFICATION ABSTRACT A34188

NAME OF SOFTWARE
  BUSINESS SIMULATION EXERCISE-DYNAMIC HOTEL MODEL SERIES 1

TYPE OF SOFTWARE
  BUSINESS GAMES

PURPOSE OF SOFTWARE
  THE EFFECT OF ONE TEAMS DECISION IS MODIFIED BY THE OTHER
  COMPETITORS IN EACH MARKET.THERE ARE EFFECTIVELY INTERRELATED
  MARKETS FOR ROOMS,MEALS, AND BAR ACTIVITIES WHICH FURTHER
  MODIFY TEAMS INDIVIDUAL MARKET POSITION.
  TEAM INPUT-SELLING PRICES,SERVICE,ADVERTISING,LOANS,
  PRODUCTION ESTIMATES,DECOR,MARKET RESEARCH ETC.
  CONTROLLER INPUT-COSTS,OVERALL MARKETS CHARACTERISTICS,
  LABOUR MOBILITY,CREDIT,MARKETS SENSITIVITY TO PRICE,SERVICE,
  ADVERTISING,IMAGE,DECOR
  ONE OF A SERIES OF GRADED EXERCISES

CONFIGURATION AND OPERATING SYSTEM
  ICL 1900

  HAS RUN SUCCESSFULLY ON ICL 1903A
  AMOUNT OF PRIMARY STORAGE 9K-16K WORDS
  2 MAGNETIC TAPE DRIVES
  1 LINE PRINTER
  1 CARD READER
  RUN UNDER OPERATING SYSTEM GEORGE 2 MK 9B

MODE OF USAGE
  BATCH

LANGUAGE
  FORTRAN IV

AVAILABILITY
  PROGRAM AVAILABLE AS A BUREAU SERVICE

      COPYRIGHT NCC 1972   PRINTED ON 19/04/72

NCC STAGE 1 SOFTWARE VERIFICATION ABSTRACT A34190

NAME OF SOFTWARE
   THE ZEUS HERMES REAL TIME EXECUTIVE FOR THE CTL MODULAR ONE
   PROCESSING RANGE

TYPE OF SOFTWARE
   OPERATING SYSTEM

PURPOSE OF SOFTWARE
   ZHEXEC IS A REAL TIME SOFTWARE EXECUTIVE FOR MODULAR ONE
   OFFERING COMMUNICATIONS, MULTI-PROCESSOR, LARGE RANDOM
   ACCESS STORE HANDLING AND CONCURRENT MULTI-PROGRAMMABLE
   BATCH OPERATING CAPABILITIES.

CONFIGURATION AND OPERATING SYSTEM
   CTL MODULAR ONE

   HAS RUN SUCCESSFULLY ON CTL MODULAR ONE (MINIMUM CONFIGURATION
   IS 1.21 + 1.11 + 1.31 + 1.32/1.72)
   AMOUNT OF PRIMARY STORAGE 4K-8K WORDS
   1 PAPER TAPE READER
   1 TELETYPE

   HAS RUN SUCCESSFULLY ON CTL MODULAR ONE, LARGE THREE PROCESSOR
           CONFIGURATION
   AMOUNT OF PRIMARY STORAGE 129K-256K WORDS
   2 DISC DRIVES,>100M WORDS STORAGE
   2 LINE PRINTERS
   3 PAPER TAPE READERS
   2 PAPER TAPE PUNCHES
   15 VDU'S
   2 COMMUNICATIONS MULTIPLEXORS
   2 REAL-TIME CONTROLLERS
   2 INTER-PROCESSOR LINKS

MODE OF USAGE
   BATCH
   INTERACTIVE
   REAL-TIME

LANGUAGE
   CTL ASSEMBLER VSN-3

AVAILABILITY
   PROGRAM MAY BE AVAILABLE FOR USE OUTSIDE SUPPLIERS
   ORGANISATION

SUPPLIERS COMMENT
   THE ZHEXEC SOURCE MODULE SET MAY, VIA SELECTION AND PARAMET-
   ERISATION, BE CONFIGURED TO SUIT MODULAR ONE SYSTEMS.
   THE FACILITY FOR ADDITION AND INTERFACE OF EXTRACODE
   TO SUIT PARTICULAR CUSTOMER APPLICATIONS IS PROVIDED AT A
   FUNDAMENTAL LEVEL

NCC STAGE 1 SOFTWARE VERIFICATION ABSTRACT A34192

NAME OF SOFTWARE
  BURROUGHS PRODUCTION CONTROL SYSTEM

TYPE OF SOFTWARE
  PRODUCTION CONTROL

PURPOSE OF SOTWARE
  PRODUCTION CONTROL; BILL OF MATERIAL PROCESSING,REQUIREMENT
  PLANNING,WORK-IN-PROGRESS MONITORING,INVENTORY ACCOUNTING,SHOP
  LOADING.

CONFIGURATION AND OPERATING SYSTEM
  BURROUGHS B500 SERIES

  HAS RUN SUCCESSFULLY ON B2500, B3500, B4700
  AMOUNT OF PRIMARY STORAGE 17K-32K BYTES
  1 DISC DRIVE.101K-1M BYTES STORAGE
  2 MAGNETIC TAPE DRIVES
  1 LINE PRINTER
  1 CARD READER
  1 CARD PUNCH
  1 VDU
  CARD PUNCH AND VDU ARE OPTIONAL
  RUN UNDER OPERATING SYSTEM MCP

MODE OF USAGE
  BATCH

LANGUAGE
  COBOL

AVAILABILITY
  PROGRAM AVAILABLE AS A BUREAU SERVICE

    COPYRIGHT NCC 1972   PRINTED ON 19/04/72

NCC STAGE 1 SOFTWARE VERIFICATION ABSTRACT A34193

NAME OF SOFTWARE
  BURROUGHS PROMIS SYSTEM- PROJECT ORIENTED MANAGEMENT

TYPE OF SOFTWARE
  PERT,CRITICAL PATH

PURPOSE OF SOFTWARE
  PROJECT CONTROL;PERT AND CPM, PROJECT COSTING, RESOURCE
  ALLOCATION

CONFIGURATION AND OPERATING SYSTEM
  BURROUGHS B500 SERIES

  HAS RUN SUCCESSFULLY ON B2500,B3500,B4700
  AMOUNT OF PRIMARY STORAGE 33K-64K BYTES
  1 DISC DRIVE, 101K-1M BYTES STORAGE
  1 MAGNETIC TAPE DRIVE
  1 LINE PRINTER
  1 CARD READER
  1 TELETYPE
  TELETYPE IS OPTIONAL
  RUN UNDER OPERATING SYSTEM MCP

MODE OF USAGE
  BATCH
  INTERACTIVE

LANGUAGE
  COBOL

AVAILABILITY
  PROGRAM AVAILABLE AS A BUREAU SERVICE

    COPYRIGHT NCC 1972   PRINTED ON 19/04/72

NCC STAGE 1 SOFTWARE VERIFICATION ABSTRACT A34195

NAME OF SOFTWARE
  EMPLOYMENT TAPE ANALYSIS

TYPE OF SOFTWARE
  STATISTICAL APPLICATION(COMMERCIAL)

PURPOSE OF SOFTWARE
  STORES EMPLOYMENT SURVEY ON TAPE.PRODUCES SUMMARY TAPE.
  LISTS DETAILS OF SELECTED FIRMS.PRODUCES FREQUENCY DISTRIBUTION
  BY EMPLOYMENT CATEGORIES

CONFIGURATION AND OPERATING SYSTEM
  IBM 360

  HAS RUN SUCCESSFULLY ON IBM 360/40
  AMOUNT OF PRIMARY STORAGE 65K-128K BYTES
  1 DISC DRIVE,<10K BYTES STORAGE
  2 MAGNETIC TAPE DRIVES
  1 LINE PRINTER
  1 CARD READER
  RUN UNDER OPERATING SYSTEM DOS G LEVEL

MODE OF USAGE
  BATCH

LANGUAGE
  FORTRAN IV

AVAILABILITY
  BY CONSULTATION WITH SUPPLIER

      COPYRIGHT NCC 1972   PRINTED ON 19/04/72

NCC STAGE 1 SOFTWARE VERIFICATION ABSTRACT A34196

NAME OF SOFTWARE
  RETAIL SALES ALLOCATION MODEL

TYPE OF SOFTWARE
  OPERATIONAL RESEARCH APPLICATION

PURPOSE OF SOFTWARE
  PERFORMS AN EXPONENTIAL LAKSHMANAN-HANSEN MODEL
  INCORPORATES PROCEDURES FOR CALIBRATION AND ATTRACTOR HYPOTHESIS
  TESTING

CONFIGURATION AND OPERATING SYSTEM
  IBM 360

  HAS RUN SUCCESSFULLY ON IBM 360/40
  AMOUNT OF PRIMARY STORAGE 65K-128K BYTES
  1 DISC DRIVE, <10K BYTES STORAGE
  2 MAGNETIC TAPE DRIVES
  1 LINE PRINTER
  1 CARD READER
  RUN UNDER OPERATING SYSTEM DOS G LEVEL

MODE OF USAGE
  BATCH

LANGUAGE
  FORTRAN IV

AVAILABILITY
  BY CONSULTATION WITH SUPPLIER

SUPPLIERS COMMENT
  AT PRESENT USED ONLY FOR ALLOCATION OF DURABLE TRADE
  MAY BE DEVELOPED LATER TO FORECAST CONVENIENCE TRADE

NCC STAGE 1 SOFTWARE VERIFICATION ABSTRACT A34197

NAME OF SOFTWARE
  LOWRY MODEL

TYPE OF SOFTWARE
  OPERATIONAL RESEARCH APPLICATION

PURPOSE OF SOFTWARE
  HIERARCHICAL FORMULATION OF LOWRY MODEL
  DESCRIBED IN DETAIL IN C.E.S. WP64, 'AN OPERATIONAL URBAN
  DEVELOPMENT MODEL OF CHESHIRE' M.CORDEY-HAYES ET AL., 1971
  MINCOST PROVIDES SHORTEST PATH COST MATRIX FOR MODEL

CONFIGURATION AND OPERATING SYSTEM
  IBM 360

  HAS RUN SUCCESSFULLY ON IBM 360/40
  AMOUNT OF PRIMARY STORAGE 65K-128K BYTES
  1 DISC DRIVE,<10K BYTES STORAGE
  2 MAGNETIC TAPE DRIVES
  1 LINE PRINTER
  1 CARD READER
  RUN UNDER OPERATING SYSTEM DOS G LEVEL

MODE OF USAGE
  BATCH

LANGUAGE
  FORTRAN IV

AVAILABILITY
  BY CONSULTATION WITH P.R.A.G. L.G.O.R.U.

SUPPLIERS COMMENT
  PROGRAM WAS THE RESULT OF A JOINT PROJECT WITH C.E.S.

NCC STAGE 1 SOFTWARE VERIFICATION ABSTRACT A34198

NAME OF SOFTWARE
  URBAN PLAN EVALUATION PROGRAM

TYPE OF SOFTWARE
  OPERATIONAL RESEARCH APPLICATION

PURPOSE OF SOFTWARE
  PERFORMS AN EVALUATION OF ALTERNATIVE URBAN PLANS
  DESCRIBED IN DETAIL IN L.G.O.R.U. REPORT C70,'SYSTEMS
  DESIGN PROJECT:A COMPUTER PROGRAM TO EVALUATE URBAN
  LAND USE PLANS', PILGRIM,B AND CARTER,R, MAY 1970

CONFIGURATION AND OPERATING SYSTEM
  IBM 360

  HAS RUN SUCCESSFULLY ON IBM 360/40
  AMOUNT OF PRIMARY STORAGE 65K-128K BYTES
  1 DISC DRIVE, <10K BYTES STORAGE
  2 MAGNETIC TAPE DRIVES
  1 LINE PRINTER
  1 CARD READER
  RUN UNDER OPERATING SYSTEM DOS G LEVEL

MODE OF USAGE
  BATCH

LANGUAGE
  FORTRAN IV

AVAILABILITY
  BY CONSULTATION WITH L.G.O.R.U.

SUPPLIERS COMMENT
  PROGRAM WAS THE RESULT OF A JOINT PROJECT WITH L.G.O.R.U.
  BUT HAS BEEN DEVELOPED FURTHER BY CHESHIRE COUNTY PLANNING
  DEPARTMENT

        COPYRIGHT NCC 1972   PRINTED ON 19/04/72

NCC STAGE 1 SOFTWARE VERIFICATION ABSTRACT A34199

NAME OF SOFTWARE
  POPULATION FORECASTING

TYPE OF SOFTWARE
  OPERATIONAL RESEARCH APPLICATION

PURPOSE OF SOFTWARE
  TO PROJECT THE POPULATION OF AN AREA,DIVIDED INTO FIVE YEAR
  AGE GROUPS, BY FIVE YEAR STAGES UP TO FORTY YEARS FROM BASE YEAR
  USING THE RELEVANT BIRTH, DEATH AND NETT MIGRATION RATES.
  FACILITIES INCLUDE MAINTENANCE OF POPULATION ON DATA FILE.

CONFIGURATION AND OPERATING SYSTEM
  IBM 360

  HAS RUN SUCCESSFULLY ON IBM 360/30
  AMOUNT OF PRIMARY STORAGE 33K-64K BYTES,OVERLAYS USED.
  1 DISC DRIVE,10K-100K BYTES STORAGE
  2 MAGNETIC TAPE DRIVES
  1 LINE PRINTER
  1 CARD READER
  RUN UNDER OPERATING SYSTEM DOS RELEASE 23

MODE OF USAGE
  BATCH

LANGUAGE
  FORTRAN IV, ASSEMBLER

AVAILABILITY
  BY CONSULTATION WITH SUPPLIER

SUPPLIERS COMMENT
  USES COHORT SURVIVAL TECHNIQUE. MIGRATION RATES CAN BE
  ESTIMATED FROM EXTRA POPULATION DATA FOR TENTH YEAR PRIOR TO
  BASE YEAR. COMPUTES NUMBERS OF HOUSEHOLDS IF GIVEN MARRIAGE
  RATES AND HOUSEHOLD FORMATION RATES,ALSO NUMBERS OF
  ECONOMICALLY ACTIVE PERSONS IF GIVEN ECONOMIC ACTIVITY RATES.

NCC STAGE 1 SOFTWARE VERIFICATION ABSTRACT A34200

NAME OF SOFTWARE
  SHOPPING MODEL

TYPE OF SOFTWARE
  OPERATIONAL RESEARCH APPLICATION

PURPOSE OF SOFTWARE
  TO DISTRIBUTE AND SUM THE RETAIL EXPENDITURES OF ZONAL
  POPULATIONS ACCORDING TO GRAVITY. EFFECTS OF ATTRACTION
  AND DISTANCE.

CONFIGURATION AND OPERATING SYSTEM
  IBM 360

  HAS RUN SUCCESSFULLY ON IBM 360/30
  AMOUNT OF PRIMARY STORAGE 33K-64K BYTES
  1 DISC DRIVE, <10K BYTES STORAGE
  1 LINE PRINTER
  1 CARD READER
  RUN UNDER OPERATING SYSTEM DOS RELEASE 23

MODE OF USAGE
  BATCH

LANGUAGE
  FORTRAN IV

AVAILABILITY
  BY CONSULTATION WITH SUPPLIER

SUPPLIERS COMMENT
  USES THE MATHEMATICAL MODEL FOR RETAIL MARKET POTENTIAL
  DEVELOPED BY LAKSHMANAN AND HANSEN FOR THE BALTIMORE
  REGIONAL PLANNING COUNCIL. NUMBERS OF RESIDENTIAL AND
  SHOPPING ZONES LIMITED TO SIXTY FOUR. UP TO NINE EQUAL INCREMENTS
  CAN BE SPECIFIED TO EXPONENTS ON DISTANCE AND ATTRACTION TO GIVE
  UP TO ONE HUNDRED SETS OF SALES PREDICTIONS IN ONE RUN

NCC STAGE 1 SOFTWARE VERIFICATION ABSTRACT A34201

NAME OF SOFTWARE
  EMPLOYMENT STATISTICS

TYPE OF SOFTWARE
  STATISTICAL APPLICATION(COMMERCIAL)

PURPOSE OF SOFTWARE
  TO PROVIDE DETAILS OF INSURED EMPLOYEES ANNUALLY BY
  EMPLOYMENT EXCHANGE, INDUSTRY TYPE, AND TO COMPARE THEM
  WITH NATIONAL FIGURES

CONFIURATION AND OPERATING SYSTEM
  IBM 360, IBM 370

  HAS RUN SUCCESSFULLY ON IBM 360/30, IBM 370/145
  AMOUNT OF PRIMARY STORAGE 33K-64K BYTES
  3 DISC DRIVES, 10K-100K BYTES STORAGE
  2 MAGNETIC TAPE DRIVES
  1 LINE PRINTER
  1 CARD READER
  RUN UNDER OPERATING SYSTEM DOS 23

MODE OF USAGE
  BATCH

LANGUAGE
  BASIC ASSEMBLER

AVAILABILITY
  BY CONSULTATION WITH SUPPLIER

      COPYRIGHT NCC 1972   PRINTED ON 19/04/72

NCC STAGE 1 SOFTWARE VERIFICATION ABSTRACT A34202

NAME OF SOFTWARE
  SUB REGIONAL ACTIVITY ALLOCATION MODEL

TYPE OF SOFTWARE
  OPERATIONAL RESEARCH APPLICATION

PURPOSE OF SOFTWARE
  TO ASSESS IMPACT OF DECISIONS TO MODIFY STRUCTURE OF AREA
  ASSUMING GIVEN LOCATION OF BASIC EMPLOYMENT, AND INTERACTIONS
  BETWEEN COMPONENTS OF STRUCTURE.

CONFIGURATION AND OPERATING SYSTEM
  HONEYWELL SERIES 200

  HAS RUN SUCCESSFULLY ON H125
  AMOUNT OF PRIMARY STORAGE 17K-32K CHARACTERS,OVERLAYS USED
  4 MAGNETIC TAPE DRIVES
  1 LINE PRINTER
  1 CARD READER
  RUN UNDER OPERATING SYSTEM MOD 1 (TR)

MODE OF USAGE
  BATCH

LANGUAGE
  FORTRAN IV

AVAILABILITY
  PROGRAM MAY BE AVAILABLE FOR USE OUTSIDE SUPPLIERS ORGANISATION
  PROGRAM AVAILABLE AS A BUREAU SERVICE

SUPPLIERS COMMENT
  MODEL IS BASED ON LOWRY MODEL.GIVEN BASIC EMPLOYMENT,MODEL
  ALLOCATES EMPLOYEES TO RESIDENTIAL LOCATIONS, GENERATES
  DEPENDENT POPULATION AND AMOUNT OF SERVICE EMPLOYMENT REQUIRED
  WHICH IS ALLOCATED TO SERVICE CENTRES. SERVICE EMPLOYEES ARE
  ALLOCATED TO RESIDENTIAL LOCATIONS AND DEPENDENT POPULATION
  CALCULATED.

NCC STAGE 1 SOFTWARE VERIFICATION ABSTRACT A34203

NAME OF SOFTWARE
  GRAVITATIONAL ATTRACTION AND INTERACTION MODEL

TYPE OF SOFTWARE
  OPERATIONAL RESEARCH APPLICATION

PURPOSE OF SOFTWARE
  TO MAKE QUICK ASSESSMENTS OF INTERACTIONS BETWEEN LOCATIONS
  GIVEN VARYING ASSUMPTIONS.

CONFIGURATION AND OPERATING SYSTEM
  HONEYWELL SERIES 200

  HAS RUN SUCCESSFULLY ON H125
  AMOUNT OF PRIMARY STORAGE 17K-32K CHARACTERS, OVERLAYS USED
  4 MAGNETIC TAPE DRIVES
  1 LINE PRINTER
  1 CARD READER
  1 PAPER TAPE READER
  RUN UNDER OPERATING SYSTEM MOD 1(TR)

MODE OF USAGE
  BATCH

LANGUAGE
  FORTRAN IV / COBOL

AVAILABILITY
  PROGRAM MAY BE AVAILABLE FOR USE OUTSIDE SUPPLIERS ORGANISATION
  PROGRAM AVAILABLE AS A BUREAU SERVICE

SUPPLIERS COMMENT
  MODEL IS A BASIC GRAVITY MODEL USING A 200 X 200 ZONE TIME
  -DISTANCE MATRIX.ANY SMALLER SIZE MATRIX MAY BE SPECIFIED.

NCC STAGE 1 SOFTWARE VERIFICATION ABSTRACT A34204

NAME OF SOFTWARE
  COMPONENT SCORE PROGRAM

TYPE OF SOFTWARE
  STATISTICAL APPLICATION(SCIENTIFIC)

PURPOSE OF SOFTWARE
  CALCULATES COMPONENT SCORES BY AREA/OBSERVATION USING AS
  DATA INPUT THE PRIMARY FACTOR LOADINGS MATRIX FROM A
  PRINCIPAL COMPONENTS MATRIX

CONFIGURATION AND OPERATING SYSTEM
  HONEYWELL SERIES 200

  HAS RUN SUCCESSFULLY ON H125
  AMOUNT OF PRIMARY STORAGE 17K-32K CHARACTERS
  1 DISC DRIVE, 1.1M-10M CHARACTERS STORAGE
  1 MAGNETIC TAPE DRIVE
  1 LINE PRINTER
  1 CARD READER
  RUN UNDER OPERATING SYSTEM MOD 1(TR)

MODE OF USAGE
  BATCH

LANGUAGE
  FORTRAN IV

AVAILABILITY
  PROGRAM MAY BE AVAILABLE FOR USE OUTSIDE SUPPLIERS ORGANISATION
  PROGRAM AVAILABLE AS A BUREAU SERVICE

SUPPLIERS COMMENT
  PROGRAM CONSISTS OF TWO PARTS - 1 COLLAPSING OF MATRIX,
  2-MAIN PROGRAM WHICH OPERATES ON COLLAPSED MATRIX.

  COPYRIGHT NCC 1972   PRINTED ON 19/04/72

NCC STAGE 1 SOFTWARE VERIFICATION ABSTRACT A34206

NAME OF SOFTWARE
   CORRELATION MATRIX

TYPE OF SOFTWARE
   STATISTICAL APPLICATION(SCIENTIFIC)

PURPOSE OF SOFTWARE
   TO PRODUCE CORRELATIONS BETWEEN SETS OF DATA IN MATRIX FORM

CONFIGURATION AND OPERATING SYSTEM
   HONEYWELL SERIES 200

   HAS RUN SUCCESSFULLY ON H125
   AMOUNT OF PRIMARY STORAGE 17K-32K CHARACTERS
   1 DISC DRIVE, 1.1M-10M CHARACTERS STORAGE
   1 LINE PRINTER
   1 CARD READER
   RUN UNDER OPERATING SYSTEM MOD 1 (TR)

MODE OF USAGE
   BATCH

LANGUAGE
   FORTRAN IV

AVAILABILITY
   PROGRAM MAY BE AVAILABLE FOR USE OUTSIDE SUPPLIERS ORGANISATION
   PROGRAM AVAILABLE AS A BUREAU SERVICE

SUPPLIERS COMMENT
   PROGRAM CALCULATES VALUE OF CORRELATION COEFFICIENT FOR EACH
   PAIR OF VARIABLES UP TO 31 AGAINST ALL VARIABLES. NO LIMIT
   ON NUMBER OF OBSERVATIONS.

NCC STAGE 1 SOFTWARE VERIFICATION ABSTRACT A34208

NAME OF SOFTWARE
   POPULATION PROJECTION PROGRAM

TYPE OF SOFTWARE
   OPERATIONAL RESEARCH APPLICATION

PURPOSE OF SOFTWARE
   TO PROJECT THE POPULATION OF ANY AREA IN FIVE YEAR STEPS
   TO A MAXIMUM OF THIRTY YEARS

CONFIGURATION AND OPERATING SYSTEM
   HONEYWELL SERIES 200

   HAS RUN SUCCESSFULLY ON H125
   AMOUNT OF PRIMARY STORAGE 17K-32K CHARACTERS,OVERLAYS USED
   2 MAGNETIC TAPE DRIVES
   1 LINE PRINTER
   1 CARD READER
   RUN UNDER OPERATING SYSTEM MOD1(TR)

MODE OF USAGE
   BATCH

LANGUAGE
   FORTRAN IV

AVAILABILITY
   PROGRAM MAY BE AVAILABLE FOR USE OUTSIDE SUPPLIERS ORGANISATION
   PROGRAM AVAILABLE AS A BUREAU SERVICE

SUPPLIERS COMMENT
   USES COHORT SURVIVAL METHOD. CAN UNDERTAKE NATURAL INCREASE
   PROJECTIONS ONLY OR INCORPORATE MIGRATION. INPUT REQUIREMENT
   -LOCAL BIRTH AND SURVIVAL RATES, BASE POPULATION STRUCTURE,
   MIGRATION AMOUNT AND STRUCTURE,INSTITUTIONAL POPULATION.
   OUTPUTS ARRAYS BY AREA AND AGE GROUP BY FIVE YEAR PERIODS.
   AVAILABLE TO LAMSAC MEMBERS

NCC STAGE 1 SOFTWARE VERIFICATION ABSTRACT A34209

NAME OF SOFTWARE
  MULTIPLE STEPWISE REGRESSION ANALYSIS

TYPE OF SOFTWARE
  STATISTICAL APPLICATION(SCIENTIFIC)

PURPOSE OF SOFTWARE
  TO CALCULATE THE VALUES OF CONSTANTS,COEFFICIENTS AND
  ASSOCIATED TESTS AND TO COMPUTE PREDICTED,ACTUAL AND DEVIATIONS
  FROM ACTUAL VALUES

CONFIGURATION AND OPERATING SYSTEM
  HONEYWELL SERIES 200

  HAS RUN SUCCESSFULLY ON H125
  AMOUNT OF PRIMARY STORAGE 17K-32K CHARACTERS
  1 DISC DRIVE,1.1M-10M CHARACTERS STORAGE
  1 LINE PRINTER
  1 CARD READER
  RUN UNDER OPERATING SYSTEM MOD 1 (TR)

MODE OF USAGE
  BATCH

LANGUAGE
  FORTRAN IV

AVAILABILITY
  PROGRAM MAY BE AVAILABLE FOR USE OUTSIDE SUPPLIERS ORGANISATION
  PROGRAM AVAILABLE AS A BUREAU SERVICE

SUPPLIERS COMMENT
  PROGRAM TAKES UP TO FIFTY VARIABLES, COMPUTING THE (N)TH
  VARIABLE AS A LINEAR FUNCTION OF THE FIRST (N-1) VARIABLES.

NCC STAGE 1 SOFTWARE VERIFICATION ABSTRACT A34211

NAME OF SOFTWARE
DYNAMIC AND STATIC ANALYSIS BY FINITE ELEMENT TECHNIQUES

TYPE OF SOFTWARE
ENGINEERING APPLICATION
SCIENTIFIC APPLICATION

PURPOSE OF SOFTWARE
THIS FINITE ELEMENT PACKAGE IS OF MODULAR DESIGN WITH A FINITE
ELEMENT LIBRARY THAT CAN BE EASILY EXTENDED. A SIMPLIFIED
INPUT PROCEDURE IS USED AND A LANGUAGE PROCESSOR IS
INCORPORATED TO PROVIDE FOR MORE THAN SIMPLE NUMERIC INPUT

CONFIGURATION AND OPERATING SYSTEM
CDC 6000

HAS RUN SUCCESSFULLY ON CDC 6600
AMOUNT OF PRIMARY STORAGE 65K-128K WORDS
7 DISC DRIVES, >100M CHARACTERS STORAGE
6 MAGNETIC TAPE DRIVES
3 LINE PRINTERS
2 CARD READERS
1 CARD PUNCH
1 PAPER TAPE READER
1 PAPER TAPE PUNCH
1 GRAPH PLOTTER
22 VDU'S
RUN UNDER OPERATING SYSTEM SCOPE

MODE OF USAGE
BATCH

LANGUAGE
ANSI FORTRAN

AVAILABILITY
PROGRAM AVAILABLE AS A BUREAU SERVICE

COPYRIGHT NCC 1972   PRINTED ON 19/04/72

NCC STAGE 1 SOFTWARE VERIFICATION ABSTRACT A34212

NAME OF SOFTWARE
   SQUIRE ASSOCIATES FINDER AND REPORTING OF
   INFORMATION SYSTEM

TYPE OF SOFTWARE
   FILE INTERROGATION AND REPORTING SYSTEM

PURPOSE OF SOFTWARE
   INTERROGATE FILES AND PRODUCE REPORTS IN VARIOUS FORMATS

CONFIGURATION AND OPERATING SYSTEM
   IBM 360, IBM 370

   HAS RUN SUCCESSFULLY ON IBM 360/30, IBM 360/40, IBM 360/50
   AMOUNT OF PRIMARY STORAGE 33K-64K BYTES
   1 DISC DRIVE, <10K BYTES STORAGE
   1 MAGNETIC TAPE DRIVE
   1 LINE PRINTER
   1 CARD READER
   RUN UNDER OPERATING SYSTEM DOS AND OS

MODE OF USAGE
   BATCH

LANGUAGE
   IBM BASIC ASSEMBLER

AVAILABILITY
   PROGRAM MAY BE AVAILABLE FOR USE OUTSIDE SUPPLIERS
   ORGANISATION. PROGRAM AVAILABLE AS A BUREAU SERVICE

SUPPLIERS COMMENT
   DESIGNED ORIGINALLY AS AN AUDIT TOOL
   HAS AN ASSOCIATED PACKAGE 'SAM',
   DESIGNED TO BE USED BY NON TECHNICAL PEOPLE
   INCLUDES USER EXITS TO LINK TO USER ROUTINES WRITTEN IN
   OTHER IBM PROGRAM LANGUAGES

NCC STAGE 1 SOFTWARE VERIFICATION ABSTRACT A34217

NAME OF SOFTWARE
  AUDITFIND

TYPE OF SOFTWARE
  ACCOUNTING , INFORMATION RETRIEVAL

PURPOSE OF SOFTWARE
  GENERAL INFORMATION ANALYSIS AND RETRIEVAL PACKAGE DEVELOPED
  FROM ICL FIND-2 WITH AUDITING REQUIREMENTS SPECIFICALLY INCLUDED

CONFIGURATION AND OPERATING SYSTEM
  ICL 1900

  HAS RUN SUCCESSFULLY ON ICL 1901,1902A,1903A,1904A
  AMOUNT OF PRIMARY STORAGE 9K-16K WORDS,OVERLAYS USED
  4 MAGNETIC TAPE DRIVES
  1 LINE PRINTER
  1 CARD READER
  RUN UNDER OPERATING SYSTEM EXEC

MODE OF USAGE
  BATCH

LANGUAGE
  PLAN

AVAILABILITY
  PROGRAM MAY BE AVAILABLE FOR USE OUTSIDE SUPPLIERS ORGANISATION

SUPPLIERS COMMENT
  CONFIGURATION IS DEPENDENT ON USER REQUIREMENTS,
  MINIMUM TAPE SYSTEM: 4 MAGNETIC TAPE DRIVES, 1 LINE PRINTER,
  CARD READER OR PAPER TAPE READER, 16K WORDS
  MINIMUM DISC SYSTEM: 1 DISC DRIVE, 1 LINE PRINTER,CARD
  READER OR PAPER TAPE READER, 16K WORDS
  OR MANY COMBINATIONS OF DISC OR MAGNETIC TAPE DRIVES,
  WILL RUN UNDER EXEC, GEORGE 2 OR GEORGE 3.

LINEAR PROGRAMMING MATRIX GENERATOR FOR DISTRIBUTION PROBLEMS **A34220**

NCC STAGE 1 SOFTWARE VERIFICATION ABSTRACT A34220

NAME OF SOFTWARE
   LINEAR PROGRAMMING MATRIX GENERATOR FOR DISTRIBUTION PROBLEMS

TYPE OF SOFTWARE
   OPERATIONAL RESEARCH APPLICATION

PURPOSE OF SOFTWARE
   GIVEN A SET OF PRODUCTS DISTRIBUTION POINTS AND CUSTOMERS
   THE PROGRAM DETERMINES WHICH DISTRIBUTION POINTS ARE POSSIBLE
   SUPPLIERS TO PARTICULAR CUSTOMERS.L.P.MATRIX ELEMENTS ARE
   PRODUCED FOR THE APPROPRIATE L.P.MODEL

CONFIGURATION AND OPERATING SYSTEM
   IBM 1130

   HAS RUN SUCCESSFULLY ON IBM 1130
   AMOUNT OF PRIMARY STORAGE 4K-8K WORDS
   1 DISC DRIVE,101K-1M WORDS STORAGE
   1 LINE PRINTER
   1 CARD READER
   NO OPERATING SYSTEM USED

MODE OF USAGE
   BATCH

LANGUAGE
   FORTRAN IV

AVAILABILITY
   PROGRAM MAY BE AVAILABLE FOR USE OUTSIDE SUPPLIERS ORGANISATION
   PROGRAM AVAILABLE AS A BUREAU SERVICE

SUPPLIERS COMMENT
   PROGRAM COST IS AVAILABLE ON REQUEST

      COPYRIGHT NCC 1972   PRINTED ON 19/04/72

NCC STAGE 1 SOFTWARE VERIFICATION ABSTRACT A34222

NAME OF SOFTWARE
   SHOPPING MODEL

TYPE OF SOFTWARE
   OPERATIONAL RESEARCH APPLICATION

PURPOSE OF SOFTWARE
   TO PREDICT THE SHOPPING SALES OF UP TO 100 CENTRES AND THE
   PROPORTION OF EACH CENTRES SALES DERIVING FROM UP TO 85
   EXPENDITURE ZONES.THE MODEL CAN BE USED TO CALCULATE DURABLE
   GOODS SALES,CONVENIENCE GOODS SALES AND TOTAL SALES

CONFIGURATION AND OPERATING SYSTEM
   ICL 1900

   HAS RUN SUCCESSFULLY ON ICL 1902A
   AMOUNT OF PRIMARY STORAGE 17K-32K WORDS
   1 LINE PRINTER
   1 CARD READER
   NO OPERATING SYSTEM USED

MODE OF USAGE
   BATCH

LANGUAGE
   FORTRAN

AVAILABILITY
   PROGRAM MAY BE AVAILABLE FOR USE OUTSIDE SUPPLIERS
   ORGANISATION
   PROGRAM AVAILABLE AS A BUREAU SERVICE

SUPPLIERS COMMENT
   THE MODEL IS BASED ON THE LAKSHMANAN AND HANSEN MODEL.
   IT REQUIRES FLOOR SPACE (DURABLE,CONVENIENCE OR TOTAL)
   FOR EACH CENTRE AND EXPENDITURE BY BLUE AND WHITE COLLAR
   POPULATION FOR EACH ZONE.DISTANCES ARE CALCULATED FROM
   NATIONAL GRID CO-ORDINATES

NCC STAGE 1 SOFTWARE VERIFICATION ABSTRACT A34223

NAME OF SOFTWARE
   POPULATION PROJECTIONS PROGRAM

TYPE OF SOFTWARE
   OPERATIONAL RESEARCH APPLICATION

PURPOSE OF SOFTWARE
   TO PROJECT THE POPULATION OF ANY AREA,EXPRESSED BY SEX
   AND BY FIVE YEAR AGE GROUPS BY FIVE YEAR STAGES TO A
   MAXIMUM OF FORTY YEARS

CONFIGURATION AND OPERATING SYSTEM
   ICL 1900

   HAS RUN SUCCESSFULLY ON ICL 1902
   AMOUNT OF PRIMARY STORAGE 4K-8K WORDS
   1 MAGNETIC TAPE DRIVE
   1 LINE PRINTER
   1 CARD READER
   NO OPERATING SYSTEM USED

MODE OF USAGE
   BATCH

LANGUAGE
   FORTRAN

AVAILABILITY
   PROGRAM MAY BE AVAILABLE FOR USE OUTSIDE SUPPLIERS
   ORGANISATION
   PROGRAM AVAILABLE AS A BUREAU SERVICE

SUPPLIERS COMMENT
   THE PROGRAM IS BASED ON THE COHORT-SURVIVAL METHOD AND CAN
   BE USED FOR BOTH NATURAL INCREASE AND WITH-MIGRATION
   PROJECTIONS.IT REQUIRES POPULATION STRUCTURE AT BASE DATE,
   SURVIVAL RATES,FERTILITY RATES, AND, AS AN OPTION,MIGRATION
   STRUCTURE.

   COPYRIGHT NCC 1972   PRINTED ON 19/04/72

NCC STAGE 1 SOFTWARE VERIFICATION ABSTRACT A34227

NAME OF SOFTWARE
   AUDITORS TIME BILLING SYSTEM

TYPE OF SOFTWARE
   ACCOUNTING

PURPOSE OF SOFTWARE
   TO MAINTAIN A RECORD OF TIME AND EXPENSES BOOKED TO CLIENTS
   JOBS

CONFIGURATION AND OPERATING SYSTEM
   HONEYWELL 200 SERIES

   HAS RUN SUCCESSFULLY ON HONEYWELL H 200
   AMOUNT OF PRIMARY STORAGE 17K-32K CHARACTERS,OVERLAYS USED
   5 MAGNETIC TAPE DRIVES
   1 LINE PRINTER
   1 CARD READER
   RUN UNDER OPERATING SYSTEM MOD-1 TR

MODE OF USAGE
   BATCH

LANGUAGE
   COBOL

AVAILABILITY
   PROGRAM MAY BE AVAILABLE FOR USE OUTSIDE SUPPLIERS ORGANISATION
   PROGRAM AVAILABLE AS A BUREAU SERVICE

      COPYRIGHT NCC 1972   PRINTED ON 19/04/72

NCC STAGE 1 SOFTWARE VERIFICATION ABSTRACT A34228

NAME OF SOFTWARE
  SALES LEDGER & ANALYSIS PACKAGE

TYPE OF SOFTWARE
  ACCOUNTING

PURPOSE OF SOFTWARE
  A SIMPLE NON-OPEN ITEM SALES LEDGER SYSTEM WITH FACILITIES
  FOR ASSOCIATED SALES ANALYSES. THE OUTSTANDING BALANCE IS AGED
  TO ENABLE COMPREHENSIVE CREDIT CONTROL REPORTS TO BE PRODUCED

CONFIGURATION AND OPERATING SYSTEM
  HONEYWELL 200 SERIES

  HAS RUN SUCCESSFULLY ON HONEYWELL H 200
  AMOUNT OF PRIMARY STORAGE 17K-32K CHARACTERS,OVERLAYS USED
  5 MAGNETIC TAPE DRIVES
  1 LINE PRINTER
  1 CARD READER
  RUN UNDER OPERATING SYSTEM MOD-1 TR.

MODE OF USAGE
  BATCH

LANGUAGE
  EASYCODER

AVAILABILITY
  PROGRAM MAY BE AVAILABLE FOR USE OUTSIDE SUPPLIERS ORGANISATION
  PROGRAM AVAILABLE AS A BUREAU SERVICE

SUPPLIERS COMMENT
  THE INPUT OF DATA ON PAPER TAPE IS ALSO POSSIBLE

      COPYRIGHT NCC 1972   PRINTED ON 19/04/72

NCC STAGE 1 SOFTWARE VERIFICATION ABSTRACT A34229

NAME OF SOFTWARE
   PURCHASE LEDGER AND ANALYSIS PACKAGE

TYPE OF SOFTWARE
   ACCOUNTING

PURPOSE OF SOFTWARE
   A NON-OPEN ITEM PURCHASE LEDGER WITH FACILITIES FOR
   ASSOCIATED PURCHASE ANALYSES.

CONFIGURATION AND OPERATING SYSTEM
   HONEYWELL 200 SERIES

   HAS RUN SUCCESSFULLY ON HONEYWELL H 200
   AMOUNT OF PRIMARY STORAGE 17K-32K CHARACTERS
   5 MAGNETIC TAPE DRIVES
   1 LINE PRINTER
   1 CARD READER
   RUN UNDER OPERATING SYSTEM MOD-1 TR

MODE OF USAGE
   BATCH

LANGUAGE
   EASYCODER

AVAILABILITY
   PROGRAM MAY BE AVAILABLE FOR USE OUTSIDE SUPPLIERS ORGANISATION
   PROGRAM AVAILABLE AS A BUREAU SERVICE

SUPPLIERS COMMENT
   THE INPUT OF DATA ON PAPER TAPE IS ALSO POSSIBLE

        COPYRIGHT NCC 1972   PRINTED ON 19/04/72

NCC STAGE 1 SOFTWARE VERIFICATION ABSTRACT A34230

NAME OF SOFTWARE
  PAYROLL PHASE 4

TYPE OF SOFTWARE
  PAYROLL

PURPOSE OF SOFTWARE
  TO CALCULATE MAKE-UP TO GROSS AND/OR GROSS-TO-NETT PAY AND TO
  PRODUCE PAYSLIPS IN AN OPTIONAL SEQUENCE ALONG WITH BACK-UP
  REPORTS AND STANDARD OPTIONAL ANALYSES.

CONFIGURATION AND OPERATING SYSTEM
  HONEYWELL 200 SERIES

  HAS RUN SUCCESSFULLY ON HONEYWELL H 200
  AMOUNT OF PRIMARY STORAGE 9K-16K CHARACTERS,OVERLAYS USED
  4 MAGNETIC TAPE DRIVES
  1 LINE PRINTER
  1 CARD READER
  RUN UNDER OPERATING SYSTEM MOD-1 TR

MODE OF USAGE
  BATCH

LANGUAGE
  EASYCODER

AVAILIBILITY
  PROGRAM MAY BE AVAILABLE FOR USE OUTSIDE SUPPLIERS ORGANISATION
  PROGRAM AVAILABLE AS A BUREAU SERVICE

SUPPLIERS COMMENT
  PAPER TAPE INPUT OF PAY DATA IS CATERED FOR TAX-YEAR-END
  DOCUMENTATION IS PRODUCED AND HOLIDAY PAY CALCULATIONS CAN BE
  DONE BY THE SYSTEM.

      COPYRIGHT NCC 1972   PRINTED ON 19/04/72

Suppliers of Information

Applied Computer Sciences
Applied Transport Simulation
Arthur Anderson & Company
Associated British Consultants Limited
Atkins Research and Development
Bath City Corporation
Bedfordshire County Council
Bell and Howell Limited
Berkshire County Council
M. J. Bevan Limited
Blyth and Blyth
British Aircraft Corporation
British Glass Industry Research Association
British Launderers Research Association
British Steel Corporation United Steel Branch
Burroughs Machines Limited
Bush Boake Allen Limited
Cambridge Computer Services Limited
Cheshire County Planning Department
Computer Consortium
CMG (Computer Management Group) Limited
Computer Systems International Inc. (G.B.) Limited
Cusdin, Burden and Howitt
Data Consultants Limited
DATASKIL Limited
Document Reading Services Limited
Durham County Planning Department
Easams
The Eastbourne Waterworks Company
E.C.C. Quarries Limited
Economic Data Services Limited
Edmunsons Electric Co. Limited
English Calico Limited
F2 Limited
Gemini Computer Systems
General and Engineering Computer Services Limited
G.K.N. Group Services Limited
Hulme House Associates Limited
Imperial Tobacco Group Limited
Industrial and Commercial Data Processing Limited
IPC Services Limited
I.S.C.O.L. Limited
Kent Data Services Limited
Leicestershire County Council
Logica Limited
Lowndes-Ajax Computer Service Limited
Management Dynamics Software Services
Management Systems and Programming Limited

Mather and Platt Limited
Maximillian Lipman and Co.
Medway Data (Systems) Limited
The Mettoy Company Limited
Midlands Computing Centre Limited
The National Coal Board
The National Computing Centre Limited
National Computing Industries (USA)
National Data Processing Service
Northern Software Consultants Limited
The Nuclear Power Group Limited
Office of the High Commissioner of Australia
Oldacres Computers Limited
Pensions and Insurance Computer Services
Peterborough Data Processing Services Limited
The Polytechnic, Wolverhampton
Port Talbot Corporation
Queens University, Belfast
Randax EDP Limited
Royal Aircraft Establishment
Royal Insurance Group
J. Sainsbury Limited
Scicon Computer Bureau
Scottish Amicable Life Assurance Society
Scottish Special Housing Association
Seat Reservation Systems Limited
S.I.A. Limited
SIRA Institute
Smiths Industries
Software Design (U.K.) Limited
Software Licencees Limited
Squire Associates
Staflex International Limited
Stirling Maynard and Partners
Systems Designers Limited
Touche Ross and Co.
U.K.A.E.A. (United Kingdom Atomic Energy Authority)
U.K. Atomic Energy Authority (Reactor Group)
Variable Model Programming Limited
Western Data Processing
Zeus Hermes Company Limited

Appendix

The Information Service and its Publications

Work on formal Information Services at NCC started in April 1969, although information has been provided since 1966 on a less formal basis.

The objective of Information Division can be stated as follows:

"To promote an increased and more effective use of computers within the U.K. and to promote the computing industry in all its aspects by the provision of prompt, accurate, authentic, complete and unbiased information on computing methods, equipment, education and services available to users."

Enquiries for information can be made by correspondence, by telex or by telephone. The telephone answering service is now operated from a specially planned Information Desk.

The telephone is manned continuously by the staff of Information Operations Centre during normal office hours and provides information from a number of indexed sources which are:

— software index
— hardware index
— installation index
— services and background index
— literature and abstracting index
— education index

Publications

NCC publishes a number of books many of which are particularly concerned with basic computing information, including:

Factfinder 1: Visible record computers
Factfinder 2: Keyboard/Printer terminals

World list of computer periodicals
International computer bibliography
The NCC Thesaurus of Computing Terms

190373 NRL

Other
"Factfinders"

Factfinder 1: Visible Record Computers

Factfinder 2: Keyboard/Printer Terminals

Factfinder 3: Computer Courses — Post Graduate & First Degree

Factfinder 4: Computer Courses — Qualifying

Factfinder 5: Computer Courses — Systems Analysis & Programming

Factfinder 6: Computer Courses — Introduction & Appreciation

Factfinder 7: Computer Courses — Manufacturers & Consultants

Factfinder 8: Program Testing Aids

Factfinder 9: Generalised Data Management Systems

Factfinder 10: Analysis of Computer Usage in the U.K. in 1971

All obtainable from:
NCC Publications, Quay House, Quay Street,
Manchester M3 3HU